THE CASE FOR GOLIATH

Also By Michael Mandelbaum

*The Nuclear Question: The United States
and Nuclear Weapons, 1946–1976* (1979)

*The Nuclear Revolution: International Politics Before
and After Hiroshima* (1981)

The Nuclear Future (1983)

Reagan and Gorbachev (Co-author, 1987)

*The Fate of Nations: The Search for National Security
in the Nineteenth and Twentieth Centuries* (1988)

The Global Rivals (Co-author, 1988)

The Dawn of Peace in Europe (1996)

*The Ideas That Conquered the World: Peace, Democracy
and Free Markets in the Twenty-first Century* (2002)

*The Meaning of Sports:
Why Americans Watch Baseball, Football and Basketball
and What They See When They Do* (2004)

The Case for Goliath

How America Acts
as the World's Government
in the Twenty-first Century

Michael Mandelbaum

PublicAffairs *New York*

Book design and composition by Mark McGarry, Texas Type & Book Works
Set in Janson

Library of Congress Cataloging-in-Publication Data
Mandelbaum, Michael.
The case for Goliath : how America acts as the world's government in the 21st
century / Michael Mandelbaum.—1st ed.
p. cm.
Includes index.
ISBN–13: 978–1–58648–360–9
ISBN–10: 1–58648–360–9
1. United States—Foreign relations—2001- 2. Security, International. 3. International relations. 4. World politics—21st century. I. Title.
JZ1480.M3258 2005
327.73′009′051—dc22
2005048897

FIRST EDITION
10 9 8 7 6 5 4 3 2 1

To Leslie H. Gelb, Vartan Gregorian,
and David A. Hamburg:
scholars themselves and inspirers of scholarship in others;

and to Anne Mandelbaum,
with my love.

It was like an anchor to the floating world.

PLUTARCH ON ANCIENT ROME

It is not done well; but you are surprised
to see it done at all.

SAMUEL JOHNSON ON A DOG WALKING ON HIS HIND LEGS

Contents

Acknowledgments

My principal debt of gratitude in the writing of this book, which I am happy to acknowledge, is to the Carnegie Corporation of New York, which made me part of the Carnegie Scholars Program for 2004–2005, thereby enabling me to complete the book. That fellowship is only one of a number of Carnegie programs in which I have had the good fortune to participate over the course of two decades, all of which have enriched my understanding of the subjects addressed in the pages that follow. My gratitude for the support I have received from Carnegie is reflected in the book's dedication to the Corporation's president, Vartan Gregorian, and his predecessor, David A. Hamburg, who, along with a third dedicatee, Leslie H. Gelb, president emeritus of the Council on Foreign Relations, have provided inspiration, encouragement, and guidance to me that have greatly enhanced my scholarship and my life.

In addition to the two presidents, I should like to acknowledge other people at the Carnegie Corporation who have made my association with it both intellectually rewarding and personally congenial: Deana Arsenian, Stephen Del Rosso, Neil Grabois, Susan King, Frederic A. Mosher, Patricia Rosenfield, Astrid Tuminez, Jane Wales (now president and chief executive officer of the World Affairs Council of Northern California), and particularly David C. Speedie III.

My home institution, The Johns Hopkins University School of Advanced International Studies (SAIS), has furnished a stimulating environment for teaching and writing. At SAIS I am particularly grateful to Dean Jessica Einhorn, Associate Dean John M. Harrington Jr., and my late colleague Frederick Holborn for facilitating the leave of absence during which I wrote this book, and to Frances Galante and Timothy Juliani for research assistance.

Some of the ideas in this book began as newspaper columns for *Newsday*. I am grateful to James Klurfeld, editor of *Newsday*'s editorial pages, for encouraging them and to Noel Rubinton, editor of its op-ed page, for commissioning them. I also benefited greatly from discussing many of the ideas in *The Case for Goliath* with Thomas L. Friedman of *The New York Times*.

I am grateful to my agent, the peerless Morton L. Janklow, for placing the book, and to my splendid publisher, Peter Osnos, and his superb team at PublicAffairs, especially Nina D'Amario, David Patterson, Melissa Raymond, Steven Strasser, and Gene Taft, for bringing the book expertly to publication.

Last but certainly not least, I am deeply grateful to my

wife, Anne Mandelbaum, to whom this book is also dedicated. Her enthusiastic encouragement and support, and her
brilliant editorial advice, were indispensable to the writing of
this book, as they have been to everything that I have written
over the past thirty years.

Introduction

When the Cold War ended, a question arose: What would succeed that great political, military, economic, and ideological conflict as the central issue in international relations? By the middle of the first decade of the twenty-first century, the question had been answered. The enormous power and pervasive influence of the United States was universally acknowledged to be the defining feature of world affairs.

In the eyes of many, American supremacy counted as a great misfortune. The foreign policy of the world's strongest country, in this account, resembled the conduct of a school yard bully who randomly assaults others, steals the lunch money of weaker students, and generally makes life unpleasant wherever he goes. The United States was seen as the world's Goliath.

In some ways the United States in the early years of the twenty-first century does resemble the Philistine giant whom David, the son of Jesse, felled with a sling and a stone according to the Bible and thereby saved Israel. Like Goliath, the United States surpasses all others in military might. And just as Goliath was, by virtue of his size and power, the logical candidate to represent his tribe in its confrontation with the people of Israel, so the United States has undertaken broad responsibilities that redound to the benefit of others.

Although the United States looks like Goliath, however, in important ways the world's strongest power does not act like him. If America is a Goliath, it is a benign one. Unlike the case of Goliath, moreover, no David, or group of Davids, has stepped forward to confront the United States. This book explains other countries' acceptance of the American role in the world by painting a different and more benign picture of that role than the one implied by the comparison with Western civilization's archetypal bully. As portrayed in the pages that follow, it has something in common with the sun's relationship to the rest of the solar system. Both confer benefits on the entities with which they are in regular contact. The sun keeps the planets in their orbits by the force of gravity and radiates the heat and light that make life possible on one of them. Similarly, the United States furnishes services to other countries, the same services, as it happens, that governments provide within sovereign states to the people they govern. The United States therefore functions as the world's government. The origins, the details, and the implications of this twenty-first-century American international role are the subjects of the five chapters that follow. Together, they present the case for Goliath.

Chapter 1 sets out the book's thesis and explains how the

United States came to assume the responsibilities of global governance. Chapter 2 describes the ways in which the United States performs, within the international system, the first duty of all governments: providing security. One of the principal American policies during the Cold War—deterrence—was transformed, in the wake of that conflict, into a related but distinct mission: reassurance. Another Cold War policy, preventing the spread of nuclear weapons, gained in importance in the post–Cold War period. The United States has introduced two new purposes for the use of force: preventive war and humanitarian intervention. Both led to yet another governmental undertaking, popularly called nation-building.

Chapter 3 concerns the American foreign policies that correspond to the economic tasks that governments perform within sovereign states. One is the enforcement of contracts and the protection of property in their jurisdictions. America's international military deployments have these effects on transactions across borders. Governments also supply the power and water without which industrial economies cannot function. Similarly, the United States helps to assure global access to the economically indispensable mineral, oil. Governments supply the money used in economic transactions: The American dollar serves as the world's money. At the outset of the post–World War II period and thereafter, the United States fostered the conditions in which yet another major economic activity—trade—flourished and expanded. Finally, just as, in the twentieth century, governments took it upon themselves to sustain the level of consumption within their societies in order to support a high level of production and thus of employment, so the huge American appetite for consumer products has helped to sustain economic activity the world over, especially in East Asia.

If the United States provides useful, indeed necessary services to the rest of the world, why does American foreign policy provoke such frequent, widespread, and bitter criticism? Chapter 4 addresses that question, exploring the multiple sources of discontent and explaining the difference between other countries' words and their deeds where the American role in the world is concerned. Whether the United States continues to function as the world's government depends on whether the American public continues to support the policies involved, and this chapter sets out the basis on which the public will make its judgment.

That judgment is not necessarily destined to be favorable. Chapter 5 therefore examines the consequences of a far more modest American global role and investigates the possible alternatives to the United States in providing governmental services to the world. In particular, this chapter explains why Europe, despite its size, wealth, rich historical legacy, and ambitions for global influence, will neither supplant nor support the United States as the world's government. The case in favor of the United States continuing to act as the world's government—the case, that is, for Goliath—therefore rests ultimately on a version of Winston Churchill's argument in favor of democracy. He said it was the worst form of government except for all the others. The United States is the best source of global governance because, in the first decade of the twenty-first century, there is no other.

Understanding the functions that the United States performs beyond its borders as constituting the role of the world's government puts American foreign policy in a new perspective. From this perspective, some things that are widely believed about America's relations with other countries turn out to be misleading or inaccurate. At the same time, some American policies appear less consequential than they are often taken to be, while others, usually unnoticed, assume greater importance.

- Although the term "empire" is routinely used to describe the American role in the world, in most important ways the United States does not resemble the empires of the past. The single indisputably imperial task it regularly carries out—nation-building—has played a relatively small part in its overall foreign policy, has been undertaken with great reluctance, and has been performed, on the whole, badly. (This point is discussed in Chapters 1 and 2.)
- The governmental services that the United States provides that affect the largest number of people— reassurance and enforcement—are the least controversial because they are the least noticed. They go unnoticed because they arise simply from America's global presence. They are vital but also unappreciated; and they are unappreciated because they are invisible. (Chapters 2 and 3)
- The foreign policies of the first two post–Cold War American administrations, those of Bill Clinton and George W. Bush, have more in common than is generally recognized. The innovations in international practice with which each is identified—humanitarian intervention in the first case, preventive war in the second—are like fraternal twins: different on the surface but sharing some basic features. Both are the products of American power, American values, and a particular American sense of international responsibility. Both encountered difficulty in gaining international support because they stretch the boundaries of international law. Both had difficulty in winning sup-

port within the United States as well, because each led
to a task unpopular with the American public: nation-
building. (Chapter 2)

- The worst twenty-first-century international offense
of the United States—the American policy that put
the largest number of people in jeopardy—was not the
occupation of Iraq: It was and is the American pattern
of energy consumption, which far exceeds that of
other countries on a per capita basis and makes virtually every other country more vulnerable than it
would otherwise be to economic damage in both the
short and long term. (Chapter 3)

- For all their criticisms of it, the American role in the
world enjoys other countries' tacit consent. More
important than what others say about it is what they
do, or rather what they choose not to do. They have
chosen not to mount serious opposition to what the
United States does in the world, something that they
would do if they considered the United States dangerous to their interests. (Chapter 4)

- The greatest threat to the American role as the world's
government comes not from the discontent it generates
in other countries, or from the assaults of terrorists, but
from the huge bill for social spending that the American public will have to pay in the twenty-first century, a
responsibility that has the potential to transform American politics in ways unfavorable to the continuation of
that role. (Chapter 4)

- The most consequential problem in European-Ameri-
can relations is not the failure of the United States to
consult with European governments but rather the
failure of those governments to muster the resources

to make major contributions to global governance. Their failure means that when the United States acts unilaterally, it does so as much by default as by design. The Europeans endeavor to induce good behavior on the part of potentially dangerous countries by the force of their example, but not by force of arms. They see their global mission as embodying civilization but not defending it. (Chapter 5)

The United States did not become the functional equivalent of the world's government deliberately. It exerted itself in pursuit of one goal—defending itself against the Soviet Union and international communism—and in the process of achieving that goal gained a position of international supremacy.

That position is not sustained by enthusiasm for it in the United States. Americans generally find their global status to be a burden, a chore, or a duty, rather than an opportunity or a reward. No American holiday or monument, or even a commemorative postage stamp, is devoted to celebrating the position of international primacy that the United States occupies or the services that it provides to other countries.

Nor do the recipients and beneficiaries of these services manifest enthusiasm either for what the United States does for them or for the American power that makes the services possible. If anything, the American global presence is unpopular. The approval ratings of the United States in some parts of the world were, in the first decade of the twenty-first century, as low as Goliath's would have been among the people of Israel had opinion polls been a feature of life in biblical times.

Still, in the world outside the United States, the case for Goliath enjoys at least tacit support. For while others may consider that presence annoying, even infuriating, they do not, apparently, find it intolerable. They do tolerate it, and for the same reason that Americans are willing to pay for it. Americans and non-Americans, whatever their differences, find the American international role to be convenient. The world needs governance and the United States is in a position to supply it. Just what it is that Americans are willing to provide and that the world finds convenient to accept is the subject of this book.

THE CASE FOR GOLIATH

Chapter One

THE WORLD'S GOVERNMENT

And I know it's hard on America, and in some small corner of this vast country, out in Nevada or Idaho or these places I've never been to, but always wanted to go ... I know out there there's a guy getting on with his life, perfectly happily, minding his own business saying to you, the political leaders of this country, "Why me? And why us? And why America?" And the only answer is, "Because destiny put you in this place in history, in this moment in time, and the task is yours to do."

TONY BLAIR,
ADDRESS TO THE UNITED STATES CONGRESS, JULY 17, 2003

Empire

At the beginning of the twenty-first century, a term came into use to refer to the American role in the world that conjured up images of Roman legions with helmets, metal breastplates, and sharp lances keeping order in the ancient world, bearded Habsburg grandees riding on horseback along cobblestone streets in Central Europe, and British colonial officials in pith helmets presiding over tropical kingdoms. The term was "empire."[1] Many books and articles appeared advancing and exploring the proposition that the United States had become, without officially acknowledging it, what the largest and most powerful political units of the past had proudly proclaimed themselves to be.[2]

Applied to the United States, the term "empire" had a jarring effect. For empire had seemed, as the twenty-first century began, the dinosaur of international history, having dominated the planet for much of recorded history but then become extinct, its place taken everywhere by the more cohesive and legitimate nation-state. The ideas that had underpinned the empires of the past—the glory of war and conquest, the commercial advantages of political monopolies, the natural hierarchy of the human race that made some people fit to govern others—had all fallen decisively out of favor.

The United States seemed a particularly unlikely candidate for an imperial role. Although America had once had an empire, it had been acquired later, had been given up earlier, and even at its zenith had been considerably smaller than the empires of the British, the French, the Austrian Habsburgs, the Russian Romanovs, or the Ottoman Turks. Moreover, the United States had been founded in revolt against empire, and even when it *was* an imperial power had harbored powerful anti-imperial sentiment. Its first and most expansive exercise in imperial conquest, the Spanish-American War of 1898 and the direct possession of the Philippines and indirect control of Cuba that resulted from its victory in that war, aroused considerable opposition in the United States Congress and among such eminent private citizens as Mark Twain and Andrew Carnegie.[3]

What accounts for the revival of a seemingly obsolete and, in the case of the United States, inappropriate term? Behind the use of the word "empire" to describe American relations with other countries lay two motives—one descriptive, the other derisive.

The global status of the United States at the outset of the twenty-first century seemed to require a new term because the American presence in the world had changed. It was an unprecedentedly powerful one. The range of the military, economic, and cultural influence that the United States could bring to bear was impressively wide. Even more impressive was the margin of power that separated America from every other country.[4] The American economy produced 30 percent of the world's output; no other country was responsible for even half that much.[5] The American defense budget exceeded, in dollars expended, the military spending of the next fifteen countries combined,[6] and the United States had some military assets—its highly accurate missiles, for example—that no other country possessed.[7]

As a term to describe this latter-day colossus, "empire" did have some advantages. America's global role did bear some resemblance to the empires of the past. Its military forces were deployed in many countries—upward of 150 by one count.[8] As with the great empires of the past, the language most frequently employed in international discussions was the one Americans spoke: English.[9] The American government itself noticed the similarity: The Department of Defense commissioned a study of the great empires of the past, with particular emphasis on how they had maintained their dominant positions—or failed to do so.[10]

Moreover, if the word "empire" seemed, in some ways, to capture the reality of the twenty-first century American global presence, more familiar and recent terms did not. The United States had surely become more than a great power, which is what the major European countries (many of them, to be sure, also empires) had been called in the nineteenth century and at the beginning of the twentieth. It had outgrown the status that, along with the Soviet Union, it had enjoyed during the Cold War, when both were called nuclear "superpowers." The great powers and even the superpowers of the past had, after all, had international peers: The twenty-first century United States had none.

Because it suggested a greater, grander status than either of the other two terms, it was empire that came to seem to many the most appropriate way to describe America's international status.

If one reason for using this term was to describe America's role in the world, another was to denounce it. By the twenty-first century, the word "empire" had ceased, in all but the most academic discourse, to be purely descriptive. It carried a negative connotation. Like slavery, dictatorship, and discrimination, it was widely understood to refer to a political practice that, while once common and acceptable, had come to be seen as an odious exercise in wrongful subordination. Two of the most powerful ideologies of the twentieth century, nationalism and Marxism, defined their respective historical missions as prominently including the defeat and abolition of imperialism.[11] To call the American role in the world imperial was, for many who did so, a way of asserting that the United States was misusing its power beyond its borders and, in so doing, subverting its founding political principles within them.

The use of the term "empire" to describe the American role in the world in the twenty-first century, whatever its advantages, has one major shortcoming: It is inaccurate. Many criticisms may plausibly be leveled at the United States for the way it conducts its foreign policy, but the charge that that policy is essentially an imperial one is not among them.

Empires are "relationships of political control imposed by some political societies over the effective sovereignty of other political societies."[12] Over the centuries the many empires that have risen and fallen all have shared three features. One is subordination: Every empire is an unequal relationship, with one party superior, the other inferior.[13] The second is coercion. Whereas most empires have involved cooperation, sometimes extensive cooperation, between the rulers and the ruled, behind the relationship always stood the threat, and sometimes the use, of force by the imperial power to maintain its control. The third defining feature of empire is an ethnic, national, religious, or racial difference—or some combination of them—between the imperial power and the society it controls. Empire is a form of dictatorship, but a particular form: a dictatorship by foreigners.

Like other forms of dictatorship, empire violates a basic norm of political justice—self-government—that commands virtually universal allegiance, at least rhetorically, in the twenty-first century. That is why it has come to be a term of disapproval. But it does not apply to the relations of the United States with other countries, vast and varied though these are.

American influence in the world is certainly considerable, but the United States does not control, directly or indirectly, the politics and economics of other societies, as empires have always done, save for a few special cases that turn out to be the exceptions that prove the rule. Where it has exercised direct control it has sought, as in the Balkans in the 1990s, to share this control with other countries, unlike classical imperial powers.[14] It has also sought to divest itself of this responsibility as quickly as was feasible, as in Haiti in the same decade. By contrast, the empires of history generally tried to perpetuate themselves and often, as in the case of France in both Indochina and Algeria after World War II, invested a great deal of blood and treasure in this effort.

If the twenty-first-century United States is not an empire,

what is it? Words matter, especially words defining complicated political arrangements, because they shape perceptions
of the events of the past, attitudes toward policies being carried out in the present, and expectations about desirable
directions for the future. The use of the term "empire" leads
to erroneous conclusions about the nature and the distribution of the costs and benefits of American foreign policies,
the origins of these policies, and the most important influ-
ences on their future course. There is a word that better con-
veys the realities of all of these. That word is government.
America acts as the world's government.

Government

The term "government," from the Greek for "to steer," is
older than "empire," which derives from the Latin word for
"command." It is more nearly neutral, without the negative
baggage that "empire" has come to carry. It is a more general
concept: Empire is but one of many forms of government.

As a description of America's relations with other countries the word "government" is even more jarring, and may at
first seem even less apt, than "empire." There are, after all,
many governments in the world and the global role of the
United States, expansive though it is, does not look much like
any of them.

The reason for this is that government everywhere is
identified with what the world lacks: a state. A state has three
defining properties. It encompasses a formally delineated territory. It employs specialized personnel, usually bureaucrats
and soldiers. And it is recognized as independent on its territory; that is, it is sovereign.[15] Government is the instrument
of the state, established by and acting on behalf of it. Govern-

ment is what the state's specialized personnel do within its territory—and sometimes outside it.

States do not necessarily last forever—the Soviet Union and Yugoslavia disappeared in the last decade of the twentieth century—but they have proven more durable than particular configurations of government. Five different republics and two empires have governed France since the revolution of the late eighteenth century, but the French state has endured.

States are not only durable, they are ubiquitous. Every member of the United Nations is a sovereign state. Every inhabitant of the Earth belongs to one or another of its almost 200 states. World history is by and large the collective and individual histories of the world's sovereign states. But there is no single overarching world state of which world government could be the instrument. The UN is the trade association of the world's states, not an entity that governs them.

Government may also be understood, however, as a provider of services for a society. A society is a collection of interconnected yet independent units that are in regular contact with one another. By this definition the world's sovereign states qualify as a society, for they, like the human inhabitants of societies, interact regularly. The society of states, like societies of individuals, requires services. Economists refer to the kind of service that societies need and that governments provide as public goods. The United States furnishes them to the society of sovereign states.

A public good is something that, once it is provided to a group, cannot be denied to any member of that group. National defense is one example; clean air is another. When a military defends a country's borders, it protects everyone who lives within them; when air is clean, everyone gets the benefits of breathing it.

The most basic of all public goods is personal safety. Governments are able to provide public safety because they have a monopoly of force. That monopoly is crucial for the supply of other public goods as well: Public goods are costly, and a government, because of its monopoly, can force people to pay for them.

Without the government doing so, no one has any incentive to contribute to the cost of a public good because no one can be excluded from receiving its benefits. Once the air is clean, anybody can breathe it whether or not he or she has contributed to the cost of purifying it. It is, in purely economic terms, rational to be a "free rider," enjoying the benefit without paying the cost, like the person who sneaks on to a bus without paying a fare. Thus, in the absence of the compulsion that government supplies, no one will voluntarily contribute to cleaning the air and it will remain dirty.

While the provision of public goods depends on the coercive power that government wields within individual states, in the society of sovereign states the United States does *not* have a monopoly of force and does *not* practice the kind of coercion that domestic governments routinely employ. Indeed, it is the absence of this characteristic governmental practice that distinguishes the twenty-first-century United States from the empires of the past. How, then, is the United States able to supply public goods to the world?[16]

It is able to do so because public goods can be supplied even in the absence of an authority to compel payment from the benefiting group when one of the group's members is large enough, wealthy enough, and, most importantly, has a great enough stake in the public good in question to pay its entire cost.[17] For example, the owner of a large, expensive, lavishly-furnished mansion surrounded by more modest homes may pay to have security guards patrolling his street, and their presence will serve to protect the neighboring houses as well, even though their owners contribute nothing to the cost of the guards. That is what the United States does in the world of the twenty-first century. It is in this sense that the United States functions as the world's government.[18]

Like the creation and maintenance of empires throughout history, the provision of international public goods by the United States is not an act of altruism. Self-interest motivates the world's strongest power to undertake its twenty-first-century global tasks, just as self-interest lay behind the expansion of Roman, Habsburg, and British imperial power. But in other ways the American global role differs dramatically from—indeed is the opposite of—imperial rule.

Empire stands condemned in the twenty-first century because it has always rested on an imbalance of power between the ruling and the ruled societies. Inequality of any kind, once considered a normal, natural part of human existence, came to be seen in the course of the twentieth century as increasingly illegitimate. For the provision of international public goods, however, inequality is desirable. Indeed, it is essential. The advantage over all other countries in wealth and power that the United States enjoys, and that those who term it a latter-day empire decry by their use of the term, is the necessary condition for the American role as the world's government.

That role also reverses the distribution of benefits commonly attributed to empire. Traditionally, the imperial power has been seen as a predator, drawing economic profit and political gain from its control of the imperial possession, while the members of the society it controls suffer; or, if they do benefit from the relationship, the ruled gain far less than their imperial masters. In its role as the provider of international public goods, by contrast, it is the United States that pays and the rest of the world that benefits without having to pay.[19] The biblical Goliath served the Philistines but not the people of Israel. The twenty-first-century United States does both. It is not the lion of the international system, terrorizing and preying on smaller, weaker animals in order to survive itself. It is, rather, the elephant, which supports a wide variety of other creatures—smaller mammals, birds, and insects—by generating nourishment for them as it goes about the business of feeding itself.

To understand the United States as the world's government rather than as an empire, finally, suggests a different future for the American international role. Empires vanished because they became too expensive. The cost of imperial rule rose sharply in the twentieth century because the societies that imperial powers governed mobilized to oppose their rule. Internal resistance by the governed raised the cost of controlling them beyond what the metropolitan societies could or would pay.[20]

Whether, and for how long, the United States will remain the world's government is an open question, the answer to which will depend on the willingness of the American public, the ultimate arbiter of American foreign policy, to sustain the costs of this role. Because the rest of the world benefits from the services that the United States provides, however, the world's other major countries are unlikely to act deliberately, as societies under imperial rule did, to raise those costs.

Why has the United States assumed the role of the world's government? America has sufficient power, as no other country does, for this purpose. But the role arises from demand as well as from supply. The world has a greater need for governance in the twenty-first century than ever before, and the developments that increased this need are the same ones that shaped the modern history of government within sovereign states.

Society

Over the course of history, and at a steadily accelerating pace in the nineteenth and twentieth centuries, governments within societies expanded both their scope and their areas of competence. They took on an increasing number of tasks, which they discharged with ever greater effectiveness. Thus, both the demand for and the supply of government services within states grew, and the principal force underlying their growth was the same: technological change. People became ever more closely connected to one another through the extraordinary improvements in transportation and communication that the Industrial Revolution brought to the world. The avenues of contact among people grew wider, and the traffic along them increased exponentially in volume.

With these changes the traditional tasks of government became more urgent, complicated, and expensive, and new ones appeared as well. The government's original task, keeping order, became more difficult. Growing numbers of people lived closer and closer together in cities, creating increased threats to public order. The apparatus for safeguarding public tranquillity—a police force and judicial and penal systems—therefore expanded in size, strength, and reach virtually everywhere.

To the task of assuring public safety governments added economic responsibilities. Markets cannot function unless those who participate in them are confident that their property will be protected and the contracts into which they have entered will be honored. Government provides that assurance by serving as an instrument of enforcement. As markets expanded, as exchanges increasingly involved people who did not meet face to face, and as transactions spanned weeks, months, and even years, the government's role grew in scope and importance.

The Industrial Revolution also gave rise to new economic roles for governments, roles that went beyond the enforcement of contracts to regulate economic activity, developing specialized agencies and complicated sets of rules for this purpose. Governments assumed responsibility for coping with the consequences of industrial activity that affect all members of society but that no one has a sufficient incentive to address privately, such as air pollution. Many of the public goods that governments provide are supplied in response to such consequences. Governments also undertook to provide a social safety net: old-age pensions, medical care, and compensation for people unable to work regularly.

The revolutions in transportation and communication had the same impact on the global society of sovereign states that they had on national societies: Global society, too, came to require more services. Interactions among sovereign states, like those that take place within them, can be divided into two broad categories: conflict, of which the most significant international variety is war; and cooperation, above all economic cooperation, of which the oldest form is trade. Both evolved in ways that expanded the need for global governance.

Societies, like individuals, require security. Order is desirable internationally just as it is domestically. Throughout history, relations among sovereign states have, of course, included a characteristic and recurrent form of disorder. For most of recorded history, war was a common and legitimate instrument of statecraft. But the inventions of the Industrial Revolution, when applied to warfare, raised its costs far beyond what was acceptable or even tolerable. The industrial conflict that was waged in the two world wars of the twentieth century, with its tanks, mechanized artillery, and fighter and bomber aircraft, caused death, destruction, and social dislocation on a far larger scale than ever before.

At the end of World War II, American and British scientists harnessed, for military purposes, the energy locked in the heart—the nucleus—of matter. Two atomic bombs, with explosive power equal to tens of thousands of tons of TNT, crushed the Japanese cities of Hiroshima and Nagasaki in August 1945. Over the next four and one half decades, the United States and the Soviet Union acquired thousands of nuclear explosives, most of them far more powerful than the first two. Other countries also equipped themselves with nuclear arsenals. During the second half of the twentieth century, it came to seem a matter of the utmost importance to keep a war among the strongest countries, like World Wars I and II, and a nuclear war of any kind, from occurring. Not coincidentally, the security policies of the United States at the outset of the twenty-first century were designed to prevent either from occurring.

Economic activity across borders, like war, has taken place for millennia, but like the techniques of combat that made warfare widely unacceptable, a truly global economy requiring governmental services on a global scale did not emerge until the modern era. When such an economy first came into existence in the nineteenth century, during the first age of globalization, Great Britain supplied both the confidence required for transactions to proceed across borders and the mechanism of payment for those transactions. The British navy patrolled the sea lanes along which much of the world's commerce passed. The British-supported gold standard provided the financial underpinnings of this commerce. In the second half of the twentieth century, the United States succeeded Britain, assuming the responsibility for providing secure geopolitical conditions for trade and playing the leading part in the international monetary system that replaced the gold standard. These American global roles carried over into the twenty-first century.

In the twentieth century, governments within societies took on an additional economic obligation. The Great Depression of the 1930s demonstrated the need to sustain an appropriate level of demand for what the workforce produced in order to maintain the economic health of industrial societies. The experience of the Depression, and the interpretation of its causes by the English economist John Maynard Keynes, led to the widely shared Western conviction that governments should contribute to keeping demand at a sufficiently high level. The provision of consumption—supplying, so to speak, demand—became yet another service for which governments assumed responsibility. The global economy similarly requires the maintenance of demand, and in the twenty-first century it is the United States that does far more than any other country to supply it.

For the sake of global order and prosperity, therefore, the United States has come to perform for the society of sovereign states some of the tasks that governments carry out within them. To be sure, the American global role is not as large, intrusive, or ambitious as government's is within states. A government's responsibility for keeping order extends throughout the society: The police monitor, at least in theory, every type of violation from jaywalking to murder. By contrast, the United States does not attempt to keep order throughout the entire international system, avoiding many pockets of disorder entirely and concentrating instead on a limited but extremely important set of problems.

Similarly, governments in the twentieth century took it upon themselves to protect and promote the well-being of individual citizens. They turned into mechanisms for redistributing some of society's output from taxpayers to beneficiaries. The pensions, health care, and unemployment compensation that they provide have become far more expensive than the cost of keeping order.

The United States does not provide comparable services to the other members of the society of sovereign states. The American government, and governments of other wealthy countries, do transfer money, in the form of foreign aid, to poorer countries, but on a far smaller scale than the transfers within their own countries. Neither the United States nor any other country or agency redistributes the world's wealth on a large scale from the rich to the poor, or from the young to the old, or from the fortunate to the unlucky, as governments within societies do. There is no global social safety net—nor is there a substantial constituency within the United States for providing one.

The ongoing processes of technological change set in motion by the Industrial Revolution created an ever greater demand for global governance. These same processes, in combination with the features of American life that made it possible to take advantage of them—a large, resource-rich continent available for settlement as well as political and economic systems that attracted immigrants and rewarded enterprise and industry—made the United States the logical candidate to provide it.

The fact that the United States is the country best placed

to provide the world with government-like services does not, however, in and of itself account for the American role as the world's government. American power is a necessary but not a sufficient condition. No iron law of history or immutable tendency in international society impels the strongest member of the international system to supply it with public goods.[21]

How then did the United States come to act as the world's government? The answer to that question is an historical one. The twenty-first-century role of the United States evolved from a set of tasks undertaken, beginning at the end of World War II, for a specific purpose. The long-term trends that the Industrial Revolution brought to the world made it possible for the United States to take up these tasks, but it was a particular kind of event that persuaded Americans that it was necessary for their country to do so. Here the history of global governance follows the pattern of government within states. Rather than growing at a slow, steady pace, each experienced moments of rapid expansion, in both cases brought on by the same event: war.

History

Throughout history, governments have grown larger and more powerful in order to meet the needs of warfare. Waging war requires recruiting, training, equipping, and paying soldiers, historically on an ever larger scale and at increasing expense. To defend and expand their domains, governments have increased the size of their bureaucracies, expanded the reach of their powers, and raised the proportion of the society's wealth they have commanded.[22] "War made the state," goes a saying about the rise of the great powers of Europe, "and the state made war."

This was true of the United States as well. The American government relies for the revenues that fund its many activities on the income tax. That tax originated as a method of financing the Civil War, was discontinued when that war ended but was revived, for the same purpose, during World War I and has remained in place ever since.[23] War also gave rise to the policies that formed the basis for the twenty-first-century American role as the world's government. They were begun in response to two wars in particular: World War II and the Cold War.

World War II was the single most destructive war ever fought. It had a profound impact on the Americans who lived through it. In its wake, they, like others who experienced it, were determined to do whatever was necessary to avoid another such conflict. This meant avoiding the mistakes that had paved the way for it, of which two in particular seemed especially damaging: the series of economic policies that had allowed the Great Depression to take place, and the sequence of concessions to Hitler's Germany in the 1930s known as appeasement.

In the aftermath of World War II, understanding and avoiding the missteps that had produced it became an urgent matter, for the United States found itself confronting another powerful, dangerous adversary. Between 1945 and 1950, the American wartime partnership with the Soviet Union was transformed into a global rivalry. Americans came to see Stalin and the country he ruled as following in the footsteps of Hitler and Nazi Germany, bent on conquest, domination, and the imposition of their political and economic systems wherever possible. Like Nazi Germany, the Soviet Union came to be seen as a mortal threat to the United States, its friends, and its political values.

The American government consequently adopted policies

and helped to build institutions designed to meet that threat by incorporating the perceived lessons of World War II.[24] Those policies and institutions cohered into two international orders, one involving security, the other economics.

While other countries—and their numbers grew over the course of the second half of the twentieth century—affiliated themselves with these orders, the United States assumed the principal responsibility for designing, organizing, and maintaining them. A German word aptly describes the American role: *ordnungsmacht*—order-maker. These security and economic orders, with modifications that accumulated over six decades, endured into the twenty-first century and form the bases of the global American role. What began as emergency measures to fortify its coalition partners in the Cold War became, over time, services that the United States provided to the world as a whole.

The economic order took shape even before World War II ended, at a 1944 Anglo-American conference in Bretton Woods, New Hampshire. The goal of the arrangements that emerged from that conference and other meetings after the war's end was to avoid what Americans and others had identified as the great economic blunder of the interwar period, the retreat from liberal (meaning free of government control) economic practices, especially fixed monetary exchange rates and free trade, a retreat that had made the economic downturn of the 1930s unprecedentedly severe.

The Bretton Woods monetary system established stable exchange rates and created an organization—the International Monetary Fund (IMF)—to help keep them stable. For trade, the General Agreement on Tariffs and Trade—the GATT—came into existence. Its main precept was that international commerce should not be subject to barriers set up by countries to protect their home markets, a principle central also to the GATT's post–Cold War successor, the World Trade Organization (WTO).

Economic activity is important even in the absence of international conflict, of course, but the advent of the Cold War made these arrangements seem particularly important in American eyes. The highest priority of American foreign policy in the early years of that conflict was to strengthen the economies of Western Europe—a purpose that American economic policies and the new international economic institutions were designed to serve—lest economic failure incubate pro-Communist sentiment in Europe. Economically successful countries, Americans further believed, would make more robust and reliable allies in the struggle against the Soviet Union.

More the creation of the United States than of any other single country, the new liberal international economic order enjoyed active American sponsorship. Washington coaxed and cajoled others to follow its rules. American economic assistance to Europe to help with the recovery from the devastation of war, including the multi-billion dollar Marshall Plan, came with conditions designed to encourage liberal economic practices as well as the kind of international economic cooperation that ultimately produced the European Union (EU). And the smooth functioning of the post–World War II economic order depended heavily on the participation of the United States. The American dollar stood at the center of the international monetary system that emerged from the Bretton Woods conference. Access to the American market, by far the largest and richest in the world, made it possible for other countries to begin to export again and for world trade therefore to resume and flourish.

The American-centered international economic order changed during the decades of the Cold War. The Bretton Woods system collapsed in 1971, but the dollar remained central to the world's economic transactions. A series of multilateral negotiations spearheaded by the United States reduced barriers to trade around the world. Over the decades the number of countries subscribing to liberal economic principles and belonging to the institutions that embodied them expanded. By the outset of the twenty-first century, in fact, both had become all but universal.[25]

Unlike the economic order, the need for a security order with the United States at its center was initially unforeseen. It took shape later than the economic arrangements that emerged from World War II, in response to what came to be seen as a severe threat from the Soviet Union and international communism. The security order was designed to avoid the mistakes that the democracies had made in dealing with Nazi Germany. They had conceded one after another of Hitler's demands, believing—or hoping—that each concession would satisfy him and thus avoid war. Instead, appeasement whetted his appetite for further conquest and the democracies eventually had to fight, but in less advantageous circumstances than if they had resisted earlier.

As a result of this experience, the Western powers were determined to confront the Soviet Union immediately and firmly. They carried out a policy of deterrence—prevention by threat—which had two components. A large multinational army with a major contingent from the United States and with an American commander was deployed along the dividing line between East and West, the middle of divided Germany, to deter an attack westward by the even larger army the Soviet Union and the Communist countries of Eastern

Europe assembled. Simultaneously, the United States built up its arsenal of nuclear weapons and successfully sought to deter a Soviet nuclear attack by threatening a devastating nuclear salvo in retaliation.

As with the economic order, the security order rested on several major institutions. The Western army in Europe was assembled under the auspices of the North Atlantic Treaty Organization (NATO), which brought together the United States and the Western European democracies in common cause against the Soviet Union and served as the instrument of deterrence in Europe. In East Asia, the Japanese-American Security Treaty served the same purpose. The United States deployed military forces in Europe and East Asia (and elsewhere as well,[26] notably, toward the end of the Cold War, in the Middle East) and these, along with the American nuclear arsenal, provided the muscle behind the policy of deterrence.

Over the decades of the Cold War, the architecture of the security order did not change as much as the design of the economic order did, because the circumstances that had called it into existence persisted. Europe remained divided, the political goals of the two military and political blocs remained incompatible, and the two large armies remained in place, facing each other. In the course of the Cold War, the United States did undertake two additional security tasks, and both increased in importance when that conflict came to an end.

One of them, reassurance, had been implicit from the outset. The founding purpose of what became NATO, before it assumed its anti-Soviet mission, was safeguarding Western Europe against the possibility of a resurgent Germany, something that, in view of the three wars Germany had fought between 1870 and 1914, did not seem, as World War II ended, an unlikely prospect. West Germany eventually joined

NATO, and its membership in an American-led alliance reassured its neighbors that the Germans would not embark on yet another campaign of aggression. Throughout the Cold War, NATO practiced "double containment," keeping its adversary, the Soviet Union, at arm's length and its ally, the German Federal Republic, locked in a friendly but also binding embrace. The Japanese-American Security Treaty similarly reassured Japan's neighbors, which, like Germany's, had been its victims in World War II, that they no longer had cause to fear Japanese aggression.

The other security task that the United States undertook during the course of the Cold War was preventing the acquisition of nuclear weapons by countries that did not already possess them. The effort to stem nuclear proliferation did not achieve complete success: A number of countries did acquire these armaments. But the atomic bomb spread less far and less rapidly than might otherwise have been the case, and the effort to keep it from spreading seemed important enough and feasible enough to justify investing the time and resources of the American government in the effort.

The international tasks that the United States undertook during the Cold War for the purpose of avoiding another ruinous armed conflict survived the end of the rivalry with the Soviet Union—and the end of the Soviet Union itself—and persisted into the twenty-first century. One reason for this was the character of the Cold War. It lasted so long that it came to define what was normal for international relations and American foreign policy. World Wars I and II had interrupted the routines of the countries that took part in them. The Cold War did not interrupt national routines: It established them.

When the two world wars ended, the belligerent countries demobilized. The enormous armed forces they had raised disbanded and the proportions of their national outputs devoted to military purposes fell sharply.[27] But the United States did not have to mobilize to the same extent during the Cold War. The defense burden, even when the country was engaged in shooting wars in Korea and Vietnam, did not exceed 10 percent of the Gross Domestic Product, and usually amounted to 6 to 7 percent of it. In further contrast to World War II, only a small fraction of the population served in the military and worked in defense industries during the Cold War.

The need for the international economic order, of which the United States continued to be the mainstay, persisted: Economic activity carries on in wartime and peacetime alike. In fact, the economic tasks for which the United States had assumed responsibility became, if anything, even more important after the Cold War because the formerly Communist countries sought to join the American-centered international economic order. The success of that order, and the attraction it consequently came to hold for countries outside it, had made a substantial contribution to the collapse of communism in Europe, which put an end to the Cold War.[28]

Like the economic order, the security order that the United States had taken the lead in constructing and maintaining persisted, in modified form, into the twenty-first century. This was a less predictable development than the continuation of the Cold War's economic arrangements. After all, the principal reason for the security order disappeared with the collapse of the Soviet Union. The need for the secondary responsibilities that the United States had assumed remained, however. Indeed, the demand for these particular services increased. More countries sought the kind of reassurance about their neighbors that an American military presence provided. And nuclear weapons in the hands of governments deemed aggressive, or unreliable, or both, emerged as perhaps the greatest threat to American and global security in the twenty-first century.

Still, the habit-forming character of Cold War policies and the continuing demand for American services in the international system do not fully explain the persistence, in the absence of a mortal threat to the United States, of policies created and sustained for the purpose of coping with such a threat. The fact that the Cold War lasted for almost half a century did not entirely erase the distinction, for Americans, between wartime and peacetime. While the country did not mobilize as extensively between the late 1940s and the early 1990s as it had during the first and especially the second world wars, it did spend an appreciable part of its national wealth on policies beyond its borders that seemed necessary for its own safety and that, after the Cold War ended, could not be fully justified on that ground. The American public wished to spend less on international pursuits, especially defense, after the Cold War, and the government did in fact cut the defense budget, as a percentage of annual output, in half.[29] Yet even in domestic circumstances less favorable to it, the United States continued to sustain its role as the world's government. It did so in part because that role became appreciably less costly. What made it so was the kind of world that emerged from the end of the Cold War.

Consensus

The world of the twenty-first century is marked by a broad and unprecedented consensus in favor of three great ideas:

peace as the optimal condition of international relations and the proper aim of foreign policy; democracy as the best form of government; and the free market as the only satisfactory way of organizing economic affairs.[30]

To be sure, the three were not firmly embedded and faithfully practiced in every corner of the planet. Determined, active opposition to all three ideas did exist, as the attacks by Islamic fundamentalist terrorists on New York City and Washington, D.C., on September 11, 2001, demonstrated. Even when not explicitly opposed to these ideas, not all countries had genuinely democratic governments or successful free market economies. Russia and China in particular, which for much of the twentieth century had been ruled by an ideology opposed in principle to all three, had abandoned orthodox communism but had not fully and unreservedly embraced peace, democracy, and free markets.

Nor had the world become entirely peaceful—far from it. But the most powerful countries in the world did endorse and practice these three ideas. What was equally significant for their global supremacy, no alternative ideas qualified as plausible bases for the organization of political and economic life. Asked where in Paris he would most like to live, a French architect is said to have replied the Eiffel Tower, on the grounds that this was the only place in the city from which he would not have to look at it.[31] Peace, democracy, and free markets are for the world of the twenty-first century what the Eiffel Tower is for Paris: towering, dominant, not universally loved but impossible to ignore and without any serious rival.

Their dominance was a result of the course of world history in the modern era, the period that began politically with the French Revolution and economically with the Industrial Revolution, in which those three ideas were first introduced as the basis for organized social life. In the first two centuries of that era, the nineteenth and twentieth, a struggle took place between those ideas and alternative methods of social organization.

The nineteenth century pitted them against the traditional way of life, according to which war was normal, power rested in the hands of monarchs who had inherited it, and economic life was, as it had always been, stagnant. The forces of tradition lost ground steadily in the nineteenth century and were swept away by the defining event of the twentieth century, World War I, but in their place, in opposition to peace, democracy, and free markets, there arose communism and fascism. Although different in important ways, both these ideologies glorified war, imposed oppressive government by a self-selected elite, and practiced extensive—in the communist case almost total—government control of economic life. Fascism was defeated in World War II and communism in the Cold War, leaving democracy and free markets, for the first time, without serious rivals.

As for war, along with the decline of communism in the second half of the twentieth century there occurred for the first time the rise of a principled aversion to this age-old practice. The sentiment of "warlessness" put down deep roots only in the Western democracies. But many other countries where it had not taken firm hold, notably Russia and China, if not rejecting in principle armed conflict as a technique of international relations, did place far greater emphasis on domestic pursuits and less on ambitions beyond their borders—in the Russian and Chinese cases far less than during their days as Communist powers. In general, and in conjunction with their common embrace of free markets, Russia and China devoted themselves to becoming rich at home, not powerful abroad.[32]

At the outset of the twenty-first century, the qualified global consensus in favor of peace, democracy, and free markets buttressed the American role as the world's government by keeping down the costs of playing that role. While the dominance of these ideas owed a great deal to the power of the United States, which embraced and espoused them, the reverse was also true: American power rested in no small part on the dominance of these ideas. Here the contrast with empire is particularly instructive.

In the twentieth century, empires disappeared because, among other reasons, the subjects of imperial rule resisted them, raising their price beyond what the imperial power was willing, or able, to pay. Although the United States does not, with a few exceptions, rule other countries, it does have a considerable presence beyond its own borders. But this presence is to a great extent economic in character and so, because of the dominance of free markets and in contrast to imperial rule, is almost entirely welcome.

Classical imperial powers generally sought to maximize the territory they controlled. Their rivals and potential victims did their best to prevent this. The most powerful and ambitious powers inspired the formation of coalitions of other countries to check them. This was the fate of Napoleonic France in the nineteenth century and Wilhelmine and Nazi Germany and the Soviet Union in the twentieth. But because the United States does not seek conquest, and because other important countries in the international system do not fear that it will, no such countervailing coalition, which would raise the costs of the American international presence, has been formed. To be sure, others have not offered universal support for American foreign policies. Some of these policies have aroused fierce criticism, but they have not evoked active opposition of the kind that great powers with an expansive international agenda normally encountered in the past.

Such powers sometimes fell victim to a self-liquidating syndrome that the historian Paul Kennedy has called "imperial overstretch." Their activities beyond their borders grew so expensive, and at the same time, because these foreign commitments diverted resources from investments to raise output at home, so reduced their economic capacities, that they were unable to sustain their international roles.[33]

The twenty-first-century United States is not necessarily immune to this syndrome, but the global consensus in favor of peace, democracy, and free markets mitigates its effects by removing potential sources of principled, active, effective opposition to America's global role. In this way the dominance of these three ideas functions as a kind of subsidy for the international services that the United States renders; and for this there is an historical parallel of sorts.

In the nineteenth century, Great Britain was able to maintain and expand its overseas empire, which was by far the world's largest, because the other European powers did not muster effective opposition to it. They did not threaten the British Empire because they were preoccupied with checking one another's ambitions on the European continent. In this way the continental balance of power subsidized the British Empire. Similarly, at the outset of the twenty-first century, the expansive American global role has produced no serious opposition from the most capable members of the international system because the shared commitment to peace, democracy, and free markets has both concentrated their attention on internal matters and made the American role seem, if not entirely benign, at least not threatening enough to be worth the cost of the active opposition that they certainly could have mounted had they chosen to do so.

The global consensus in favor of these three ideas is responsible for the way in which the American governmental role in the world comes closest to the normal functioning of governments within sovereign states. Although there is no world state, those parts of the world where these three ideas are most solidly entrenched do collectively resemble, in two particular ways, the most orderly and best governed members of the community of sovereign states—the Western democracies and Japan.

The first point of similarity between the community of democracies and individual democratic countries is that, because of the dominion of these three ideas, within both there is broad agreement on fundamental matters. This is not to say that disagreement is unknown. To the contrary, among the democracies as well as within them sharp and often bitter disputes are common. Democracy does not, after all, offer a formula for perfect and eternal agreement. It is rather a method for expressing, mediating, and resolving disagreement. In stable democracies, discord concerns secondary, not fundamental, questions. The form of government, the location of the state's borders, and the definition of its citizenship are settled.

The second way in which the broad allegiance to peace, democracy, and free markets causes the international community, or at least part of it, to resemble some of the sovereign states that comprise it, is that disputes within that community, however sharp, do not lead to armed conflict. War among the democracies, in the first decade of the twenty-first century, had become as unlikely—indeed as unthinkable—as civil war within any one of them.

These two statelike features of the community of the world's democracies were on vivid display during the 2003 war with Iraq. That war divided the democracies sharply, even bitterly, but the division concerned means, not ends. None believed that Saddam Hussein's regime ought to possess weapons of mass destruction. They disagreed about whether and when war should be waged to achieve that goal. Nor was there ever the slightest chance that the disagreement about the war in Iraq would lead to war between and among the democracies.

Of the three dominant twenty-first century ideas, free markets were more widely embraced and practiced than peace or democracy. So popular had this method of organizing economic life become that it was perhaps the most widely accepted cultural institution in all of human history. The American international efforts to promote free markets, therefore, while not without difficulties, moved very much in the direction of one of history's most powerful tides.

Peace and democracy, by contrast, although without powerful, principled opposition—no major country touted the universal validity of undemocratic politics or advocated war, as had been the case in the nineteenth and twentieth centuries—had less universal currency. They proved more difficult to establish than free markets, and as a result, American international efforts on their behalf at the outset of the twenty-first century were taxing, controversial, and not always successful.

Chapter Two

INTERNATIONAL SECURITY

A policeman's lot is not a happy one.

W. S. GILBERT, *The Pirates of Penzance*

Reassurance

During the Cold War, the United States deployed major military forces in Europe and East Asia, the two regions where World War II had been chiefly fought and where, Americans believed, without the presence of those forces yet another bloody, destructive conflict would erupt. The purpose of those deployments was deterrence: the prevention, through the promise to repulse and retaliate against it, of the campaign of aggression and conquest that, in the absence of American military forces, the Soviet Union and China would be powerfully tempted to launch.

These deployments followed from the lesson that American leaders had learned from World War II: the need to deter aggressors before they could attack. The Western democracies had delayed in mobilizing to confront fascism until it was too late to prevent a costly war. After that war, American leaders were determined to avoid making the same mistake with the other branch of twentieth-century totalitarianism, communism. By putting in place the forces necessary to wage World War III, they sought to avoid having to do so, and they achieved their goal. In the last decade of the twentieth century, the circumstances that had made the maintenance of a military presence in Europe seem imperative disappeared entirely, and without a shot being fired.

The dramatic post–Cold War transformation of the international relations of Europe stemmed from three interlocking, overlapping, and, in geopolitical terms, revolutionary developments: a great political upheaval, a long-term change in attitudes toward armed conflict, and a series of negotiated accords covering armies and weapons.

Changes within the Communist bloc led first to the end of the Cold War, as the Soviet Union withdrew from the European countries it had dominated since 1945 and their Soviet-imposed governments fell from power, and then, in 1991, to the end of communism in Europe and of the Soviet Union itself. Unlike in previous great wars, the victorious countries of the West had no interest in capitalizing on the collapse of their adversary. Contrary to what had been normal in relations between and among the sovereign states of Europe for centuries, the winners did not seek to expand the territory they controlled and their citizens increasingly believed that war for any purpose other than self-defense was politically irrational and morally unacceptable.[1]

The end of the aggressive ideology of communism in Eastern Europe and the growing sentiment of warlessness in the West underpinned a series of negotiated agreements that reconfigured armed forces throughout the continent according to two principles: Those armed forces became suitable for defending their own countries but not for attacking others; and each country was aware at all times of just how large the forces of all the others were and what the other governments were doing with those forces. The first principle, "defense dominance," made launching an attack highly problematic. The second, "transparency," gave each country confidence in the sturdiness of the first principle.

The "common security order" that defense dominance and transparency created, and the aversion to war that underlies it, converted what had been for five centuries the cockpit of international politics, the place where the most devastating battles had been fought, into an oasis of tranquillity. Yet while Europe had become, by the beginning of the twenty-first century, a place where war was all but unthinkable, American armed forces remained on station there. Why was this so?

The force of habit partly accounts for American military forces outstaying the circumstances that brought them to Europe in the first place. Moreover, the bases for these forces continued to be useful for launching military operations in nearby regions where wars still were fought—the Middle East, above all. But American armed forces also remained in Europe, albeit in substantially reduced numbers,[2] because they assumed a new role, one that contributed to the transformation of the continent from the center of great-power rivalry into a zone of peace. The American military deployments at the outset of the twenty-first century provided reassurance to the governments and the people of Europe.

Reassurance involves instilling confidence in countries so that they can conduct their domestic affairs and foreign policies without feeling intimidated.[3] The same American military forces that had once deterred the Soviet Union reassured all Europeans by serving as a buffer between and among countries that, while at peace with one another, harbored suspicions that their neighbors might be tempted to launch dangerous policies if circumstances changed. The American armed forces reassured one and all that no sudden shifts in Europe's security arrangements would occur.

Reassurance had a precedent in the Cold War period. Then, Western Europe's security organization, the North Atlantic Treaty Organization (NATO), had, in the words of its first secretary-general, Lord Ismay of Great Britain, three purposes: "to keep the Americans in, the Russians out, and the Germans down." The third purpose reassured the other countries of Western Europe, which were Germany's allies but had recently been its adversaries and victims, that, because they were closely tied to the United States, the Germans would not threaten them again.

Reassurance ensures against what *might* happen, and the need for it arises from the structure of the system of sovereign states. Because no superior power controls relations among them, an attack by one against another is always possible. Governments therefore tend to take steps to prepare to defend themselves. In foreign policy, wariness, suspicion, and preventive measures are the norm. But military preparations that one country undertakes for purely defensive reasons can appear threatening to others, which may then take military measures of their own and so set in motion a spiral of mistrust and military buildups.

The American military presence in Europe acts as a barrier against such an undesirable chain of events. It reassures the Western Europeans that they do not have to increase their armed forces to protect themselves against the possibility of a resurgent Russia. American forces can protect them if this should become necessary. At the same time, the American presence reassures Russia that its great adversary of the first half of the twentieth century, Germany, will not adopt policies of the kind that led to two destructive German invasions in 1914 and 1941.[4] The troops, tanks, and planes that the United States keeps in Europe, that is, provide the Europeans with a hedge against the kind of uncertainty about the security arrangements of the continent that could set in motion a series of events that would make all the countries there less secure.

No one wants a war in Europe, and the contribution that the United States makes to preventing one—or, more properly, to preventing the advent of circumstances in which war in Europe would once again loom as a possibility—is similar to the services that governments provide within sovereign states. Here reassurance differs from the deterrence of the Cold War era, which was not undertaken for the benefit of all Europeans. Although the effect of deterrence was to prevent war, its primary purpose was to forestall the Soviet Union and the Communist bloc from achieving the domination of the entire continent.[5] American deterrence thereby conferred a benefit—freedom—on some Europeans (those in NATO) at the expense of others (Communist officials) who desired to revoke it. In the wake of the Cold War, however, like the services of governments within states, all the countries of Europe approved of—or at least did not actively oppose—what American forces were doing there, as the Soviet Union certainly had opposed America's European policy during the Cold War.

With the end of communism and the spread of the sentiment of warlessness, war came to be seen not as a plausible, if increasingly expensive, instrument of policy but rather as a disaster for everyone concerned, to be avoided at all costs. It acquired the same status as an infectious disease, and by providing reassurance to all Europeans, which inoculated the continent against such a war, the United States functioned as the equivalent of something that domestic governments supply: a public health service.

A major war in Europe would have disastrous consequences not only for the people of the continent but for the entire world. The contribution the American military forces stationed there make to preventing such a conflict therefore has some claim to being the most important service the United States provides to the world. Yet it is scarcely recognized or even mentioned, let alone fully appreciated. For this there are several reasons.

Reassurance arises from the suspicion that countries and governments that conduct peaceful, cordial relations with others might, under certain circumstances, turn out to be the international equivalents of burglars or muggers. It is indiscreet and impolite to say such things about friends and neighbors and so European governments do not say them, at least not publicly. Moreover, the American-provided service of reassurance, while important, is also invisible, in three distinct ways.

First, the American forces that carry out this mission do not actually do anything: They simply stand by. The filmmaker Woody Allen once observed that "90 percent of life is showing up." For reassurance the proportion is 10 percent higher. This was the case as well when the American military mission in Europe was deterrence; but then a large, powerful Communist army confronted the Western forces across the line of division in Europe. It was clear what was being deterred.

Second, with the end of the Cold War the purpose of deploying American forces changed, but the forces serving this new purpose did not. The American military presence in Europe in this sense resembles a building that once housed offices that were then converted to apartments without changing the building's outward appearance.

Finally, the achievement of reassurance is measured by what does *not* happen. To the extent that the subject of security in Europe, once the object of intense attention, remains uneventful and uninteresting, American armed forces are successfully carrying out their mission. But it is what is eventful that gets noticed. The great basketball player Bill Russell helped his team win many championships through his prowess at blocking the shots of opposing players. What contributed most to his teams' successes, however, was not the shots he blocked but those that the other teams did not dare to take for fear that they would be blocked. So it was and is with the reassurance that American armed forces provide in Europe. Their contribution to the peace of the continent, and to the welfare of all Europeans, is properly counted not simply in what the historically warlike countries of Europe now do not do, but also in what, partly because of this American role, they do not even *think* of doing.

During the Cold War, the United States also kept armed forces in the other part of the world in which major war has been and might be fought, East Asia. The American forces were stationed there, too, for the purpose of deterrence. In this case the threat came from two large Communist powers, the People's Republic of China as well as the Soviet Union. As with NATO in Europe, in East Asia a treaty provided the framework for the American presence—the Japanese-American Security Treaty, signed in 1950. But the American military experience in East Asia also differed from the European pattern.

In Asia, the American military deployments for most of the Cold War consisted largely of naval and air forces rather than a land army, since the principal American task was to defend the Japanese archipelago. Still, and unlike in Europe, the United States did fight two substantial wars on the Asian mainland during the first half of the Cold War, in Korea in the 1950s and in Indochina in the 1960s and 1970s.

Political changes affecting the American position in the region came earlier to East Asia than to Europe. China broke with the Soviet Union in the late 1960s and effected a rapprochement with the United States in the early 1970s that led to a measure of military cooperation, if not to a formal alliance. East Asia was therefore a less dangerous region than Europe for the United States in the second half of the Cold War. However, it became a more dangerous one in the wake of that conflict because the political transformation that the end of the global rivalry with communism brought about was less sweeping across the Pacific Ocean from North America than it was on the other side of the Atlantic.

Unlike in Europe, Communists retained power in major East Asian countries, China and Vietnam. Unlike in Europe, a principled aversion to war had not established itself, at the dawn of the twenty-first century, as central to the political cultures of the sovereign states of East Asia, with the notable exception of Japan. Unlike Europe, East Asia was home to political disputes over which countries were ready and willing to go to war: on the Korean peninsula, where a heavily armed, secretive, and fanatically oppressive Communist regime in the North threatened South Korea and the region; and between mainland China and the island of Taiwan, which the Communist government in Beijing claimed as part of its own territory and threatened to attack if it declared itself to be formally what it was in fact—an independent (and, after 1996, unlike the mainland, democratic) country.

The system of common security in Europe, based on the principles of defense dominance and transparency, had not taken hold in East Asia. There, in fact, through its tacit commitment to the defense of Taiwan against an attack from the mainland, the United States continued to practice deterrence.[6] But as in Europe, in East Asia the United States was also in the business of providing reassurance. Both during the Cold War and thereafter, the Japanese-American alliance reassured Japan's neighbors, including China, that it would not resume the campaign of conquest that the United States and its allies had gone to war to reverse between 1941 and 1945.[7] As well as deterrence, the dispute between Taiwan and mainland China gave rise to American reassurance. Deterring the People's Republic reassured the Taiwanese;[8] but while tacitly promising to help preserve the island's de facto independence, the United States insisted that Taiwan not seek to make this status formal and official, thereby reassuring the government of the mainland that it would not suffer a public setback in response to which, it repeatedly declared, it would launch an attack across the Taiwan Strait.

American forces remained in Europe and East Asia because the countries located in these two regions wanted them there, even if they did not always say so clearly or even explicitly. They wanted them there because the American presence offered the assurance that these regions would remain free of war and, in the case of Europe, free of the costly preparations for war that had marked the twentieth century. The American military presence was in both cases a confidence-building measure, and if that presence were withdrawn, the countries in both regions would feel less confident that no threat to their security would appear. They would, in all likelihood, take steps to compensate for the absence of these forces.

Those steps would surely not include war, at least not in the first instance. Instead, since the American forces serve as a hedge against uncertainty, some of the countries of East Asia and Europe might well seek to replace them with another source of hedging. A leading candidate for that role would be nuclear weapons of their own.[9] The possession of nuclear weapons equips their owner with a certain leverage, a geopolitical weight that, unless somehow counterbalanced, can confer a political advantage in dealing with countries lacking them. Like the relationship between employer and employee, the one between a nuclear-weapon state and a non-nuclear-weapon state has inequality built into it, no matter how friendly that relationship may be.

During the Cold War, the American military presence, and the guarantee of protection by the mighty nuclear arsenal of the United States that came with it, neutralized the nuclear weapons that the Soviet Union and the People's Republic of China accumulated. Russia and China retain nuclear stockpiles in the wake of the Cold War, and with the end of the American military presence in their regions, several of their non-nuclear neighbors—Germany, Poland, Japan, South Korea, and Taiwan, for example—might feel the need to offset those stockpiles with nuclear forces of their own.

Perhaps the process of replacing American nuclear armaments with those of other countries, if this should take place, would occur smoothly, with Europe and East Asia remaining peaceful throughout the transition. But this is not what most of the world believes. To the contrary, the spread of nuclear weapons to countries that do not already have them is widely considered to be the single greatest threat to international tranquillity in the twenty-first century. The United States has made the prevention of nuclear proliferation one of its most important foreign policies, and its efforts to this end constitute, like reassurance, a service to the other members of the international system.

Nuclear Nonproliferation

Nuclear weapons have had a revolutionary impact on international politics. Their invention made for a military revolution by vastly expanding the destructive power that their possessors wield. Just one weapon can level a large city in an instant. They have a potentially revolutionary effect on relations among sovereign states as well because they can flatten the hierarchy of the international system. They are the geopolitical equivalents of elevator shoes, making otherwise weak states equal to strong ones in one particular way by giving the weak what they never had before the nuclear age: the power to inflict grave damage on states superior to them in every other index of power. Nuclear weapons can turn Lilliputians into Gullivers.

By the year 2005, the nuclear age was sixty years old. Perhaps the most notable and certainly the most welcome feature of that time span was that, after the two American raids on the Japanese cities of Hiroshima and Nagasaki at the end of World War II, no nuclear shot had been fired in anger. What accounts for the nuclear abstinence of the second half of the twentieth century and beyond?

It was certainly not due to a lack of opportunity. The two great global rivals of the Cold War, the United States and the Soviet Union, accumulated large stockpiles of nuclear armaments, aimed them at each other, and asserted that they were prepared to use those weapons if need be. It was the existence and the size of each nuclear arsenal that kept the other in check, as well as the resilience of both. Each was large enough and well enough protected to survive the most massive blow the other could deliver and still mount a devastating attack in return. Each, that is, had the capacity for the "assured destruction" of the other under any circumstances. So neither side dared to launch a nuclear attack—or an attack of any kind—against its adversary for fear of a crushing counterblow. Each side deterred the other and deterrence kept the peace.

From this it might seem to follow that the antidote to nuclear weapons is more nuclear weapons, and that when one country acquires these armaments the formula for peace requires that its neighbors do so as well. The overwhelming consensus of global opinion, however, which crystallized shortly after nuclear weapons appeared and has strengthened since then, favors the opposite conclusion: Where these weapons are concerned, more are not better; fewer are better. The fewer there are, and above all the fewer the number of countries that have them—that is, the fewer independent centers of nuclear control there are—the safer the world will be.

This conviction rests on the fear that where nuclear weapons are concerned, the members of the international system are prone to herd behavior, so that the acquisition of these armaments by some countries will trigger a frantic rush to follow suit by many others, turning the entire planet into a nuclear-armed camp.[10] Even worse, in a world crowded with nuclear-armed countries, the chances of an actual nuclear war would increase substantially, for several reasons: because the technical conditions that helped keep the peace between the United States and the Soviet Union—assured destruction— would not be reproduced between every pair of rivals; because a political quarrel between two of these nuclear-armed countries could spill over into war that could then become a nuclear war, as almost happened with the Soviet-American rivalry in the October 1962 Cuban missile crisis; and because of the possibility that one or more of the new nuclear-weapon states would come under the control of an individual or group rash, or mad, or evil enough to start a nuclear war.

The global consensus that the spread of nuclear weapons poses a serious threat to the safety and well-being of all members of the international system led to an international agreement designed to prevent it: the Nuclear Nonproliferation Treaty (NPT) of 1968. The NPT has two categories of signatories, which assume different obligations. Those that have nuclear weapons at the time of their accession promise not to help others get them.[11] Those that do not have them promise not to obtain them. The purpose of the treaty is to freeze the nuclear status quo at the lowest number of nuclear-weapon states possible.

Because almost every one of the world's sovereign states adheres to the NPT, the principle that the treaty embodies, nonproliferation, has the status of a global norm, and enforcing that norm is one of the tasks of global governance in the twenty-first century. Here, as with reassurance, the United States plays a central role. It was, along with the Soviet Union, the coauthor of the NPT. The American government took an active part thereafter in coaxing and cajoling other countries to sign it. Once it was in place, moreover, the United States assumed more responsibility than any other country for promoting compliance with its terms. These American efforts count as one of the most important ways in which the United States functions as the world's government.

The world's strongest power has the same motive as all other countries for promoting nuclear nonproliferation: an interest in keeping the world as tranquil as possible and minimizing the prospects for nuclear war. But as the world's strongest power, the United States has an additional reason to try to prevent the spread of nuclear weapons. Because these armaments equalize the otherwise unequal distribution of power in the international system by giving the weak a way of standing up to the strong, the United States has the most to lose from their spread. Every new country with nuclear weapons reduces its margin of superiority over the rest of the world.

Although the NPT symbolizes the global norm of nonproliferation, it is not itself the main cause of that norm: Countries have not disavowed the acquisition of nuclear armaments because they have signed the NPT. Rather, they sign the treaty because they have decided, for other reasons, that they do not wish or need to acquire these weapons. To these other, more formidable barriers against a global stampede to nuclear-weapon status the United States makes a considerable contribution.

Nuclear nonproliferation would seem, on its face, to have the properties of a public good: Everyone wants it but no one wishes to pay for it. Specifically, whereas every country has an interest in a world with as few nuclear-weapon states as possible, each also has an incentive to make itself an exception and join the club of such states.[12] No country is entirely indifferent to the status and power that these weapons confer; and none of the countries that has formally joined the nuclear club since 1945—the United States, Great Britain, the Soviet Union (subsequently Russia), France, China, India, and Pakistan—has found itself visibly worse off in political or military terms for having done so. Why, then, have so few countries chosen to be nuclear-weapon states?

One reason is that making a bomb is neither simple nor cheap. It requires resources and technical expertise that the poorest members of the international system do not have. Another reason is that, because of their enormous, unprecedented destructive power, a taboo has come to be attached to nuclear weapons. Like pork to a Muslim and beef to a high-caste Hindu, they are widely (although certainly not universally) regarded as unclean and to be avoided: Contact with them is considered a political form of ritual pollution.[13] A third reason that nuclear weapons are not more widespread is that their acquisition by one country may prompt a neighbor and actual or potential rival to do the same, leaving the original proliferator no more and perhaps even less secure or powerful.[14] This prospect has surely deterred some would-be proliferators from acquiring such armaments.

Some nuclear-weapon-free countries, however, have neighbors that already possess nuclear armaments and so would seem, whatever their reservations about these armaments, to have strong incentives to counterbalance the neighboring arsenals with nuclear weapons of their own, yet continue to eschew them. They have felt comfortable in these circumstances because the United States has provided them with a nuclear guarantee. By extending its umbrella of nuclear deterrence over their territories, it has, in effect, enlisted its own formidable nuclear arsenal in their defense.

The United States first provided this protection to the countries of Western Europe, including Germany, through NATO, to Japan via the Japanese-American Security Treaty, and to South Korea and Taiwan with bilateral guarantees, during the Cold War, when all of them faced a common challenge from the Soviet Union and other Communist powers. The protection continued after the Cold War ended, as part of the American mission of reassurance.

By contributing in this way to the global public good of nuclear nonproliferation, the United States functions as governments do within sovereign states. American nuclear guarantees help to secure something that all countries want but would probably not get without the United States. The military deployments and political commitments of the United States have reduced the demand for nuclear weapons, and the number of nuclear-armed countries, to levels considerably below what they would otherwise have reached. But American policies have not entirely eliminated the demand for these armaments, and so the ongoing effort to restrict their spread must address the supply of them as well.

In conjunction with the NPT, several international organizations were established to control the materials and the equipment for making nuclear weapons. Since the same physical process—a nuclear chain reaction—that produces a nuclear explosion can be harnessed to generate electric power, and since, in part due to American encouragement in the 1950s through its "Atoms for Peace" program, many countries that forswore nuclear weapons acquired such power plants, the International Atomic Energy Agency (IAEA) was established to monitor these plants to ensure that their nuclear materials were not being diverted to the making of bombs. Similarly, the Nuclear Suppliers Group monitors the dissemination of the equipment that can be used both for power generation and bomb making. The Missile Technology Control Regime keeps watch on, and tries to restrict, the diffusion of the most effective vehicle for delivering nuclear weapons to distant targets—the ballistic missile.

The United States took the lead in establishing and overseeing the work of each of these organizations; and a significant part of the technical and human assets of the American intelligence community was devoted to the surveillance of nuclear-weapons-related activities around the world.[15] These organizations by themselves, however, could not be counted on to shut off completely the circulation of dangerous nuclear materials. A country bent on acquiring nuclear weapons can employ a number of methods of circumventing the rules and institutions designed to prevent this.

A state with sufficient resources, for instance, including a sophisticated cadre of scientists and engineers, can build a bomb unaided, as the United States, and for the most part the Soviet Union, France, and India, managed to do. None of these countries ever signed the NPT as a non-nuclear country. Even for a country that has signed it, moreover, it is possible to make considerable progress toward building a bomb within the confines of the treaty. A signatory may legally acquire the skills, the machinery, and the materials that require only minor modifications to be suitable for a bomb, then declare that it is opting out of the NPT, as it is legally entitled to do with six months' notice. In 2003, North Korea announced that it was withdrawing from the Treaty.

It is also possible for countries that have signed the NPT to cheat. Iran was discovered to have violated its terms, undoubtedly as part of an effort to acquire nuclear weapons in clandestine fashion. Cheaters can get around the barriers to nuclear proliferation through the international black market in nuclear materials, of which Pakistan and North Korea were discovered to be the mainstays.[16] The head of Pakistan's nuclear weapon program, A. Q. Kahn, sold plans and equipment to Iran, Libya, and North Korea. North Korea sold missiles to Iran, negotiated for their sale with Iraq, and transferred fuel for atomic weapons to Libya. In the twenty-first century, therefore, a government with a serious interest in equipping itself with nuclear weapons has, over time, a good chance of achieving this.[17]

For the purposes of American policy, the group of nuclear aspirants divides into two distinct categories, toward which the United States has pursued radically different policies. The nuclear ambitions of one group evoked disapproval but not active, effective opposition from the United States. The American government either lacked the means to prevent the countries in question from acquiring nuclear weapons at anything like an acceptable cost—this was the case with India—or had friendly political relations with them, as it did with India, Pakistan, and Israel (a presumed although not a declared nuclear-weapon state), or calculated that their possession of nuclear armaments would not seriously damage American interests, which was true in varying degrees of all three countries. To the second group none of these considerations applied. These were the "rogues," in whose hands nuclear weapons seemed prospectively dangerous enough to American policymakers to justify energetic efforts, going well beyond the NPT and its affiliated organizations, to prevent.

In his State of the Union address in 2003, President George W. Bush directly confronted the problem of rogue states. He referred to an "axis of evil" consisting of Iraq, Iran, and North Korea. Each of the three had an oppressive, dicta-

torial government that professed a radical anti-Western ideology: a form of Arab nationalism in the case of Iraq, Islamic
fundamentalism in Iran, and a particular (and peculiar) form
of communism in North Korea.[18] The acquisition of nuclear
armaments by any one of them seemed likely to spur their
neighbors, even those to which the United States furnished a
nuclear guarantee, to obtain nuclear weapons of their own,
thereby making East Asia or the Middle East, or both, less
predictable, more dangerous places.

If any of the rogue states were to become declared
nuclear-weapon states, the initial consequence would be to
thrust upon the United States the military mission that it carried out toward the Soviet Union during the Cold War:
deterrence. The purpose would be not only to protect the
rogues' neighbors but also to try to persuade them not to
acquire nuclear weapons themselves. The new mission would
not require wrenching changes in either the foreign policy or
the military deployments of the United States. American
forces were already stationed on the Korean peninsula to
deter a non-nuclear attack southward by North Korea, and
the United States had long assumed responsibility for protecting the oil-rich but militarily weak sheikhdoms of the
Persian Gulf that an Iraqi or Iranian nuclear arsenal would
threaten.

The task of deterring nuclear-armed rogues would, in one
sense, be an easier one than deterrence had been during the
Cold War, since none could accumulate the huge stockpiles
of nuclear arms that the Soviet Union assembled. In another
way, however, post-proliferation deterrence would present a
more difficult challenge. The threat of retaliation did successfully deter the Soviet Union, but the three rogue regimes
seemed sufficiently detached from the normal constraints of

decency and prudence that American officials wondered whether it would be possible to prevent them from using nuclear armaments in their possession by the same method. Moreover, even if the familiar technique of deterrence could prevent an actual nuclear attack by any of the axis countries, the mere possession of armaments of this type might embolden these regimes to blackmail or assault their neighbors, on the assumption that their nuclear arsenals would deter the United States from retaliating.[19]

Rhetorical disapproval of the rogues was virtually universal; active opposition to their nuclear aspirations, however, came, as with other global public goods, chiefly from the United States. One response to the prospect of a rogue regime equipped with nuclear weapons, and with ballistic missiles capable of delivering them to distant targets (including, ultimately, North America), is to construct defenses against missile attack.[20] Research on missile defense in the United States dates back to shortly after the initial appearance of ballistic missiles in World War II. It accelerated in 1983, when President Ronald Reagan announced the Strategic Defense Initiative, the purpose of which was to render the nuclear-armed ballistic missiles of the Soviet Union "impotent and obsolete" by building elaborate and technically advanced machinery to intercept and destroy incoming missiles.

Designing and producing defenses adequate to the task of knocking down the thousands of missiles that the Soviet Union could hurl at the continental United States proved beyond the capacity of even the scientific and engineering talent at the disposal of the United States government. But the George W. Bush administration committed itself to deploying a system capable of carrying out the far more modest but still technologically formidable mission of defending the country against the handful of missiles that a nuclear-armed rogue might one day be able to fire at the United States. The administration withdrew from the 1972 treaty with Russia that banned the construction of defenses and, in 2004, amid doubts that the technology necessary for even the scaled-down version of what Ronald Reagan had envisioned was available, began to set up a missile defense system.

The efforts by the United States to deny nuclear weapons to the members of the axis of evil went beyond the construction of a missile defense system to contemplating, and ultimately to carrying out, more active measures. In 2003, the American government organized the multinational Proliferation Security Initiative to intercept, by seizing vessels on the high seas and searching aircraft while on the ground, shipments of nuclear-relevant equipment, or even bombs themselves, to and from the targeted countries.[21] And it made clear that it was prepared to use force to deny nuclear armaments to the rogues, or to remove from power the regimes ready to put them to dangerous uses, or both. In 1994, the United States came close to war with North Korea over its nuclear-weapon program.[22] In attempting to keep nuclear weapons out of the hands of both North Korea and Iran, the United States and other countries came, although not by design, to play complementary roles. These roles corresponded to the methods by which policemen sometimes attempt to obtain information from suspected criminals by a combination of sympathy and menace.

In the case of North Korea, the neighboring countries, South Korea, China, and Japan, played the part of the "good cop," offering the prospect of economic assistance and the hand of friendship to the Pyongyang regime if only it would give up its nuclear ambitions. The United States assumed the role of the "bad cop," prepared to use far harsher tactics if the North Koreans persisted in these ambitions. In the case of Iran, it was the governments of the largest countries of Western Europe—France, Germany, and Great Britain—that communicated an interest in avoiding armed conflict and expanding economic ties in exchange for Tehran's abandoning the path toward a nuclear arsenal, with the United States reserving the right to use force if it refused.

With the third member of the axis of evil, Iraq, the United States did go to war. The outcome of that war was the removal from power of a government whose nuclear aspirations American officials regarded as intolerable. But the Iraq war did not emerge solely from the long-standing American concern about nuclear proliferation. Two other events were required to launch it: the terrorist attacks on New York and Washington, D.C., of September 11, 2001, and the promulgation of a new American strategic doctrine in response to these attacks.

Terrorism and Preventive War

On September 11, 2001, Islamic militants commandeered four American commercial airliners filled with passengers. They crashed two of them into the twin towers of the World Trade Center in Manhattan, New York's tallest buildings, which collapsed, killing 2,752 people. Another was steered into the headquarters of the American Department of Defense, the Pentagon, in Washington, D.C., causing another 189 deaths.[23]

Although the attacks of September 11 qualify as the most spectacular, and perhaps the most deadly, acts of terror in all of history, they were certainly not the first. Terrorism is a very old phenomenon. It differs from war in that it employs violence sporadically and on a far smaller scale. Like those who wage war, terrorists have political goals, which they seek to achieve through shock. An act of terror is intended to bring these goals to public attention, and terrorism is therefore sometimes called "propaganda by deed."[24]

Acts of terror have also often been designed to call forth a harsh, repressive response that, terrorists hope, will trigger a backlash and thus win support for the terrorists' cause. One of the ultimate goals of al Qaeda, the perpetrators of the September 11 attacks, was to overthrow the ruling monarchy of Saudi Arabia. The United States became a target because of its close association with that monarchy, which included the stationing of American troops within the country's borders.[25]

Historically, campaigns of terror have virtually never achieved their goals, and far from driving the United States out of the Middle East, the September 11 attacks had, at least initially, the opposite effect. Still, those attacks seemed particularly ominous, for three reasons.[26]

First, al Qaeda promised to be difficult to eliminate because, as a network rather than a centralized, hierarchically controlled organization, it had personnel or active sympathizers scattered all over the world preparing to carry out attacks.[27] Second, unlike the terrorists of the nineteenth and early twentieth centuries, who targeted the particular individuals—monarchs, presidents, and ministers—whom they held responsible for, and who symbolized, the policies and institutions they were attacking, the twenty-first-century Islamic fundamentalists aimed at killing, indiscriminately, as many people as possible. Third, that aim made the twenty-first-century variety potentially far more lethal than terrorism had been in the past if terrorists ever managed to acquire chemical, biological, or nuclear materials.[28] After September 11, evidence came to light suggesting that al Qaeda was interested in acquiring all three.

In response to the attacks, the United States dispatched a small expeditionary force to Afghanistan, where al Qaeda had its base of operations. In cooperation with local armed groups, it overthrew the Islamic fundamentalist Taliban regime that had welcomed and protected al Qaeda, destroyed the camps in which terrorists had trained, captured or killed many of them, and drove the surviving leaders into hiding in the mountain range that straddles Afghanistan and neighboring Pakistan. At the same time, the United States government stepped up its cooperation with the governments of other countries, in Europe, Asia, and Africa, in tracking down the terrorist cells that were believed to be operating within their borders.

In so doing, these governments took the most effective measure available to them for combating those terrorists: They began looking for them. They began, that is, to scan intensely the ocean of information that flows into the bureaucratic machinery of the world's governments every day for evidence of likely terrorist attacks, as they had done far less scrupulously before September 11. Modern, and especially Western, governments are large and powerful but also blunt and inflexible instruments. They are effective at performing those tasks that they are programmed to carry out, but not at operating nimbly and creatively, without guidance from above. In the wake of September 11, these powerful machines were trained on detecting and preventing terrorist activity.

No doubt at least partly as a result, in the next three years no al Qaeda attack took place on American soil. Terrorists struck at more accessible targets, on the Indonesian island of Bali in 2002 and in Casablanca, Morocco, and Istanbul in 2003, several times in Saudi Arabia, and most spectacularly in the Spanish capital of Madrid on March 11, 2004, and in London on July 7, 2005.[29] Once the Taliban were dislodged from Afghanistan, the war on terrorism that the United States declared in the wake of the September 11 attacks principally involved intelligence gathering and police work within other countries. But it also led to a more formal and elaborate military operation: The attacks gave rise to a new American strategic doctrine, on the basis of which the United States went to war in 2003 against Saddam Hussein's regime in Iraq.

When a military disaster occurs, it is normal and natural to reflect, in its aftermath, on the lessons that can be learned from it, for the purpose of avoiding having to repeat it. So it was after World War II, when American policymakers adopted the policies of deterrence and containment toward the Soviet Union in order to avoid the mistakes they believed had been made in failing to confront Hitler. So it was, as well, on a smaller scale, after September 11, 2001. American officials could see in retrospect that warnings of the attacks had been readily available. Al Qaeda had previously launched several assaults on American targets outside the United States—against American embassies in Tanzania and Kenya in 1998 and against the American ship the USS *Cole* in the Arabian Sea port of Aden in 2000. The American intelligence community was well aware of the group's activities and concerned about the possibility of attacks in North America.

While greater vigilance might have prevented the assaults on New York and Washington, the surest way to have stopped them would have been to eliminate their source by destroying al Qaeda's base of operations in Afghanistan. This, of course, is what the United States did after September 11, but by then it was too late to forestall the attacks. Moreover, if the terrorists had been able to strike the United States with chemical, biological, or especially nuclear weapons, the death toll could have been far higher than it was.[30]

The lesson that the responsible officials drew from the events of September 11 was therefore that in dealing with aggressive terrorist groups or rogue states, the better part of valor is not discretion but rather boldness. The safety of the United States and the well-being of the world, they concluded, might well require attacking these ill-intentioned and dangerous forces *before* they could strike. "The gravest danger our Nation faces," according to the National Security Strategy of the United States, a document issued over the name of President George W. Bush on September 17, 2002,

> lies at the crossroads of radicalism and technology. Our enemies have openly declared that they are seeking weapons of mass destruction, and evidence indicates that they are doing so with determination. The United States will not allow these efforts to succeed ... And, as a matter of common sense and self-defense, America will act against such emerging threats before they are fully formed. We cannot defend America and our friends by hoping for the best ... History will judge harshly those who saw this coming danger but failed to act. In the new world we have entered, the only path to peace and security is the path of action.[31]

The new doctrine was sometimes wrongly called one of "preemptive war." Preemption, however, involves attacking when the enemy is just about to attack: that is, when an assault is imminent and certain. With its new security doctrine the United States was embracing something different: *preventive* war, which involves attacking *before* an attack is imminent.[32] "I will not wait on events, while dangers gather," the president said in his 2002 State of the Union address. "I will not stand by as peril draws closer and closer. The United States of America will not permit the world's most dangerous regimes to threaten us with the world's most destructive weapons."[33] The United States, the new doctrine asserted, would act to eliminate some threats before they became imminent:

> The United States has long maintained the option of pre-emptive actions to counter a sufficient threat to our national security. The greater the threat, the greater is the risk of inaction—and the more compelling the case for taking anticipatory action to defend ourselves, even if uncertainty remains as to the time and place of the enemy's attack.[34]

The country to which this new doctrine seemed, in the eyes of President Bush and his colleagues, most aptly and urgently to apply was Iraq.[35] That country's conduct in the 1990s had confirmed its standing as an American adversary, an international outlaw, and a regional and perhaps global menace. Under the brutal dictatorship of Saddam Hussein, Iraq had initiated and waged a war against neighboring Iran from 1979 to 1988 and then, in August 1990, had attacked, occupied, and plundered the tiny sheikhdom of Kuwait on its southern border. The United States assembled and led a multinational coalition that evicted the occupying troops in February 1991. Much of the country rose up against Saddam's rule in the aftermath of his defeat, but his security forces and army crushed the rebellions and he remained in power.

By the terms of the 1991 agreement that ended the war, the Iraqi government was obliged to declare and destroy all the nuclear, chemical, and biological materials that it had accumulated. The United Nations was authorized to conduct inspections to verify compliance with these terms. Saddam's regime, however, gave the inspection teams limited and grudging cooperation, concealed materials and programs it was supposed to declare and abandon, and finally, in 1998, evicted the inspectors altogether.

For this reason, in the aftermath of the attacks of September 11, it was impossible to know just what weapons Iraq had. The regime was widely believed to have retained stores of toxic chemicals; and after the 1991 war it had been discovered to have come much closer to fabricating a nuclear weapon than Western intelligence agencies and nonproliferation organizations had estimated.[36] Historically, moreover, nuclear weapons programs around the world had progressed farther, faster, than those charged with tracking their progress had believed.[37]

The Saddam Hussein regime therefore posed precisely the kind of danger that the terrorist attacks of September 11 had persuaded American officials it was necessary to meet *before* it matured into an imminent threat.[38] With his regime, it would be better to be safe than sorry; and the path to safety lay in removing him from power before he could acquire the most dangerous weapons. He was clearly committed to acquiring nuclear armaments whenever and however he could. He had proven himself reckless and aggressive enough that, once he had them, it might not be possible to deter him from using them.

Even if he did not launch a nuclear attack, the mere possession of these weapons might embolden him to take steps radically injurious to American interests—sheltering terrorist camps, as the Taliban had done in Afghanistan, for instance, or attacking Saudi Arabia and seizing its oil fields—based on the confident assumption that neither the United States nor any other country or combination of countries would risk a nuclear attack on their forces by opposing him.[39]

In the fall of 2002, the American government therefore demanded full Iraqi compliance with the series of United Nations Resolutions on its weapons programs that Saddam Hussein had flouted. When he failed to comply fully, the United States, joined by Great Britain, attacked Iraq and by mid-April 2003 had vanquished the regime and occupied the country.

From a strictly military standpoint, the Iraq war was a resounding success. The American and British military forces achieved their objective in only three weeks, with minimal casualties. Unlike the Cold War doctrines of containment and deterrence, however, which the events of 1945 to 1950— the Marshall Plan, the Truman Doctrine, the Berlin blockade, and the Korean War—had confirmed as the central features of American foreign policy, the war in Iraq, despite its initial success, did not augur a comparable twenty-first-century status for preventive war. Indeed, the American experience in Iraq demonstrated just how limited the scope for putting this doctrine into practice was likely to be.

The two other members of the axis of evil did not lend themselves to the kind of treatment that Iraq received. North Korea had armed itself so heavily that even without nuclear weapons it was able to deter an American attack. Although the Communist regime was certain to lose a war fought against the United States, it had the military capacity to inflict vast damage on prosperous, democratic South Korea before being conquered.[40] Thus, South Korea was anxious to avoid a shooting war, as were Japan and China, neighboring countries with an interest in events on the Korean peninsula whose views the United States had to respect.

Larger and more populous than Iraq, Iran presented a more formidable military challenge. The clerical regime in power in Tehran was also far less politically isolated than Saddam Hussein's had been.

Although a sponsor of terrorism, it had not waged two wars of aggression, it was not subject to United Nations sanctions, and it was not defying a series of UN resolutions, as Iraq was in 2003. In Iran, discontent with the rule of the mullahs was widespread and visible, leading to the hope that, unlike in Iraq, the Islamic republic might ultimately be overthrown from within, without any assistance from outside the country.[41]

Furthermore, public support for the application of the doctrine of preventive war to Iraq was less than wholehearted in the United States and even thinner in Great Britain, for several reasons. For one thing, the conflict in Iraq qualified, for the United States, as a war of choice. Saddam Hussein had not attacked the United States, or any other country, as he did to provoke the 1991 war. The 2003 conflict could not, therefore, be justified on the grounds of self-defense, which is the rationale that most strongly disposes democracies to fight and provokes Western democracies to overcome their powerful twenty-first-century bias against war.

Moreover, a preventive war has a self-canceling quality to it. If it is successful it removes the threat that, were it to grow to menacing proportions, would clearly justify military action. It removes, in effect, the evidence that would convince people of the wisdom of waging war.

In addition, acting to prevent a misdeed before it takes place violates the common-sense notion of justice that is basic to democratic societies. In democracies, people may be punished for what they do but not for what they *might* do or for what and who they are. Yet preventive war against rogue regimes punishes countries on precisely these grounds.

Perhaps the best evidence of the difficulty of rallying support for a preventive war was the failure of the Bush administration seriously to attempt to do so. In its public presentations, the administration did not emphasize the need to remove Saddam Hussein from power before he could obtain weapons that would pose a serious threat to American interests. Instead, it presented the war as one waged in order to deprive him of the weapons that, it was assumed, he already had. The *causus belli* was his continued possession, contrary to the stipulations of many UN resolutions, of "weapons of mass destruction." But while the world's intelligence services were virtually unanimous in the conviction that Iraq had retained stockpiles of chemical weapons, none believed that Saddam had yet managed to build or acquire nuclear armaments. Chemical weapons have far less potential for inflicting destruction than nuclear weapons; and there were several countries that possessed these weapons and were distinctly unfriendly to the United States—Syria, for example—that the American government nonetheless did not suggest be overthrown by force.

The principal official rationale for the Iraq operation thus did not follow from the post–September 11 doctrine of preventive war, and that rationale eroded support for the war in the United States and elsewhere when it turned out to be inaccurate: Following the ouster of Saddam, no chemical weapons were found in Iraq.[42]

In the period leading up to the war, the American and British governments suggested, or hinted at, reasons for war that were more persuasive to the publics of their countries than the doctrine of preventive war but that also lacked solid bases in fact. The Bush administration did little to correct the misimpression that Saddam Hussein had had a role of some kind in the attacks of September 11, which, if true, would have made the military operations a response to these attacks and therefore an exercise in self-defense.[43] Indeed, the president himself encouraged that impression, citing, in October 2002, a number of connections between Saddam's regime and al Qaeda.[44] Earlier, in his 2002 State of the Union message, Mr. Bush had said that Iraq had tried to purchase uranium from the African country of Niger. If true, this would have indicated an active program for making nuclear weapons, for which uranium is a basic ingredient; but the report on which it was based turned out to be unsubstantiated, if not unfounded. Similarly, Vice President Cheney suggested that Saddam Hussein was close to acquiring nuclear weapons.[45]

Finally, the British government released a report saying that Iraq had the capacity to use its weapons of mass destruction on forty-five minutes' notice, which left the impression that Saddam's forces could attack European targets in this time.[46] In fact, Iraq lacked the means to launch an attack of that range even if it had had chemical weapons.

None of this involved outright lying. There is no reason to doubt that the president and his senior colleagues, along with virtually everyone else in the world with a professional interest in the matter, honestly believed in the existence of Iraqi chemical weapons. But officials on both sides of the Atlantic may well have presented the case for war in less equivocal terms than the evidence warranted.[47]

If the Iraq war evoked a measure of exaggeration and perhaps even dissembling by its sponsors,[48] it produced hypocrisy among its opponents. Two other rationales for war should have appealed to people who instead turned out to be extremely unsympathetic to the Anglo-American effort. Removing Saddam Hussein from power had an indisputably humanitarian value, given the widespread brutality and many thousands of needless deaths for which he was responsible. But those, especially in the United States, who approved in principle of conducting military operations in order to alleviate suffering and who had supported operations in the Balkans in the 1990s for that purpose, proved, if anything, more strongly opposed to the Iraq campaign than the public as a whole.

Similarly, the Iraq war could be seen as a way of vindicating the United Nations. That organization had been so closely identified with the cause of disarming Iraq, had devoted so much of its time and resources to that end, and had passed so many resolutions in support of it that Iraq's continued defiance of the UN risked saddling the organization with the same kind of reputation for feebleness that its inability to respond effectively to the crises of the 1930s—the Italian assault on Ethiopia and the Japanese invasion of North China—had affixed to its predecessor, the League of Nations. Yet those who insisted most emphatically on a central role in international affairs for the UN—notably several governments in Western Europe—refused to sanction the enforcement of the demands it had made repeatedly over the course of a decade and that they themselves had joined in supporting.

As a prospective staple of American foreign policy, the doctrine of preventive war had yet another drawback: It is, strictly speaking, illegal. The basic precept of international law is, and has been for three and a half centuries, the inviolability of national sovereignty. The violation of internationally recognized borders and the forcible interference in the internal affairs of other countries is prohibited except in self-defense. The precept is enshrined in the UN Charter, according to which, in Article 2 (4), "all Members shall refrain ... from the threat or use of force against the territorial integrity or political independence of any state" and that prohibits, in Article 2 (7), intervention "in matters which are essentially within the domestic jurisdiction of any state."

Still, this objection received less emphasis from critics of the Iraq war than might have been expected, given its centuries-long centrality to the norms of international relations. One reason for this was that the norm had already come under serious political challenge, albeit from a different political quarter than the one in which the doctrine of preventive war originated. In the 1990s, the United States had dispatched troops to a number of countries without being invited by their governments, thereby violating their sovereignty. It had done so not for the sake of preventing the development of a threat to the United States but in order to end violence against people living in those countries, which was often perpetrated or abetted by their own governments. The rationale for these post–Cold War but pre–September 11 interventions, that is, was not national security but international rescue, and here, too, the United States performed, for the international system as a whole, a role that governments sometimes play within sovereign states.

Humanitarian Intervention

The prohibition against forcible intervention in the internal affairs of other countries has often been honored in the breach. The inequality in military capability among the members of the international system makes this possible and has made it possible since ancient times. In his account of the Peloponnesian Wars of the fifth century B.C., the Greek historian Thucydides recorded representatives of powerful Athens saying to the people of smaller, less mighty Melos, in order to justify subduing them, that in relations among sovereign political entities, "the strong do what they have the power to do and the weak accept what they have to accept."[49]

From Thucydides' day to the twentieth century, the strong intruded on the weak for self-interested reasons: for plunder, or to gain territory, or as part of a larger war as in the case of the Athenians and Melians as well as that of the United States during the Cold War, which fought in Korea, Indochina, and elsewhere as part of the global conflict with the Soviet Union and international communism.

In the decade following the end of that conflict, American military forces crossed international borders even more frequently than they had while it was under way,[50] but with a major difference in many of these cases. They had no prospect of bringing the United States any benefit, or preventing any harm to Americans. The interventions of the 1990s had, on the whole, selfless rather than self-interested motives. The United States sent troops abroad not to defend its interests, as great powers had done from time immemorial, but to vindicate its values.

In 1991, the United States intervened on behalf of the Kurds of northern Iraq, who had risen in rebellion against the Iraqi dictator Saddam Hussein after the international coalition led by the United States had evicted his army from Kuwait. Despite this military defeat, Saddam retained his grip on power and unleashed his forces on the Kurds, whom the United States then stepped in to protect.[51]

In 1992, American military forces went to the African country of Somalia, where the central government had collapsed and famine threatened, to ensure the distribution of food. In 1994, American troops landed on the Caribbean island of Haiti as part of a military and diplomatic operation to remove from power the dictatorship of that country, whose political oppression and economic failures had caused thousands of Haitians to flee across the Caribbean to Florida to seek refuge in the United States.

In 1995, NATO forces, led by the United States, conducted bombing raids in support of the beleaguered Muslims of Bosnia, a multinational republic of the recently-dissolved federation of Yugoslavia, and against the Bosnian Serbs, who, with support from their compatriots in Serbia proper, had driven Muslims from their homes in large numbers, an ugly practice that had come to be known as "ethnic cleansing." In 1998, NATO waged another campaign of aerial bombardment in Kosovo, also once part of Yugoslavia but never a full-fledged Yugoslav republic and thus, with the collapse of Yugoslavia, regarded by the international community not as independent, like Bosnia, but rather as a part of Serbia. The campaign was undertaken on behalf of ethnic Albanians, who made up 90 percent of the population of Kosovo and were fighting against the Serbs who controlled it, at whose military forces and cities the bombing was directed.

American officials occasionally sought to justify these interventions in traditional terms, as military operations designed to defend American interests. The former Yugoslavia was said to be crucial to the United States because of its location in "the heart of Europe"—a curious reading of the continent's geography—and opposing the Serbs there was thus deemed necessary to protect what was, or had been during the Cold War, a vital

American interest: the integrity of the NATO alliance. In fact, however, the outcome of the wars that the collapse of Yugoslavia triggered—like the future of the Kurds, the Somalis, and the Haitians—could have had no impact on the safety or well-being of American citizens. The turmoil in those places affected the Americans and Western Europeans only insofar as it produced refugees who sought admission to their countries; and the governments of those countries could have closed their borders to these refugees—the Western Europeans to the people from the Balkans, the Americans to those fleeing Haiti— had they regarded it as an urgent matter to do so.[52]

The United States intervened in those places, which had no relevance to its strategic or economic interests, in order to relieve the palpable suffering of the people who lived in them, suffering inflicted by their own governments or as a result of the absence of effective government to protect them against their fellow citizens. While historically fear or greed, or some combination of the two, had propelled the military forces of great powers outward beyond their borders, the motive for the American humanitarian interventions of the 1990s was compassion.[53] They were acts of charity, which is in many traditions a religious duty but in almost none a political imperative.

Because the United States had no tangible interests at stake in northern Iraq, Somalia, Haiti, Bosnia, or Kosovo, the armed interventions in these places commanded relatively little public support. Americans were willing to do something to alleviate the sufferings of foreigners, but not to pay much in treasure or anything in blood for this purpose. Each of the military operations was therefore conducted so as to avoid American casualties, which limited, although it did not entirely eliminate, their effectiveness.[54]

When the practice of humanitarian intervention in the 1990s is compared with the post–September 11 doctrine of preventive war, it is, at first glance, the differences that stand out.[55] The two fall on opposite sides of the line that divides the two principal approaches to the theory and practice of foreign policy. Humanitarian intervention belongs to the idealist approach, which emphasizes the promotion of values in the conduct of foreign policy and embraces the belief that the foreign policies of particular countries, especially powerful ones, can and sometimes do change the world for the better. Preventive war, by contrast, emerged from the "realist" outlook on relations between and among sovereign states, according to which insecurity and competition are unavoidable in the international arena and the goal of individual countries is and must be the protection of their own interests, above all the paramount interest in survival. Realists stipulate as the supreme goal of foreign policy, or at least the most desirable achievable goal, order among sovereign states. Idealists aim higher, seeking to promote justice within them.

Support for the two practices in the United States came from different parts of the American political spectrum. Preventive war, a doctrine promulgated by a Republican administration, enjoyed the approval, on the whole, of those on the right side of that spectrum, the conservative part of the American public. The most enthusiastic practitioner of humanitarian intervention, by contrast, was the Democratic administration that preceded it, and it was principally liberals who believed that the practice represented an appropriate use of American military power.[56]

The proponents of preventive war and of humanitarian intervention both adduced evidence from history in support of the type of military operation they favored, citing disastrous historical episodes that the practice they favored would prevent in the future; but they were different episodes. The champions of preventive war invoked, of course, the attacks of September 11, but also the unsuccessful British and French policy of appeasing Hitler and Nazi Germany in the 1930s as evidence to demonstrate the need to act quickly and decisively to eliminate a threat before it becomes imminent. By contrast, the partisans of humanitarian intervention took as their touchstone the systematic mass murder of European Jews by the Germans during World War II—the Holocaust—other, if lesser, versions of which the use of American military power people was designed to prevent.[57]

Each of the two post–Cold War innovations in American foreign policy may be seen as an example of the United States providing a governmental service to the international community, for both correspond to something that governments do within sovereign states, although the domestic practices are, once again, different. Preventive war represents an international version of the practice (which is, to be sure, of dubious legality) of prior restraint: taking legal steps to restrain someone who otherwise, authorities have reason to believe, would commit a crime. Humanitarian intervention corresponds to the twentieth century practice, increasingly common in Western countries, of removing children from the custody of parents who are abusing them. This violates the age-old custom of vesting responsibility for their offspring in the people who brought them into the world in favor of serving, in the legal phrase, "the best interests of the child," just as humanitarian intervention violates the norm of sovereignty on behalf of what is deemed more valuable, the welfare of individuals.

For all their differences, however, preventive war and

humanitarian intervention have some basic similarities, like fraternal twins who may not look or act alike but who share fundamental characteristics. Both count as radical innovations in international affairs because, whereas the frequent intrusions of the strong upon the weak throughout history violated the norm of absolute sovereignty in practice, the post–Cold War American interventions posed a direct challenge to that norm as a constitutive principle of international order. The proponents of each assert that some circumstances other than pure self-defense justify overriding a country's sovereign prerogatives. Although this contention did not originate in the wake of the Cold War—the UN Charter makes provision for intervention in the internal affairs of sovereign states in the event of "threats to international peace and security"—these two doctrines propounded it more insistently and for more clearly defined conditions than ever before.

The conditions prevailing in the world after the Cold War made both preventive war and humanitarian intervention possible. The United States undertook both on behalf of the values that came to have wide currency: preventive war to thwart the designs of rogue states that did not honor these values, humanitarian intervention to rescue people from governments that, in violation of the global consensus, were oppressing them. The existence of a global consensus in favor of peace, democracy, and free markets meant that almost no country objected strongly enough to these American interventions to try to stop them. The wide margin of military superiority that the United States enjoyed over all other countries meant that even if any had so objected, none would have had the power to make contesting them seem advisable.

From the American point of view, preventive war and humanitarian intervention not only defended American interests and protected American values, they also served the wider international community. Indeed, these practices did more for others than for Americans, who were not exposed to the depredations of the regimes the United States removed from power and to whom the rogue states that were the objects of the doctrine of preventive war posed lesser threats than they did to their immediate neighbors. Americans certainly believed that they were acting on behalf not only of themselves but also of other countries for the purpose of making the world they shared a safer and more humane place.

The practices of preventive war and humanitarian intervention had one other feature in common: Neither was likely to establish itself as a permanent, prominent feature of American foreign policy and twenty-first-century international relations.

Neither the one episode of preventive war nor the several instances of humanitarian intervention attracted a great deal of support beyond the borders of the United States. The war in Iraq in fact provoked widespread and sometimes intense international indignation. The military operations in northern Iraq, Somalia, Haiti, and the Balkans proved less controversial, and all obtained a measure of support from other countries. The largest of them, the two Balkan interventions, were conducted under the auspices of the most powerful regional organization in Europe, NATO. Even these, however, failed to gain the approval of the United Nations, which, for all that organization's shortcomings, was generally considered to be the mark of international legitimacy.

The doctrine of humanitarian intervention, moreover, had potential relevance, and was therefore highly objectionable, to more members of the international community than the practice of preventive war. The prospective targets of the first—governments that repressed their own citizens—far outnumbered the handful of rogue states that had reason to fear the second. China, India, and Russia, for example, scarcely qualified as rogue states. All had reasonably good relations with the United States. But the Chinese government's blanket denial of political rights and its cultural assault on Tibet, India's conflict with secessionists in Kashmir, and Russia's war in Chechnya each had some of the features that had triggered American military interventions, on humanitarian grounds, during the 1990s.

Moreover, neither of the two post–Cold War innovations in American foreign policy enjoyed particularly extensive popularity within the United States itself. Humanitarian intervention received less support than preventive war because no American interests—that is, nothing that directly affected Americans—were at stake. Americans, like others, proved more willing to expend lives and resources for the sake of themselves, their families, their neighbors, and their countrymen than for strangers living in foreign countries.[58] While a resolution supporting the war in Iraq passed both houses of Congress, none of the humanitarian interventions of the 1990s received comparable congressional approval.

As it unfolded, however, the Iraq initiative lost support in the United States[59] because of a final feature that it shared with the humanitarian interventions of the 1990s. From different directions, the two types of military operation arrived, so to speak, at the same destination. In both cases, the United States decided, albeit for different reasons, to remove the government of another country. Having done so, the governance of that country became, at least for a time, an American responsibility. As a consequence, the United States found itself saddled with a task that proved difficult, more costly in each case than anticipated, and frustrating. The name commonly given to that task is nation-building.

State-Building

What the world knows as nation-building is more appropriately called *state*-building. A nation is a community of fate, a group of people who feel bound to one another by ties of history, language, religion, shared beliefs, or some combination of them. Because it has at its heart feelings of loyalty, nationalism is ultimately a property of mass psychology. What the United States attempted to do, for varying periods of time and with differing degrees of success, in Somalia, Haiti, Bosnia, Kosovo, Iraq, and Afghanistan, was to put in place what all of them lacked: the apparatus of a working, effective, decent government.[60]

The United States did not embark on any of its post–Cold War interventions for the purpose of state-building. Once having accomplished the goals for which they had intervened, however, the American authorities found themselves driven to the task of state-building by the force of circumstances.

It would hardly have been sensible, after all, to restore to power the regime that the intervention had been undertaken to remove. Nor, in most of these places, was an alternative set of political leaders, who had sufficient experience to govern effectively and were acceptable to the United States, available to step in. Nor was the task at hand simply one of identifying a more suitable group of political leaders than those the United States had dislodged. To one degree or another, each of the objects of American intervention lacked the governmental institutions necessary to maintain a decent political order, underpin a flourishing economy, and guard against the return of the kinds of policies that had prompted the United States to act in the first place. To prevent the return of the conditions that had led to the interventions, the United States felt obliged to try to promote these institutions.

In none of the cases, however, did the American effort to do so succeed. Of all the post–Cold War American interventions, the one that led to the most promising political developments was the first, in northern Iraq. The Kurds formed a government that was, especially by the standards of the Middle East, tolerably effective and relatively democratic. This achievement, however, stemmed almost entirely from the Kurds' own efforts rather than from those of the United States, whose contribution to state-building consisted of patrolling the skies above the Kurdish territory to ensure that Saddam Hussein could not send his army to reconquer it.[61]

In Somalia, despite the boast of the American ambassador to the United Nations, Madeleine Albright, that the United States was engaged there in "an unprecedented enterprise aimed at nothing less than the restoration of an entire country as a proud, functioning and viable member of the community of nations,"[62] the killing of eighteen American troops caused Washington to withdraw all its forces from the country, which reverted to the clan-dominated anarchy the United States had found when it first intervened.

In Haiti, when American forces left after eighteen months, political turmoil, violence, and economic deterioration resumed. Jean-Bertrand Aristide, the elected president who had been deposed by a coup in 1991 and whom the United States restored to power in 1994, was elected again in 2000 but governed so badly that in 2004, he was once again driven from office, this time with the tacit approval of the American government.

After five years of bitter fighting, the American-led NATO intervention brought a truce to Bosnia. But the subsequent occupation did not fulfill the intervention's stated goal: the creation of a stable, harmonious, multiethnic country. With the Serbs, Croats, and Muslims each dominating their own areas and having little to do with one another (and with renewed communal violence likely if the foreign peacekeepers left), Bosnia was effectively partitioned into distinct, quasi-sovereign sections. So, too, was the Serbian province of Kosovo, between the majority Albanians and the minority Serbs. Six years after the American-led intervention, Kosovo was a place where corruption was widespread, where communal violence occasionally erupted, and from which more than 100,000 Serbs had been driven, in an outbreak of ethnic cleansing, *after* American and European forces had compelled Serb military forces to leave and had occupied the province themselves.[63]

In Afghanistan, with the Taliban ousted, a moderate, capable, pro-Western leader, Hamid Karzai, presided over the central government in Kabul, the country's capital city. Outside the capital, however, a patchwork of local leaders—warlords, the press usually called them—exercised the dominant influence, as had been the case for most of the country's modern history. And in Iraq after the overthrow of Saddam, despite the presence of 130,000 American troops, the United States could not supply the most basic of all public goods: civil order. The American forces did not manage to prevent terrorist violence on a disturbing scale.

These shortcomings make for an ironic counterpoint to the frequent references, in the early years of the twenty-first century, to the United States as an imperial power. For of all the American international tasks in the wake of the Cold War,

state-building most closely conformed to the normal work-
ings of the empires to which it was being compared. Yet of all
the American international activities, this most imperial of
them was the one at which the United States had the least
success.

The world's strongest state did poorly at the imperial
undertaking because several of the conditions that historically
had made empires possible no longer existed. The will to
empire had faded. The United States was considerably less
willing, and in some ways less able, to supply governance to
foreign peoples than traditional imperial powers had been.
Unlike the European imperial powers of the nineteenth century, for example, the United States did not welcome, take
pride in, or in any way draw its national identity from governing faraway territories. Nor did Americans believe, as had the
imperial states of Europe and of other times and places, that
their own security depended on preventing other powerful
states from seizing the territories that they had come to control. Unlike empires of the past, the United States eagerly
sought to share responsibility for administering the societies
it found itself governing.

Americans thought of the responsibility for the governance and well-being of others that they had inherited
through their exercises in preventive war and humanitarian
intervention as a burden and a distraction, not an honor or a
privilege. In the first decade and a half of the post–Cold War
era, despite the frequency with which it found itself trying to
build viable political institutions in foreign countries, the
government of the United States did not embrace this mission. Rather than developing a governmental agency devoted
exclusively to it, responsibility for state-building was dele-
gated largely to the armed forces. They gave it a name that

bespoke its distance from what the military felt comfortable in doing and competent to do: "MOOTW"—Military Operations Other Than War.[64]

Nor was state-building a paying proposition, as traditional empires were, or at least were often thought to be. American taxpayers, not the local economy, subsidized the American presence in Somalia, Haiti, the Balkans, Afghanistan, and Iraq.

Nor, finally, could the United States employ the tactic that had done most to reduce the costs of ruling rebellious subjects in the past: brutality. When Indians mutinied against the British in 1857, when Iraqis did the same in 1920, when Filipinos opposed the imposition of American authority after the United States had evicted Spain from the Philippine archipelago in 1898, the uprisings were harshly suppressed, with the imperial power killing many of those who resisted its rule. The regimes that the post–Cold War American interventions unseated often maintained their grip on power by murdering large numbers of their own citizens, thereby intimidating the rest. But the standards of political propriety and decency that prevailed in the United States, as well as one of the purposes of these interventions—to replace vicious, oppressive governments with kinder, gentler ones—precluded the American use of this tactic.

If Americans were less inclined to provide governance, the peoples of the societies in which the United States intervened were, in comparison with the subjects of history's empires, less willing to accept it. They acted under the influence, as subject peoples for most of history had not, of the most powerful political sentiment of the twentieth century: nationalism.

Nationalism is the desire, often an intense one, of particular groups to govern themselves rather than submit to the rule of foreigners. In the age of empire, a venerable saying summarized the political attitudes of most people in most parts of the world: "Better a hundred years of tyranny than one day of anarchy." Rule by outsiders was generally accepted insofar as it provided order. Once nationalism swept the world, however, the prevailing view of governance changed. The new attitude could be summarized as "Better a hundred years of indigenous misrule than one day of governance, even good governance, by foreigners." It was that shift in attitude, more than anything else, that put an end to the great European overseas empires. The same kind of nationalist sentiment that dissolved these empires in the first half of the twentieth century, along with equally powerful allegiances to tribal, religious, and ethnic groups, often undercut post–Cold War American efforts at state-building in the wake of the Cold War.

The disruptive impact of nationalism should not have come as a surprise. The severest American setbacks during the Cold War occurred when the adversaries of the United States managed to mobilize nationalist feeling in an anti-American cause. The Communists defeated the American-sponsored Kuomintang in the Chinese civil war in the second half of the 1940s in this way. Fidel Castro seized and held power by casting himself as the defender of Cuban independence against the Yankee colossus to the north. The mullahs of Iran rallied their countrymen against the Shah in 1979 by portraying him as a puppet of the United States.

With the Cold War at an end, American efforts at state-building bumped up against the same obstacle. The United States and its European allies had difficulty constructing effective governments in Bosnia and Kosovo because the Serbs and Croats in the first case and the Albanians in the second did not wish to belong to the state that the United States was proposing to build. They wanted states of their own instead.[65] Similarly, tribal and ethnic loyalties in Afghanistan and religious and national divisions in Iraq complicated the efforts to create a state apparatus that would function effectively throughout each country.

To the problems arising from American diffidence and local resistance was added another obstacle to state-building in the twenty-first century, perhaps the most formidable obstacle of all: the inherent difficulty of the task and, even in the best of circumstances, the necessarily protracted time scale for it.

States are effective to the extent that they have effective institutions. These include a governmental bureaucracy, a legal system with courts, police, judges and prisons, and, in private hands, standing outside the government but regulated and protected by it, a financial system for channeling resources to the places where they can spur economic growth. Democratic institutions are particularly difficult to fabricate because they must strike a delicate balance between the strength needed to function effectively and the restraint required to safeguard political and economic liberty.[66] None of the requisite institutions, even nondemocratic ones, can be called into existence by fiat. All require personnel with the skills necessary to operate them, which cannot be acquired overnight.

The term "state-building" implies a similarity to architecture, in which the builder can control every part of the process: drawing up the plans, gathering the building materials, hiring the workers, and supervising the construction. State-building, however, more closely resembles horticulture. It is a collaboration between human agents and forces beyond short-term human control. In the case of horticulture, the independent collaborator is nature. The equivalent for state-building is culture—the values, attitudes, and beliefs of the society in which the effort to build a state takes place.[67]

Some cultures lend themselves to the construction of effective, decent states more readily than others. Where the cultural soil for such states is fertile, they probably already exist, which means that the American efforts at state-building almost by definition are undertaken in the least promising places. In none of these places are the prospects for implanting and cultivating sturdy institutions entirely hopeless. Cultures can and do change, but they change relatively slowly. The relevant unit of time is not the month, the year, or the life of a particular government: It is the generation.

Here, too, state-building resembles horticulture, not architecture. While careful planning and appropriate management can help to promote the flowering of a garden or the growth of a forest, neither can occur according to a man-made schedule. People can plant the seeds, and water and tend what springs up out of the ground, but they cannot advance the rate of growth beyond nature's schedule. Similarly, while the proper policies can improve the chances for establishing a stable government, an effective legal system, and working financial institutions, there are limits to how rapidly these can be created, limits set by the political cultures of the societies in which they are being created. In Somalia, Haiti, Bosnia, Kosovo, Afghanistan, and Iraq, even the United States, for all its power, was bound by these limits. The tools of foreign policy, even when wielded by the world's strongest state, cannot, by themselves, create a working state apparatus, let alone the apparatus of a democratic state, any more than a gardener's tools can, by themselves, create a garden.

The post–Cold War American efforts at state-building evoked references, and explicit comparisons, to the two most successful such exercises in American history, the rebuilding and rehabilitation of Germany and Japan after World War II.[68] The transformation, under American occupation, of the two aggressor powers of World War II into peaceful, prosperous, democratic members of the international community count, however, as exceptions that prove the rule. The conditions for state-building in these two countries can be seen, in retrospect, as extraordinarily favorable, certainly far more favorable than in any of the societies in which the United States attempted, in the last decade of the twentieth century and the initial years of the twenty-first, to repeat its experiences there.[69]

Germany and Japan were homogeneous societies, without the kinds of social divisions that plagued state-building in Bosnia, Kosovo, Afghanistan, and Iraq. More importantly, Germany and Japan had already constructed powerful, effective states, so powerful and effective that they came close to conquering Europe and Asia, respectively. The Germans and the Japanese did not have to learn from scratch how to administer their countries, manage a system of justice, and operate a market economy. They had already done these things, and had used the same social skills to amass the world-class military forces that had made them formidable adversaries. State-building involved reassembling what had been constructed and then, briefly, broken.

Indeed, the German and Japanese cases suggest that there is an inverse relationship between the ease with which a country can be defeated militarily and the ease with which a new and better government can be established after its defeat. The Haitian, Balkan, Afghan, and Iraqi regimes proved relatively easy to dislodge once the United States decided to do so, but putting stable, democratic systems of governance in their place turned out to be prohibitively difficult. By contrast, defeating Germany and Japan militarily in World War II required stupendous efforts by the United States and its allies, but once the two had been conquered, model governments were established in both countries—although not immediately and certainly not without difficulties.

Finally, the United States was able to maintain a large military and administrative presence in both countries for years after the end of the war, with support rather than opposition from the German and Japanese people, because, with the advent of the conflict with the Soviet Union, America was transformed from occupier to protector. The Cold War underwrote an enduring American role, which gave the United States the opportunity to oversee the emergence and consolidation of democratic governments in both countries.

The American difficulty with state-building has a parallel with the experience of governments within states the world over. For the United States as the world's de facto government, as with governments within sovereign states, the more ambitious the task, the less successful the efforts to carry it out are likely to be. The more a governmental initiative attempts to change deeply rooted patterns of human behavior—the further, that is, it seeks to go beyond the traditional, familiar task of keeping order—the longer are the odds of success.[70]

The most ambitious modern form of government, communism, produced the most decisive—and monstrous—failures. In democratically governed Western societies, a similar pattern has obtained. Governments can make people less poor by the simple expedient of giving them money but have not managed to eliminate poverty, which would require inculcating habits of thrift, self-reliance, and foresight throughout the society. Many people do have these qualities of character, and over time, it is probably safe to say, more and more have acquired them, thanks in part to the programs and exhortations of governments—but only in part. Individuals absorb the habits and beliefs with which they go through life from the societies in which they grow up, above all from their families rather than from their governments, just as a country's political culture exercises the most extensive influence on the shape and strength of its institutions.

Societies everywhere would no doubt benefit if their governments had the capacity to instill virtue in their citizens, and the world would surely be a better place if the United States could build prosperous democracies in countries that lack them. Every threat to international order for which the United States bore responsibility after the Cold War involved a government that fell short of Western political and economic standards. Every security problem that the American government felt called upon to address would be alleviated, if not solved altogether, if the regimes responsible for them could be remade to American specifications. A genuinely democratic China would find it easier to come to an accommodation with Taiwan acceptable to the Taiwanese. A democratic Iran or North Korea would be less likely to seek nuclear weapons, and nuclear weapons in the possession of these countries would seem less threatening to the rest of the world, were they governed according to democratic principles. The Middle East would likely breed fewer terrorists if the countries there offered their citizens meaningful political participation, economic opportunity, and the rule of law.[71] And merely competent government would serve as an antidote to much of the civil strife that had erupted in the poorest parts of the world in the wake of the Cold War.[72] Accordingly, both post–Cold War presidential administrations, those of Bill Clinton and George W. Bush, put the promotion of democracy at the center of their foreign policy goals.[73] If the United States had a grand strategy in the wake of the Cold War, it was to spread the blessings of liberty the world over.

Although it was neither naive nor foolish to believe that the establishment of functional, and especially functional democratic states across the planet would make the world of safer place, however, the capacity of the United States, or indeed any group of countries, to achieve this worthy goal was, unfortunately, considerably more modest than official rhetoric often implied.[74] Still, the American capacity to cause states to be built was not entirely negligible.

Occupying a country does have an effect on its governing structures. It is not accidental that many of the world's democracies, including the United States, were once governed by the world's oldest democracy: Great Britain. British imperial possessions often, although not always, retained the institutions and practices, above all the rule of law, that the British had brought to them. The effort by one country to build state institutions, particularly democratic institutions, in another does not always succeed, and the American record is not an impressive one;[75] but neither are outside powers entirely without influence in this matter.

The United States has probably exercised more indirect than direct influence on state-formation around the world. In the long run the most effective American power is the power of its example as a stable, open, affluent, well-governed society. People, after all, tend to act on what they notice rather than on what they are told. Imitation—voluntary, not coerced—is not only the sincerest form of flattery, it is also the motor of history. At the outset of the twenty-first century, it was impossible not to notice that power and prosperity went hand in hand with democracy and free markets, and the global impact of this fact was all the more powerful because it was true not only for the United States. All other advanced industrial countries had democratic politics and free market economics. The American example was potent precisely because it was not a uniquely American example.[76]

At the outset of the twenty-first century, the United States promoted state-building in another indirect way: by its role in the international economy. The global networks through which trade and investment flowed had attained a special, almost exalted status through the powerful appeal of the free market as a system of economic organization. Of the three main elements of the post–Cold War global consensus—the other two being peace as the appropriate aim of foreign policy and democracy as the optimal form of government—the free market as the organizing principle of economic activity enjoyed the broadest and deepest acceptance. War and civil violence still afflicted all too many parts of the world, and many governments eschewed democracy in practice even while paying lip service to it; but the market held sway almost everywhere. Only a few marginal, recalcitrant, and, not coincidentally, impoverished countries—North Korea and Cuba were the most notable—held out against it, and even they found themselves forced to adopt modest market reforms in order to avoid complete economic collapse.

The reason for the market's popularity was obvious: it emerged, over the course of the second half of the twentieth century, as the royal road to prosperity, and prosperity was a condition to which every society aspired and that every government therefore felt obliged to promise. To work effectively, free markets require what state-building is intended to create: institutions, in particular the financial structures at the heart of a market economy and the governmental institutions necessary to secure property rights and enforce contracts.

Moreover, working free markets tend, once established, to promote the democratic politics that promise to alleviate the security problems for which the United States had assumed responsibility in the twenty-first century. This is so for several reasons: because once people make their own economic choices, as they do in free market economies, it is natural for them to make political choices, which is the essence of democracy; because the private economy that the free market creates provides a base for political activity independent of state sponsorship and control, which democracy requires; and because the affluent citizens that a successful market economy produces have the time and the inclination to participate in politics, which is yet another hallmark of democracy.[77]

At the outset of the twenty-first century, the formula for achieving material well-being through market institutions and practices included not only establishing free markets within the borders of sovereign states but also participating in the international economy in order to take full advantage of the products, the money, the technology, and the expertise available from other countries. A major incentive for constructing proper market institutions and adopting proper market practices was that these were necessary prerequisites for gaining access to the global economy. A number of countries—Ireland, Portugal, and the formerly Communist countries of Central Europe, for example—implemented serious reforms so as to qualify for membership in the European

Union. China promised to do the same to gain admittance to the World Trade Organization.

Here the United States played an important role, a role comparable, once again, to that of governments within states. Just as the world's most powerful country had assumed responsibility for a variety of aspects of international security, so, too, it undertook, in a number of ways, to keep the international economy in good working order. For the global economy, as for international security, the United States functioned, in the wake of the Cold War, as the world's government.

Chapter Three

THE GLOBAL ECONOMY

As treasury secretary, I observed that the global economy depended on the U.S. economy, that the U.S. economy depended on the consumer, that the consumer depended on the stock market, and that the stock market depended increasingly on 30 or 40 stocks. I also remarked that the main thing we had to fear was the lack of fear itself, and that the world economy could not fly forever on a single American engine.

LAWRENCE H. SUMMERS, "AMERICA OVERDRAWN"[1]

Enforcement

A country's security depends on its economy: People must pay for the police and the soldiers who keep them safe.[2] The reverse also holds true and is just as important: Economic activity requires security. Within countries it is the government that provides the secure political framework for producing, buying, and selling.[3] In the international economy much of the confidence needed to proceed with transactions and the protection that engenders this confidence come from the policies of the United States. Thus, in matters of international economics, as with international security, the world's strongest country functions as the world's government.

The need for security in economic affairs can be seen in

the two meanings of the word "market." It is the physical place where people go to exchange some goods for others, or for money, but it is also a *system* of exchange, one that extends in both time and space. Trade takes place over great distances among people who never see each other. The time between the making of a contract and the delivery of what has been contracted for, and between delivery and payment, can stretch beyond days and weeks into months and even years.

In order for a market system to operate successfully, those involved must have confidence that the seller will deliver what he or she has promised, that the buyer will pay, and that no third party will seize either the product or the payment. By enforcing property rights, contracts, and laws against theft, government engenders this confidence. Most transactions proceed smoothly, with all parties fulfilling the obligations they have undertaken, because the parties know that if one of them defaults, the government will step in and put things right. This is one of government's basic functions: to serve as a kind of commercial guarantor.[4]

The absence of a supreme global authority to provide enforcement for economic transactions across sovereign borders was of relatively little consequence for most of human history because the volume of such transactions was modest. For most of human history, economic activity was local in scope, not national, let alone international. International commerce, such as it was, took place mainly by sea. Ships armed themselves for protection against raiders or relied on the naval forces of the countries from which they had embarked. When they did reach faraway destinations, much of their trade was by barter.

In the second half of the nineteenth century, however, the revolutionary advances in transportation—the steamship and the railroad—considerably expanded the flow of cross-border trade. This first great age of globalization brought with it an increasing need for the kind of enforcement upon which domestic economic activity already depended. The country that was then the world's strongest commercial and naval power, Great Britain, provided it.

With the world's largest empire, Britain actually governed much of the planet, giving intra-imperial commerce the same protection that trade and investment within well-governed nation-states enjoy. As the world's most powerful maritime force, the Royal Navy supplied protection to seaborne commerce, much of which originated or terminated in one part or another of the British Empire.[5] The British navy also occasionally compelled foreign governments to fulfill economic commitments they had made by threatening bombardment or occupation, a practice known as "gunboat diplomacy." By the second half of the twentieth century, the British had lost their empire and with it their commercial and naval primacy. The country that succeeded Britain as the world's richest and most powerful, the United States, stepped in to provide a secure political framework for international economic activity.

In the second half of the twentieth century, the second great age of globalization, most cross-border economic transactions took place within what came to be known as the trilateral world, which consisted of Western Europe, North America, and Japan.[6] Not coincidentally, the trilateral countries were those to whose security the United States was most strongly committed. International trade and investment—in general, not only by the United States—followed the American flag.

The American navy, the most powerful in the world, patrolled both the Atlantic and the Pacific Oceans, the great trade routes connecting North America to Europe and Asia, assuring the safe passage of the growing volume of commerce along these routes. The treaties that the United States signed to protect Western Europe and Japan, and the American troops stationed within their borders to fulfill the terms of these treaties in case of attack, ensured that governments well-disposed to, and well-equipped for, international commerce—market-friendly, property-protecting governments rather than Communist regimes hostile to both—would hold power in these countries. In this way American military power performed for the wealthy parts of the international system the task that governments carry out within sovereign states: enforcement.

In the second age of globalization, a particularly sharp rise in the transborder flow of goods and capital took place in Western Europe, the result of the carefully negotiated process of European integration that led to the establishment of the six-member European Economic Community (EEC) in 1958, which had become, by 2005, the twenty-five-country European Union. The United States helped to launch this process, and so contributed to the expansion of international economic activity, in two ways.

In 1947, two years after the end of World War II, Washington offered economic assistance to the war-ravaged countries of Europe. A condition of receiving funds from the European Recovery Program, which came to be known as the Marshall Plan after George C. Marshall, the American secretary of state who first announced it, was that the recipient countries cooperate economically with one another. The habit that the Marshall Plan sought to foster became institutionalized with the 1957 Treaty of Rome that established the EEC.

The presence of American military forces in Europe also

fostered economic cooperation by removing what had been, historically, one of the chief obstacles to it, the security competition among the countries of the continent. On two occasions in the twentieth century, that competition had erupted in wars that, among other things, had put a stop to international commerce on any appreciable scale. France and Germany each felt freer to trade with and invest in the other when neither had to be concerned with protecting itself from an attack by the other. In this sense NATO made the EU possible.

While the trilateral world remained the core of the international economic system, in the course of the second half of the twentieth century other countries became important parts of it, and those countries usually had close political and often military ties with the United States. In the century's last three decades, a number of Asian countries achieved remarkable rates of economic growth, in no small part through exports. Of these, South Korea played host to American troops, Taiwan was an informal ally of the United States, Indonesia had close American connections, and the American navy made port calls at Singapore and the British colony of Hong Kong. The Asians' close association with the United States both helped to protect the trade in which they engaged and made them seem to investors reliable destinations for capital. The American security treaty with Japan made it easier for other Asians to establish economic ties with that country, which had attacked, conquered, and occupied them in the 1940s, just as the American presence in Europe had eased its neighbors', and erstwhile victims', fears of Germany. Similarly, the decision of the world's two most populous countries, by China in the 1980s and India in the 1990s, to involve themselves far more deeply in the international economy coincided in both cases with an upgrading of their political and military relations with the United States.

The American role in supplying the necessary service of enforcement for the international economic order is similar to the American provision of reassurance in security affairs. Both roles arise from the global deployment of American military forces, the original mission of which was neither economic enforcement nor reassurance but rather the deterrence of the Soviet Union and other Communist countries. The United States Navy patrolled the world's two greatest oceans principally to keep the sea lanes of communication open in case of war: The protection this afforded commercial shipping came as a by-product of that mission.

The parallel between reassurance and enforcement goes even further. The purpose of each is to foster confidence, the confidence that normal, desirable political and economic activity will proceed uninterrupted. Because they guarantee what is normal and therefore not usually considered worthy of note, the two roles are not visible and for that reason not appreciated. They are taken for granted. They are being successfully carried out if and when nothing noteworthy happens.

This does not, however, mean that they are unimportant. To the contrary, to the extent that reassurance keeps at bay the kind of political conflict that produced the two world wars of the twentieth century, and enforcement permits the international economy to flourish, nothing the United States does in the world is more important. In this way the Goliath of the twenty-first century serves to soothe the nerves and ease the everyday lives of the inhabitants of weaker countries, rather than terrifying them as the original Goliath did.

It is conceivable that an American military presence in Europe, if not Asia, is no longer necessary to stifle the historically familiar and occasionally devastating impulse for security competition among the sovereign states of these regions because they have become so strongly invested in peaceful international relations—although no country there has appeared anxious to evict the United States in order to discover whether this might be so.

Similarly, the habits of compliance with economic commitments may have become so deeply ingrained since the end of World War II that the international economy would function smoothly without the American military standing by. Europeans, after all, were transporting goods and capital beyond their borders on a large scale well before the United States had a global military presence on the continent. The diminished need for the United States to supply the services of enforcement to the global economy is at least a debatable proposition—although, again, the countries that benefited from those services did not insist, in the early years of the new century, on conducting that debate.

One crucial international economic activity, however, indisputably continued to require American protection. This was the trade in one of the world's most valuable commodities, for which protection continued to be needed because it was located in one of the world's most volatile regions. The commodity is oil, the region the Middle East.

Oil

The world runs on oil. Without a reliable supply, the industrial economies would cough, sputter, and in some cases grind to a halt.[7] The supply of oil is an international matter because of a geographic mismatch: The places where the planet's

major reserves are located are different, and sometimes distant, from the places where the rates of consumption are
highest.

Almost no major industrial country, including, since the
1970s, the one where the first huge oil well was discovered in
1901 and that once produced more than any other—the
United States—has enough oil within its own borders to sustain its economy. Oil moves, and must move, across sovereign
borders in huge quantities for the global economy to keep
turning over.

It is the United States that has undertaken the principal
responsibility for safeguarding this movement, thereby assuring an adequate supply of oil to the world, in much the same
way that formally constituted governments have the responsibility for delivering water and electricity within their jurisdictions. American naval forces patrol the sea lanes over which oil
is transported, with particular attention to places where the
flow is vulnerable to disruptions.[8] During the second half of
the twentieth century, the United States established friendly
political relations, and sometimes close military associations,
with governments of most of the major oil-producing countries: Mexico and Venezuela in Latin America, Indonesia in
Asia, and Nigeria in Africa.[9]

By far the highest concentration of the world's proven oil
reserves, an estimated 60 percent to two-thirds of them, lies
in countries in the Persian Gulf region of the Middle East.[10]
In 1980, in the wake of the overthrow of the pro-Western
shah of Iran by Islamic radicals and the Soviet invasion of
neighboring Afghanistan, the United States made formal its
commitment to assuring the continuing flow of oil from that
part of the world with what came to be known as the "Carter
Doctrine." President Jimmy Carter announced that "an

attempt by any outside force to gain control of the Persian Gulf region will be regarded as an assault on the vital interests of the United States of America, and such an assault will be repelled by any means necessary, including military force."[11] Of the countries of the region, the one richest in oil, with between 20 and 25 percent of the world's total reserves, is the Kingdom of Saudi Arabia, with which the United States maintained a special relationship.

In most important ways the two countries could hardly be more different: the one a sprawling, open, tolerant, law-governed, outward-looking, secular democracy with a strong Christian heritage; the other a sparsely populated, culturally rigid tribal autocracy governed by a combination of Islamic law and the most radical and xenophobic of Islamic traditions. Despite these deep social, cultural, and political differences, the two managed to establish a partnership that controlled the global market for the world's indispensable commodity.

The official U.S.-Saudi relationship began with a 1945 meeting between the American president Franklin Roosevelt and the Saudi king, Ibn Saud, on an American warship as Roosevelt was traveling back to Washington from a meeting with his World War II allies, Winston Churchill and Joseph Stalin, at Yalta, a Black Sea port in what was then the Soviet Union. The United States and Saudi Arabia shared a postwar antipathy to communism, and in the 1950s and 1960s the United States supported the Saudi monarchy against the challenge to its rule mounted by Egypt's leader, Gamal Abdel Nasser, who sought to extend his own power throughout the Arab world under the guise of pan-Arab solidarity. The two oil shocks of the 1970s, which sent world oil prices soaring, changed but also ultimately solidified the relationship between the two countries.

The shocks had political causes: The first grew out of the embargo the Arab oil-producing countries tried to impose on the United States and the Netherlands as punishment for their support for Israel in its October 1973 war with Egypt and Syria; the second came after the revolution in Iran that drove the pro-American monarch, the Shah, from power and replaced him with radical clerics led by the Ayatollah Ruhollah Khomeini—an upheaval that interrupted Iranian oil production. Both events led to the withdrawal of oil supplies from the world market, which, with demand unchanged, drove up the price.

Global oil supplies declined in each case because the United States no longer had the capacity to compensate for the shortfall. Seven decades of expanding production in North America had depleted the once-vast American reserves of easily accessible oil. Now it was Saudi Arabia, with its even larger reserves, that had become the world's "swing" producer, able to increase or decrease its output on short notice.[12] Saudi oil abundance formed the basis for the partnership with the United States that emerged in the wake of the two oil shocks.

For its part, the United States provided the kingdom with military protection against external threats, which meant guaranteeing the perpetuation of the power of the al-Saud tribe, from which the ruling family came and that appropriated to itself a large share of the revenues from the sale of oil. Although the Saudi regime spent lavishly on expensive (and usually American-made) weapons, there was no expectation, either within Saudi Arabia or elsewhere, that the kingdom would be able to defend itself against a serious attack. In the 1980s, the Saudi rulers needed protection from the Islamic Republic of Iran, which proclaimed the Saudi regime (and the

others of the region) insufficiently faithful to religious principles and therefore deserving of removal from power. Accordingly, the United States aligned itself informally with Iran's
Arab neighbor, Iraq, in the bloody war between the two that
lasted from 1980 to 1988.

The Saudi monarchy, in turn, undertook to keep the world
price of oil stable, pumping more when supplies tightened and
the price rose but also on occasion cutting back on production
to try to put a floor under the price. Consumers of oil had a
major economic interest, for the short term, at least, in a
steady (or a declining) oil price. Stability served Saudi interests
as well. Although low oil prices—and in real terms the price of
oil did decline in the 1980s and 1990s—reduced the revenues
at the regime's disposal,[13] sustained high prices would reduce
consumption and ultimately revenue by encouraging conservation and making commercially viable hard-to-extract non-
Saudi oil as well as non-oil sources of energy.

In 1991, the American side of the bargain involved the
United States in a war in the region. While Iraq's clear violation of international law in transgressing an internationally
recognized border and seizing control of Kuwait gave the
operation to reverse its aggression a firm legal foundation, the
moving force behind the American decision to act was a concern about the fate of the region's oil. Had Saddam Hussein
been allowed to remain in Kuwait unchallenged, he would
have controlled that country's oil as well as the considerable
reserves of Iraq itself, which together amounted to approximately 17 percent of the world's total.[14] In addition, he would
have been in a position to threaten and intimidate Saudi Arabia and perhaps even manipulate the Saudis' oil policy.

From the American point of view, the 1991 Gulf conflict
was, at its heart, a war to defend Saudi oil.[15] A reckless, ruth-

less dictator holding sway over more than 40 percent of the world's oil reserves was an outcome the United States was unwilling to permit and so went to war to prevent. The Saudi royal family held up its end of the bargain with the United States by pumping enough oil to keep the world price steady throughout the crisis that the invasion of Kuwait triggered, by opening its territory to the American military forces that used it as a base from which to launch their attack on the Iraqi troops in Kuwait, and by contributing, out of its own treasury, some 60 billion dollars to the cost of the war.

Contrary to the expectations of most governments, Saddam's resounding military defeat in Kuwait did not lead to his overthrow in Iraq, so in the decade following the war the United States undertook to protect Saudi Arabia, and the smaller oil-producing sheikhdoms of the Persian Gulf, from both Iraq and Iran, a policy known in Washington as "dual containment." That policy, and the Saudi-American partnership, received, however, another shock on September 11, 2001.

The terrorist attacks on the World Trade Center in New York and the Pentagon in Washington qualified, in a number of respects, as Saudi attacks on the United States. Most of the attackers, fourteen of the nineteen men who seized the four planes that were commandeered, were Saudi nationals. Osama bin Laden, the leader of the organization, al Qaeda, that had recruited, trained, and dispatched them, came from a wealthy Saudi family and used his own money and that of other affluent Saudis to finance his terrorist network. Al Qaeda's animating ideology, a fanatical form of Islam known as Wahhabism, also had Saudi roots. Its founder was Ibn Abd al-Wahhab, an eighteenth century cleric in the Arabian peninsula whose ideas the al-Saud tribe adopted to justify and guide its rule there.[16]

The attacks had contradictory effects on the relationship between Saudi Arabia and the United States. On the one hand, they cast the kingdom, in American eyes, in a distinctly unfavorable light—as a theocratic successor to the Soviet Union as the world headquarters of a murderous, totalitarian, anti-American ideology.[17] Americans, most of whom had known little about Saudi society before September 11, learned, among other things, that it relegated women to second-class citizenship and prohibited worship in any faith other than Islam. Neither practice was well regarded in the United States and both had the effect, when Americans became aware of them, of calling into question the wisdom and morality of defending, with American blood and treasure, the regime that imposed them.

The attacks of September 11 not only revealed the Saudi regime to be, by the standards of most Americans, an odious one, but they also pointed to the conclusion that the close American association with that regime was at least partly responsible for those attacks. For al Qaeda's principal grievance against the United States was the ongoing American support for the Saudi monarchy, which bin Laden denounced, not entirely inaccurately, as corrupt, hypocritical, impious, and generally unfit to rule.[18] Accordingly, the American government moved to distance itself from the regime, withdrawing the troops it had stationed in the kingdom since the 1991 war (and relocating some of them to the nearby sheikhdoms).[19]

On the other hand, the attacks made the perpetuation of the rule of the al-Saud family on the Arabian peninsula seem an even more important American interest. The events of September 11 did not, after all, change the distribution of petroleum reserves on the planet, nor did they eliminate the global economy's appetite for oil.[20] The attacks did, however, reveal the character of the forces that aspired to replace the al-Saud tribe as the rulers of the country with the world's largest oil deposits. Unattractive as the Saudi royal family was by American standards, it was at least committed—for its own reasons, to be sure—to extracting and exporting that oil. As the world's demand for oil rose in the early decades of the twenty-first century, that commitment would become ever more important for the health of the international economy, since the largest pool of readily accessible untapped oil lay beneath the sands of the kingdom. By contrast, people capable of organizing and exulting in the murder of almost 3,000 civilians, as were al Qaeda's leaders, seemed equally capable of shutting off the flow of oil altogether if they managed to seize control of Saudi Arabia, as they aspired to do. Bad as America's Saudi partners appeared to be in the light of the events of September 11, the alternative loomed as worse.[21]

The United States therefore confronted a dilemma: The Saudi regime was both unacceptable and indispensable. Supporting it risked expanding the global pool of terrorists; abandoning it risked shrinking the global supply of oil. An American strategy for resolving the dilemma emerged from the events that September 11 set in motion.

In the wake of these attacks, the United States first overthrew the Taliban regime that had sheltered al Qaeda in Afghanistan and then, in 2003, removed Saddam Hussein from power in Iraq. The second Iraq war had a conservative aim: to prevent Saddam from acquiring weapons with which he could overturn the status quo in the region and establish himself as its overlord. The United States also proclaimed what was, by the standards of the Middle East, a radical goal for the Iraq war: the establishment of a democratic government in Iraq that would, over time, by the force of its example, catalyze a democratic transformation in the rest of the hitherto entirely undemocratic Arab world.

In 2004, as the United States struggled to help Iraqis form a stable, open, liberal, representative government, the administration of George W. Bush announced the Greater Middle East Initiative, a program designed to promote, over the course of several years and perhaps as long as a generation, the growth of democracy in that part of the world. From the American, Western, and global standpoint, the democratic transformation of the Arab world was a logical aspiration. Democratic countries tend, on the whole, to be more peaceful and prosperous than undemocratic ones.[22] A democratic Saudi Arabia in particular could be expected to cease propagating the murderous religious ideology that had led to the September 11 attacks because its government would have a different, sturdier, and far more benign basis for political legitimacy. Democracy had the potential to transform the repository of the planet's largest deposits of oil from the rogue state that it had seemed to be, in the wake of September 11, into a reliable partner for the United States and the rest of the world.

Desirable though such a transformation was in theory, however, the project to bring it about in practice raised three formidable difficulties. First, as the state-building efforts of the post–Cold War period had made painfully evident, neither the United States, nor the United Nations, nor any other country or organization possessed a formula for effecting this transformation. No one knows how to turn Saudi Arabia into Denmark.[23]

Second, the effort to do so risked unintended and unwelcome consequences. Pressing the Saudi regime to reform might have the effect of toppling it from power, to be replaced by a fundamentalist regime even more dangerous to American and global interests. This possibility reproduced a foreign policy problem familiar from the Cold War era. With a number of undemocratic but also anti-Communist regimes, the United States had faced the "friendly tyrant" dilemma: whether to be true to American values, above all democracy, by opposing (or at least refraining from embracing) them or to pursue its interest in maintaining the broadest possible anti-Soviet coalition by supporting them.[24]

In several such countries, notably the Shah's Iran and the Nicaragua of Anastasio Somoza, a pro-American dictator was forced from power with little or no resistance by the United States, only to be succeeded by a government—the Islamic Republic in Iran, the Marxist Sandinista regime in Nicaragua —no more democratic than the one it replaced but considerably more hostile to the United States. The interests of the United States and the health of the global economy would not be served by a repetition, in Saudi Arabia, of what had happened in Iran and Nicaragua in the 1970s.

Third, even the successful conversion of Saudi Arabia and the rest of the Arab world into Middle Eastern versions of the democratic, peaceful countries of Western Europe would not address the principal long-term problem associated with oil that the world would eventually have to confront, a problem rooted not in geopolitics but in geology. That problem stems from the fact that the amount of oil stored beneath the earth's surface and available for extraction is finite. Some day it will run out. Just when this will occur cannot be forecast with any confidence. It depends on the rate of consumption, itself subject to wide swings over time, and on the unpredictable development of new and more sophisticated techniques for finding and extracting oil.[25] At least several decades' worth of oil remains untapped. At some point toward the end of the twenty-first century or the beginning of the twenty-second, however—if not before—the global economy will have to run on other sources of energy.

The transition away from reliance on oil has several precedents. Human history is, among other things, the history of the transition from one source of energy to another: from the calories expended by human labor to wood, to coal, and ultimately to oil.[26] Nature offers a number of candidates to succeed oil: other fossil fuels, notably coal and natural gas, both in extensive use at the outset of the twenty-first century; nuclear energy, perhaps one day using the process of fusion that takes place in the sun and is a potentially limitless source but that was not, in the new millennium's first decade, close to being harnessed for human use; hydrogen; and the so-called "renewables"—natural steam, wind, solar power, and energy from plants known as biomass.[27]

The replacement of oil will in one way be easier than the previous transitions: The relevant basic scientific information—how much energy is available from which sources—is well known. In another way, however, this transition promises to be unprecedentedly difficult. Technologies must be developed, and infrastructure built, to extract energy from hydrogen, the sun, and the other potential sources, and make it available for transportation and the generation of electricity, in ways that are commercially viable. At the beginning of the twenty-first century those technologies, and therefore that infrastructure, were not well developed. Hydrogen-fueled cars and solar heating were novelties or pilot projects, neither of them capable of fulfilling a substantial part of global demand at affordable prices.

In the world's long-term transition away from an oil-based energy system, the United States has an important role to play, and once again it is a role that resembles what governments often do within sovereign states. Research and development on a large scale will be required to devise and produce the technologies to make non-oil sources of energy sufficiently plentiful and accessible to replace petroleum altogether. In many cases the costs of what needs to be done will be too high, and the prospects for a commercial payoff from the technologies too distant, to induce private industry to undertake it.[28] If it is to be done, governments will have to do it. Because the United States is the world's richest country, with the largest share of its scientific and engineering talent, the American government is a logical candidate to sponsor the creation of alternative energy technologies.[29]

Even with the active financial support of the American government, however, the task of devising an alternative energy system will be a formidable one. It will have something in common with two well-known government-sponsored undertakings in the twentieth century, the Manhattan Project, which produced the first atomic bombs during World War II, and the Apollo Project, which sent a man to the moon for the first time in the 1960s. In both cases the government organized, managed, and paid for a massive, complex, and expensive exercise in engineering and construction, which required inventing a whole host of new technologies. Fostering the transition to a new energy system differs from bomb making and manned space flight, however, in two ways that make it more complicated.

First, the goal is broader. The Manhattan Project developed two different kinds of atomic explosives, but a new energy system will require many different ways of extracting and using energy. Second, the Manhattan and Apollo Projects remained entirely outside the commercial economy, but the new energy system will have to be fully integrated into it; indeed, in some sense it will have to underpin it. The space program did not have as its goal earning enough money by ferrying passengers to and from the moon to pay for itself, but new energy technologies, to replace existing ones, will have to be profitable, just as extracting, refining, and selling oil are.

Although governments, and especially the American government, have an important part to play in promoting the transition from an oil-based global economy to one that draws the energy it requires from other sources, much of the burden of carrying the world from one to the other will rest on one of the central features of a commercial market economy: the price mechanism. Price mediates between supply and demand. When the supply of something diminishes or fails to keep pace with the demand for it, its price rises. Consumers, in response, find ways to save money by using less of it—by greater efficiency in its use or by substituting other things for it, or both. The world switched to oil from coal because oil was cheaper and easier to use.

Although when it will begin and at what rate it will proceed cannot be precisely known, the price of oil will likely rise in the twenty-first century, and ultimately will rise substantially. Oil production will reach its peak—the point at which half of all the Earth's reserves have been used—and after that, some students of geology and energy believe, extraction will become more difficult and therefore more expensive.[30] Whether it comes at this halfway point or later, sometime in the present century the cost of extraction is likely to move sharply upward.

The demand for oil, meanwhile, is certain to increase, as a consequence of the economic growth that all countries seek in the twenty-first century. The greater the rate of growth, the higher the consumption of energy, and in particular of oil, tends to be. The surging output of the world's two most populous countries, China and India, will exert particularly strong upward pressure on the global demand for the world's favorite source of energy. By one estimate the demand for energy will double in the three decades between 2004 and 2035.[31]

In the early decades of the twenty-first century, this will increase reliance on output from Saudi Arabia in particular, which in turn will require multi-billion-dollar investments to expand the Saudi capacity for oil production. (The price spike of 2005, with oil rising above $70 per barrel, stemmed from a shortage of capacity rather than from political disturbances.) International investors may shy away from committing such sums to a country and a region that seem politically unstable, while the Saudi government, for its own reasons, may be reluctant to expand the capacity of its oil industry as much as global oil demand would warrant. In any case, over time the combination of tightening supply and rising demand will boost the price of oil, triggering a shift away from the extensive reliance on it characteristic of the second half of the twentieth century and the early years of the twenty-first.

The price mechanism by itself, however, may not provide a smooth transition from one energy system to another. For one thing, the price of oil, especially in the United States, did not, at the outset of the new millennium, fully reflect its true cost. The use of oil involved costs for which the consumer did not pay. These include the pollution that burning oil to produce energy generates, which imposes the extra cost of removing it from the air, and, for Americans, the money they spend on the military forces that assure access to oil located outside the country, especially in the Persian Gulf.[32] By one estimate, if all the costs of gasoline consumption were imposed at the pump, Americans would pay a full dollar more for a gallon of gasoline than they actually do.[33]

Moreover, the price mechanism does not work perfectly for oil because the market for oil is not an entirely free one. It is partly controlled by an oligopoly, the Organization of Petroleum Exporting Countries (OPEC), which, among other things, prevents the oil that is cheapest to pump from being extracted before deposits that are more expensive to tap are exploited.[34]

For this and other reasons, and because the supply of oil is subject to politically-driven interruptions of the kind that occurred in 1973 and 1979 and could happen again—with turmoil in Saudi Arabia, for instance—it is possible that the rise in the price of oil will not be gradual and will not give the world time to make the necessary adjustments in the pattern of its production and consumption of energy. Instead, the rise may occur abruptly, administering a grievous shock to the global economy.[35] The second case would inflict damage on all economies that depend on imported oil, which is to say virtually all of the world's major economies. It would likely cause both inflation and a decline in output and could lead to political and even military competition among countries for access to oil.[36]

The difference between the two scenarios for moving from one energy system to another may be compared to two ways of changing homes. The first, the protracted and relatively smooth transition, corresponds to the normal, and preferable, way in which people move. They decide that they want a new home, search the real estate advertisements, with the help of a realtor visit homes for sale to find the right one, purchase it, sell their old home, and then pack, transport, and install their possessions in the new place. This is ordinarily a months-long process, and while seldom free of tensions and difficulties, it is something that millions of people do every year.

By contrast, a sudden, sharp shift upward in the price of oil would visit upon the world an experience comparable to a far less desirable way of changing residences: a fire destroys a house and everything in it. To add to the trauma of what amounts to a sudden eviction from comfortable lodgings, insurance does not cover the full cost of what was lost. The new, hastily purchased home therefore lacks the size and the comforts of the old one. Many years are required to earn enough money to buy a home comparable to the one that was lost. So might it be with the level of global output that a plentiful supply of oil has made possible, if the transition away from dependence on oil turns out to be a rocky one.

Governments can take steps to make the transition smoother, longer, and less abrupt than relying exclusively on market forces would likely make it. They can impose energy-saving regulations, in particular high mileage requirements for moving vehicles. They can raise the price of gasoline by taxing it. In response to these steps consumers would use less oil, the higher price would render other, more expensive sources of energy more attractive for investment and production, and the supply of the two things needed for a smooth transition—time and alternative sources of energy—would increase.[37]

In addition to easing the transition to a new energy system, decreased energy consumption, especially of oil, would bring short-term benefits. It would make the world less vulnerable to politically-induced interruptions in the supply of petroleum. It would reduce the flow of money to the Persian Gulf and thus shrink the pool of resources available to finance Islamic terrorism. By depriving the governments of that region, particularly the Saudi regime, of some of their oil revenues, it would encourage economic and perhaps even political reform, in order to keep the local standard of living from plummeting. It would reduce the trade deficit of the United States, the size of which posed a threat to the international economy as a whole. Government-mandated regulations to conserve energy and subsidies for alternative sources of energy are in fact official policy in Western Europe, where, in addition, taxes on energy and especially gasoline are considerably higher than in the United States, and per capita energy use is accordingly considerably lower.[38]

Because it is by far the largest consumer of oil of any country in the world, accounting for about one-fourth of the global total, the United States could make an enormous contribution to assuring a smooth, manageable energy transition by taking these steps.[39] Here, as in other areas of international affairs, it is in a position to perform a service for the international system as a whole. But deliberately reducing its consumption of oil is one global service that the United States has refused to furnish.

Its refusal to do so has several causes. Perhaps the most important of them is the fact that the issue of energy usage creates a conflict, or at least a trade-off, between long-term and short-term economic well-being. Over the long term, the United States, and other countries, would be better served by a high price for oil, to encourage conservation and the shift to other sources of energy. But a rise in the price of oil would have, and on occasion has already had, an adverse short-term economic effect, which even a carefully controlled price increase might not avoid. In the last three decades of the twentieth century, every significant increase in the price of oil was associated with a recession in the industrial countries.[40]

Moreover, in the United States far more than in any other Western country, taxation of any kind arouses substantial political opposition. Americans, more than most other people, also bridle at accepting limits of almost any kind. To base national energy policy on the assumption, scientifically grounded though it is, that the world's oil supply will someday become exhausted smacks of pessimism, which runs counter to the national ethos. Where energy was concerned, in the early years of the twenty-first century the prevailing American sentiment echoed the motto of Wilkins Micawber, a character in Charles Dickens's novel *David Copperfield*, who moved through life unfazed by mounting debts, operating on the cheerful principle that to meet any difficulty "something will always turn up."[41]

Indeed, after the shocks of the 1970s the balance between supply and demand shifted so that over the two decades beginning in the mid-1970s oil was relatively cheap. In response, rather than continuing the trend, which the oil shocks began, of conservation and energy efficiency, the United States had resumed, by the mid-1980s, what was, in comparison with the patterns in other industrial democracies, its prodigal use of energy.[42] In this sense the energy problem resembles the rationale behind the doctrine of preventive war: By the time the problem is glaringly apparent, it will be too late to deal with it at a reasonable cost.

Even if the United States were to reduce its oil consumption to European levels—even, that is, under the most favorable circumstances—the transition away from oil would encounter difficulties. One of the largest of them would arise from the fact that the readiest substitutes for oil are other fossil fuels, principally coal and natural gas. These are plentiful, they are more accessible than oil to large consumers of energy—including two of the largest, the United States and China, where coal is abundant—and they are already extensively used around the world.[43] If these fuels are superior from a political standpoint to oil as it is currently obtained and closer in price to oil than any of the nonfossil sources of energy, however, they are in one important way equally undesirable. They have a comparably deleterious impact on the Earth's environment. Fossil fuels aggravate a problem that affects the entire planet and has its roots not in politics or geology but in geophysics, the problem of climate change.[44]

The presence of "greenhouse gases" such as carbon dioxide in the Earth's atmosphere makes life on the planet possible. They trap some of the heat that radiates from the sun, raising, as in a greenhouse, the planet's temperature to the point at which plants and animals, including human beings, can survive.[45] In the case of the greenhouse effect, however, it is possible to have too much of a good thing. The burning of fossil fuels produces these gases, and since the outset of the Industrial Revolution, which began the ever-increasing human use of such fuels, they have accumulated in the atmosphere. The heavier the concentration, the more heat gets trapped and, eventually, the hotter the Earth and its atmosphere become. Toward the end of the twentieth century, scientists began to notice such a trend and calculated that, as industrial activity accelerated throughout the world, the greenhouse effect would increase as well, raising the average temperature of the planet by several degrees.[46]

The effects would be far-reaching and in some cases dire.

The list of consequences reads like a latter-day version of the plagues visited on the ancient Egyptians as recounted in the biblical book of Exodus. Weather patterns would change, making some regions less suitable (and some more so) for agriculture, thereby disrupting the world's food system. Polar ice caps would melt, causing the sea level to rise, which would swamp coastal communities and perhaps even entire inhabited islands. Storms would become fiercer and more frequent, inflicting more extensive damage than ever before.

To avoid these unwelcome and potentially catastrophic global effects requires limiting the concentration of greenhouse gases in the atmosphere, which means limiting and ultimately giving up altogether the use of the fossil fuels that generate them. It requires, that is, the same Herculean, long-term effort that the prospect of the ultimate exhaustion of the planet's oil necessitates, but on a faster schedule. It therefore requires an extensive American role, which the United States, in the first decade of the twenty-first century, was not playing.

The reasons for the American disinclination to treat global warming as an urgent matter requiring substantial changes in its pattern of energy consumption included both the causes of the national indifference to the specter of the end of oil—notably the absence of the kind of concrete evidence of imminent danger that could mobilize the public for corrective action—and some additional motives.[47] The scientific calculations underlying the warnings about climate change included some gaps. While there is little doubt that the global temperature is rising, that man-made emissions contribute to this,[48] and that above some level of concentration greenhouse gases would have serious adverse consequences for life on Earth, it is not clear precisely where the threshold of danger is,[49] when it might be reached, what the exact consequences will be, and which parts of the world will be most seriously affected.[50]

Moreover, the international community's organized response to the prospect of global warming, the Kyoto Protocol of 1997, has serious flaws that have made it unacceptable to the United States. While it mandated reductions in greenhouse gas emissions, it was drafted so that the burden of making them would fall mainly on the United States. The poorer countries, including one of the planet's leading polluters, China, were excused from reductions, and the quotas for the countries of Europe were set at totals that, for various reasons, they could easily achieve. Furthermore, while the treaty assigned reductions in greenhouse gases to the signatory parties, it said nothing about the complicated technical and economic problems of making them. It was, that is, a treaty whose terms the signatories did not know how to fulfill at the time they signed it. Finally, although—and perhaps because—they were set at levels that most countries would not experience difficulty in meeting, the reductions in greenhouse gases, even if they were achieved, would do little to restrain the rise in the Earth's temperature. The global warming accord would not, therefore, prevent global warming.[51] The reluctance of the United States to subscribe to it was therefore only one reason, albeit an important one, that as a mechanism for coping with the problems presented by the increasing accumulation of greenhouse gases in the Earth's atmosphere, the Kyoto Protocol was inadequate.

Preventing global warming by leading the transition from an energy system relying heavily on oil to one making extensive use of other sources of energy is an immense, long-term task that involves replacing the very foundations of the international economy. It is a task for which a major American role is necessary, not least in supporting the expensive research and development necessary to find substitutes for fossil fuels—another way in which the United States would be performing a service for the entire international system similar to one that governments routinely carry out for the societies they govern.[52] At the outset of the twenty-first century, the United States did not seem inclined to assume this responsibility. It did, however, provide other economic services to the world. Their purpose was not to create a new international economy but rather to keep the existing one functioning smoothly. One of these services duplicated something that every government does within the society over which it presides: the provision of money.

Money

Money has the same function in economic life as enforcement: it makes possible transactions that extend in time and space beyond face-to-face encounters. For most of human history precious metals, primarily gold and silver, served as the units of nonbarter exchange. Readily portable, they were universally regarded as having value and therefore universally acceptable.

In the modern era—that is, from the latter part of the eighteenth century on—governments began to issue money on an expanding scale. They were frequently motivated by the felt need for more purchasing power, above all to finance wars, than the precious metals at their disposal gave them. The result was often a familiar economic malady of the modern world: inflation. But the role of money creation that governments assumed also had a beneficial effect. It produced enough liquidity to support an increasing volume of transactions, which the slow-growing supply of gold and silver would otherwise have restricted. Government money (sometimes called "fiat" money) has thus contributed to the economic growth that sets the modern era apart from the previous stages of human history.

While there is, and has been for many centuries, a world economy, there is no world government to issue a global currency. In the first great age of globalization in the nineteenth century, when commerce conducted across borders grew rapidly, because every government issued its own money—this had come to be a mark of sovereignty—a method had to be found to convert one country's money to that of another when transactions between the two took place. The gold standard, the first comprehensive international monetary system, served this purpose. All parties to it used gold to back their currencies and for international exchange.[53]

The gold standard had several advantages. It knit the world's major trading partners together into a system of clear rules. It fixed the value of every currency in relation to all the others, thereby imparting predictability about costs to international transactions. By fixing the value of each currency, the gold standard prevented inflation. Finally, and not least importantly, it provided a more or less automatic mechanism for countries to adjust to surpluses or deficits in their transactions with the rest of the world.

The mechanism of adjustment ultimately doomed the gold standard, however. It dealt with a payments deficit by lowering the level of economic activity in the country involved, which, while reducing the deficit, also drove down wages and pushed up unemployment. In the nineteenth century, with the franchise limited, the people who suffered from the operation of the gold standard carried little political weight and so could not effectively oppose it. In the twentieth century, with universal suffrage, they could and they did.

World War I interrupted the gold standard—and the international economy in general—and in the wake of the war, political pressures thwarted governments' efforts to reinstate it. After World War II, they did not even try to do so. Instead, in 1944 at a conference in Bretton Woods, New Hampshire, the United States and Great Britain devised a new monetary system that sought to combine some of the advantages of fixed exchange rates with greater flexibility, and thus less automatic economic distress, than the gold standard had imposed. The new system had the American dollar at its center. The United States came to supply money to the entire world, just as governments do within countries.

The Bretton Woods system put the world on a gold-exchange standard. Dollars, but not other currencies, could be exchanged for gold, at the rate of $35 per ounce. The values of the world's other currencies were pegged to the dollar. In practice, this made the dollar the world's currency. It became the international "vehicle" currency, used for trade and investment even when the United States was not involved. It also became the world's "reserve" currency, with countries holding it to back their own money and to pay for their international obligations.

The special, and privileged, international role of the dollar conferred economic advantages upon the United States, which could pay its foreign bills in the currency that it itself printed.[54] Because of the extensive responsibilities for international security that the United States undertook in the postwar period, as well as because of the large American appetite for purchases of other kinds, those bills mounted.

Whereas in 1945 the world suffered from a dollar shortage, with less of the American currency available than individuals, firms, and governments the world over wanted to have, two decades later the steady issuance of it had created a dollar glut. More dollars were in circulation than the American government could redeem with its supply of gold. This led to the criticism, made most forcefully by President Charles de Gaulle of France, that the United States had abused its position at the center of the international monetary order in much the same way that governments sometimes abuse their monopoly on the issuance of domestic currencies in pursuit of their own particular goals, leading to an excess of currency and therefore to inflation. The glut of dollars similarly threatened other countries with a general increase in prices.[55]

Other countries, however, were willing to hold more dollars than they wanted or needed in purely economic terms. The largest holders were West Germany and Japan, which had two reasons for doing so. Refusing dollars would have overturned the Bretton Woods system itself, a system in which they were prospering. And the United States spent some of the dollars that they accumulated on defending them against the Soviet Union. By holding dollars beyond the economically optimal total, the two countries were, in effect, paying a tax to support a vital service, just as individuals pay taxes to their own governments to purchase the military forces that protect them.[56]

The Bretton Woods system did come to an end, but it was the United States itself, not France, Germany, or Japan, that ended it, by announcing that it would no longer pay out gold in exchange for dollars. The American government acted because the Bretton Woods system, by fixing the American exchange rate at what became, over the years, an artificially high level, made American exports less and less competitive, leading in 1971 to the first American trade deficit since 1893.[57] (The boost that fixed exchange rates of the Bretton Woods system gave to their own exports was another reason that Germany and Japan were willing to hold dollars in large amounts in order to sustain it.) To increase its exports (and please politically influential exporting industries) the United States had to lower the international value of its currency; but that meant abandoning the Bretton Woods rules, which the Nixon administration did on August 15, 1971.

In retrospect, the fundamental flaw of the Bretton Woods system was not American economic profligacy but rather a contradiction in the status of the dollar, one most prominently noted by the Belgian-American economist Robert Triffin and known as the "Triffin paradox." Its role as the world's vehicle currency, used in transactions everywhere, required an increasing volume of dollars in order to support the steady post–World War II expansion of international commerce. But its role as the world's reserve currency, used to guarantee the value of all other currencies, required restraint in dollar creation so that the United States would always be able to supply gold to countries that wanted to trade their dollars for it. It was this contradiction that ultimately doomed the Bretton Woods system.[58]

The world was unable to devise a fully articulated monetary system to replace it. In particular, the major economic powers could not agree on rules to govern exchange rates, and so the international economy functioned, after August 15, 1971, under a non-system: Countries were free to set the value of their currencies however they chose to do so. One feature of Bretton Woods did persist, however: the central role of the dollar. The world continued to use it more extensively than any other currency as a vehicle for transactions and as a reserve. Those tasks still had to be performed, and the American economy continued to be the world's largest. It was particularly attractive to holders of dollars because its financial markets were the deepest and most diversified in the world, offering many financial instruments in which dollars could be placed. The dollar had no real rival for the role of the world's money—until the outset of the twenty-first century.

In 1999, twelve members of the European Union pooled their separate national currencies to create a common European currency, the euro. They aspired for all members of the EU, which by 2004 numbered twenty-five countries, ultimately to adopt it. In that case, the euro would become the currency of an economy larger than that of the United States and therefore would be attractive as a reserve. It would provide ready access to the huge European economic sphere and would be widely, probably universally, accepted. Countries might choose to hold more euros, and use them increasingly for trade and investment, in addition to or instead of the dollar, circumscribing if not eliminating altogether the American role as the supplier of money to the world.[59]

While some Europeans, particularly the French, had precisely this goal for the euro—seeking to reduce American power and influence in the world and enhance their own—the principal motive for creating a common European currency was different. It was to restore one of the cardinal features of the gold standard, which the end of Bretton Woods had abolished—a fixed exchange rate to facilitate the intra-European trade and investment that the EU had been founded to foster by eliminating the risk stemming from uncertainty about currency values. The surest way to eliminate fluctuations in currency values among different countries is for them to have a common currency. With the euro, trade between France and Germany carried no more currency risk than exchanges within the United States between Massachusetts and California.

Although the euro had the potential to rival or even displace the dollar, the currency union that underlay it also had the potential to fall apart. A single currency deprives European governments of one of their chief tools of economic management because there can be only a single monetary policy for all of them. Economic conditions, however, will inevitably vary among them and a policy that is healthy for one may be harmful to another.

Economic conditions vary across the United States as well, of course, but two features of American economic life help to counteract these differences: The federal government can transfer funds on an appreciable scale, through a number of programs, from prospering to struggling regions; and Americans can move easily from one part of the country to another, from a state where jobs are scarce, for instance, to one where they are plentiful. Europe lacks both these mechanisms for coping with inequalities. In technical economic terms, it is not an "optimal currency area."[60] If some countries conclude that membership in the common currency is inflicting economic damage on them, political pressure will mount to withdraw from it. The euro may turn out not to be viable for the same reason that the gold standard could not be sustained, in which case the burdens, and the advantages,[61] of furnishing the world with its money will continue to belong to the United States.

Neither the absence of a constitution for the international monetary order, however, nor the political rivalry for international primacy between the well-established dollar and the upstart euro, qualified as the most serious international economic problem of the first decade of the twenty-first century. That distinction belonged to the prospect of national and international financial crises of the kind that had erupted in the 1990s, bringing serious economic damage to the countries involved. In coping with them, the United States once again assumed a responsibility for the international economy as a whole comparable to what governments routinely do within individual countries.

Modern economies depend on banks that operate on the principle of fractional reserves, keeping less money readily available than they have loaned to borrowers. This system provides the same benefit as government-issued currency: It makes possible the expansion of credit and thus the expansion of economic activity. But it also has a potential pitfall. Sudden, large-scale demands by depositors for the funds they have deposited may cause the bank to fail if it cannot meet those demands. Bank failures can damage the wider economy: A crucial trigger for the worldwide depression of the 1930s, the most devastating economic downturn of the modern era, was the failure of an Austrian bank. To cope with financial "panics,"[62] governments have established central banks with the power to create money and lend it to afflicted institutions to keep them solvent. In the twentieth century, they had occasion to do so.[63]

Governments can find themselves in the same position as distressed banks when they, or their citizens, borrow in a foreign currency. They must repay such loans in the currency in which it was borrowed or in reserves, rather than with money that they create. A sudden, large-scale demand for repayment can pose the same problem as a run on a bank. The pattern became familiar in the 1990s, when the removal of controls on the movement of capital in many countries led to a substantial increase in the volume of international capital flows, especially to countries that had not attracted much in the past. To cope with this problem, an international version of a national central bank is needed. In the nineteenth century, Great Britain, the world's strongest financial power, undertook to mitigate several financial panics by serving as the international "lender of last resort."[64] In the last decade of the twentieth century, an international organization, the International Monetary Fund (IMF), assumed some, although not all, of the tasks that central banks perform within countries, and the most powerful influence on the IMF was exercised by the United States.

The IMF was founded as part of the Bretton Woods system. Its initial missions were to make loans to countries with temporary balance of payments deficits to tide them over until they could correct the imbalances without having to resort to the unemployment and deflation that the gold standard had imposed, and to preside over what were expected to be the relatively rare changes in the official value of national currencies. By the 1990s, it had assumed a different, although related role: It made loans, the money for which was supplied by subscriptions from its member countries, to governments in the throes of currency crises. To qualify to receive these loans, the recipient countries were required to adopt policies designed to restore the confidence of bankers and investors, including steps to address the economic problems that the IMF believed had triggered the flight of capital in the first place. The required measures, such as high interest rates and the reduction of subsidies on food, often inflicted economic hardship on the societies involved.

In 1994, the IMF assembled a rescue package for Mexico,

and in 1997 and 1998 it did the same for several countries in East Asia, notably Thailand, South Korea and Indonesia. Each of these countries had received an influx of foreign capital, which, by virtue of an exchange rate "pegged" to the dollar, they promised to repay at a fixed rate. In each case, misguided economic policies—large government deficits in Mexico, bad loans by private banks in Asia—triggered a stampede to convert the loans back into the currencies in which they had originally been provided, forcing the governments of these countries to abandon the peg and devalue their own currencies, which only made foreign lenders (and domestic holders of the local currency in a position to do so) more anxious to withdraw their money. All of the affected countries suffered economic hardship as the result of these crises and the policies that the IMF prescribed in response to them,[65] but most recovered their economic health after several difficult years.[66]

In these episodes the IMF did some but not all of the things that central banks do within countries. It extended loans that came with strings—"conditions"—attached. But it could not, in the end, force the countries to fulfill these conditions.[67] Nor could it impose institutional reforms to strengthen national financial systems, as could a sovereign government. The amount of money at the disposal of the IMF was a tiny fraction of the total capital that flowed across international borders, and unlike national central banks, the IMF could not print the currency it lent. It had to rely on the funds it received from its member countries. Finally, the IMF did not act purely on its own initiative. The driving force behind its rescue efforts, the power behind the throne that wielded quasi-governmental authority in the financial crises of the 1990s, was the United States.

It was the American government, which holds the largest shares of the votes within the IMF[68] and exercises influence out of proportion to that share, that pressed the organization to act and that helped to negotiate the terms of the loans that were provided.[69] The United States had self-interested reasons for wanting the IMF to respond to these national financial difficulties. Economic collapse in the afflicted countries would have damaged American interests—social and economic interests in the case of neighboring Mexico and strategic interests in South Korea, where 30,000 American troops were stationed to keep Communist North Korea at bay. Because the United States was the world's leading financial power, moreover, many of the firms and individuals at financial risk in the crises were American.[70] The American government also acted, however, for the sake of the international economy as a whole, fearing that if the crises were unconstrained they would spread, thus infecting countries around the world and causing large-scale damage to global economic activity. Russia did, in fact, experience a financial crash in the wake, and probably as a consequence, of the Asian crises in 1998. Brazil had a comparable although not quite as serious episode in the same year. Among the reasons for American action, that is, was the same motive that spurs governments within sovereign states, using their central banks, to rescue private banks that are under pressure.

The conditions for IMF loans provoked two major criticisms. One was that by acting to rescue the distressed economies, the organization had aggravated the moral hazard problem, which is the danger that if people believe that they will be spared the consequences of bad loans and bad investments, they will be more likely to make them. The other criticism was that the economic measures that the IMF had prescribed as a condition for its loans were unduly harsh and inflicted greater hardship than was necessary or fair on the populations of the distressed countries, who were the innocent victims of bad economic choices made by their leaders.

The American government did not entirely escape these criticisms, but they were directed mainly at the IMF itself, which therefore served as a kind of heat shield for the United States. Because the IMF was a prominent international organization that was exercising nominal authority—and real authority as well; it was not simply a puppet of Washington—the United States was able to wield the kind of power associated with governments within countries without having to accept full responsibility for the consequences of doing so.

The monetary affairs in which the United States acted as the world's government constituted one of the two principal parts of all international economic activity. The other is trade. Where trade is concerned, according to the doctrine officially embraced by the United States and many other countries, governments should have no role at all. Nevertheless, in matters of international trade, as in international security and international monetary affairs, the United States has acted in ways similar to governments within sovereign states.

Trade

To trade, according to Adam Smith, is human. People have a natural tendency, he wrote in his pathbreaking 1776 treatise on economics, *The Wealth of Nations*, to "truck, barter, and exchange one thing for another,"[71] and the evidence available from societies around the world and through the ages supports his contention. Exchange is as natural across borders as within them, and the proper thing for governments to do about cross-border exchange, according to the consensus among professional students of economics, is to let it flow unimpeded.[72] They take their cue from the doctrine of comparative advantage, first formulated by the English economist David Ricardo in 1817, according to which countries benefit by trading with each other even if one of them can produce everything they exchange more cheaply and efficiently than the other. If the superior country concentrates on products in which its advantages are greatest, and the other country makes other products, both will, it can be mathematically demonstrated, be better off. Government interference with exchanges can only lower the welfare of trading countries, according to the doctrine of comparative advantage, which has withstood all intellectual challenges for almost two centuries.[73]

Because the proposition that international exchange most surely enhances welfare when it is unbound by regulations or controls is a scientifically grounded fact rather than a mere political preference, it might be expected that the sovereign states of the international system would spontaneously practice free trade among themselves. This is all the more plausible in the contemporary period, in which historically unprecedented prosperity has coincided with a vast increase in the volume of global trade. In fact, economic studies show that trade expansion contributes to economic growth.[74]

The United States played a major role in the expansion of global trade in the second half of the twentieth century and in so doing provided a particularly valuable service to the rest of the world. This role arose from the fact that, contrary to what would seem to be both logical and the lesson of actual experience, most governments do not gravitate toward policies of free trade. A concerted effort was needed to push the world in this direction, and the United States made by far the largest contribution to that effort.

Government-imposed barriers to trade have, historically, been the rule rather than the exception. For most of history, and well into the modern period, governments had as their principal purpose not fostering the well-being of those they governed but rather maximizing their own strength, and this often entailed achieving a trade surplus in order to use the precious metals thereby accumulated to purchase arms and finance armies.[75] Mercantilism, as the practice was called, had, in its classical form, ceased to be relevant for governments by the twentieth century. But the practice of interfering with imports and exports did not disappear with it, in part because of the widespread belief that exports are somehow more valuable and important than imports[76] and in no small part because of the political arithmetic of trade.

When a country imports a good made more efficiently abroad, it reaps both gains and losses. The cost of the good will be lower than for the same good produced domestically, and all purchasers of it will therefore save money. The sum of those savings invariably exceeds the sum of the losses to those, who are far fewer in number, who work in the domestic industry and lose their jobs because of the foreign competition.[77] The gain accruing to each of the winners is small, however, while the loss suffered by each of the losers is considerably larger. The losers therefore have a much greater incentive to organize themselves politically for the purpose of blocking imports in order to protect their jobs than do the winners in order to preserve the small gain that comes to each of them when trade is free.[78] Intensity affects the outcome of political struggles, especially in democratic political systems and especially struggles over trade. The forces favoring protection are often more intensely committed to their goal than are the forces supporting free trade, with the result that, despite the firm consensus among professional economists in support of Ricardo's doctrine and its implications, trade is not and never has been entirely free.[79]

In this sense, free trade qualifies as a kind of public good, something that all countries would benefit from having but that they will not achieve if left to their own devices. As with other international public goods, the policies of the United States, especially in the years immediately after World War II, helped to give the world a freer trading system than it would otherwise have had.

After World War II, the American government was determined to avoid what it saw as the mistakes that had led to war in the 1930s. In security affairs this meant acting swiftly to check aggression, as France and Britain had failed to do against Hitler. The policy of deterring the Soviet Union and global communism was the result. In economic matters, the Great Depression of the 1930s had, as the Americans saw it, paved the way for war by bringing to power in Germany and Japan governments determined to wage it. In response to the economic slump triggered by the American stock market crash of 1929 and subsequent bank failures in Europe, governments throughout the industrial world (including in the United States) had sought to sustain employment by protecting their home markets against imports. The widely adopted policy of protection had the effect of worsening economic conditions everywhere, however, and when the war ended the American government was determined to make trade as free as possible.

In the early postwar period it exerted itself to that end, coaxing and cajoling the countries of Western Europe to dismantle, or to refrain from erecting, tariffs and other obstacles to trade, using as an incentive access to its own market, by far the largest and richest in the world. With the Marshall Plan, it encouraged economic cooperation, including trade, within Western Europe. The United States played a crucial role in establishing the General Agreement on Tariffs and Trade, which enshrined the principle of free trade and served as the constitution for the world trading system for almost half a century, until it was superseded, in 1995, by the World Trade Organization.

Most importantly, the United States took the lead in launching what became the most effective vehicle for promoting free trade, a series of multilateral negotiations to lower barriers to commerce. In theory, a country benefits by practicing free trade no matter what its trading partners do. It gains by accepting imports from others even if they obstruct its own exports to them. On occasion, countries have unilaterally lowered barriers to imports, notably in 1846 when Great Britain repealed its agricultural tariffs, known as the Corn Laws, and ushered in a great age of international trade, one that brought enormous benefits to Britain itself.[80] In practice, however, overcoming the inevitable obstacles to uninhibited international exchange, which stem from the differences in political intensity between the winners and the losers from trade, requires comparable measures by other countries. In practice, freeing trade turns out to involve reciprocal reductions in trade barriers, which in turn require formal international negotiations to secure.

Political realities make the process of freeing trade similar to riding a bicycle. Just as a bicycle must keep moving forward if it is not to topple over, so it is politically difficult to reduce, or even to avoid raising, barriers to trade in the absence of ongoing negotiations in which reductions in these barriers by one country are matched by reductions by others. Acting on these realities, between 1946 and 1994 the United States led the way in launching and completing seven separate multilateral trade rounds, encouraging others to take part, setting the agendas, and making concessions at key points to ensure successful conclusions. Because of these American efforts, the world traded more freely, and thus in greater volume, after World War II than would have been the case without them.

Over the last three decades of the twentieth century, American support for free trade sometimes wavered. During the previous quarter century, following World War II, America's chief trading partners recovered from the devastation of war, the huge gap in output that had separated them from the United States in 1945 narrowed, and industries in Europe, Japan, and elsewhere began to compete with American products. This made Americans richer, but it also activated resistance to the inflow of foreign goods by workers and employers whose jobs and firms were threatened by imports.[81] At the same time, the global political and military competition with the Soviet Union, while it continued to dominate American foreign policy, came to seem less urgent. This weakened the political impulse within the United States, which had been powerful in the early years of the Cold War, to maintain and expand trading relationships with Europe, Japan, and other countries even when they did not fully reciprocate the American hospitality to their products, in order to solidify the global anti-Soviet coalition to which those countries belonged.

Japan, especially, aroused protectionist sentiment in the United States in the 1970s and 1980s, and the American government-imposed-restrictions on Japanese automobiles and semiconductors. Section 301 of the Trade Act passed by the Congress in 1974 stipulated limits on imports from countries deemed to treat products from the United States unfairly, and the provision was strengthened in 1988.[82]

The United States, along with many other countries, entered into regional and bilateral trade agreements, the most notable American one being the North American Free Trade Agreement (NAFTA) with Canada and Mexico. By conferring favored status on the products of particular countries, such agreements violated one of the cardinal principles of free trade—nondiscrimination.[83]

In the last decade of the twentieth century, demands to attach provisions governing labor and environmental standards to trade agreements became part of the global trade agenda. Those demands came mainly from groups within the United States.[84] While no doubt genuinely concerned about protecting the interests of workers and promoting clean air and water, these groups aroused the suspicion that they had an ulterior motive as well—to enact standards that poor countries could not meet and thus create a basis for excluding their products from the United States. The push to write labor and environmental standards into trade agreements, that is, seemed to some a disguised form of protectionism.[85]

If the elements of ambivalence about free trade that entered American international economic policy in the 1970s had been present in the immediate aftermath of World War II, the global trading system might have developed in a different, and less open, direction. By the 1970s, however, the principle and the practice of free trade were well established.[86] Barriers to trade continued to fall, and the volume of trade continued to expand during the balance of the century and beyond, despite diminished American support.

Although more complicated and protracted than its prede-cessors, the last major global trade negotiation of the twenti-eth century, the Uruguay Round, did reach a successful conclusion. One reason it was complicated and protracted was that many countries wished to take part in it, a sign of the global popularity of the principle of free trade that underlay it. Indeed, more and more countries not only sought to inte-grate themselves into the American-sponsored global trading system but also moved to lower their own barriers to trade unilaterally.[87]

They did so on the basis of the clear and overwhelming evidence that trade promotes prosperity. An ideologically-based resistance to trade was one of the reasons for the dismal economic performances of orthodox Communist govern-ments in the 1970s and 1980s, which in turn contributed to the collapse of those governments across Europe.

Moreover, the United States did not completely abandon its commitment to free trade. The executive branch of the federal government negotiated, and the Congress ratified, several important trade agreements: NAFTA, the Uruguay Round, the establishment of the WTO, and permanent most-favored nation (meaning normal) trade status for China.[88] With American help, a major new round of trade negotiations was launched in Doha, Qatar, in the Persian Gulf, in 2001.

In international forums, the United States led the way in broadening the trade agenda to include services, investment, and intellectual property, and pressed for freer trade in agri-cultural products. To be sure, each of these initiatives prom-ised benefits to American firms and workers if the rest of the world adopted them; but each would also enrich the citizens of other countries. Despite its occasional departures from the principle of free trade, finally, the United States maintained the largest and most open economy in the world. Its size and openness formed the basis for yet another service America provided to the other members of the international system.

Consumption

The achievement, for the first time in human history, of sustained economic growth is one of the hallmarks of the modern age. In the nineteenth century, the major source of growth was investment—capital goods used to make other products, and infrastructure, notably railroads. In the twentieth century, the major source of growth in industrial economies came to be consumption—the things that individuals buy. Consumption would seem to be permanently abundant—there is, after all, no limit to human wants—but this has turned out not to be the case.

Thrift is an economic virtue in most circumstances, but sometimes people can be too thrifty and fail to spend enough to keep the economy functioning at a high level. This is what happened in the Great Depression of the 1930s and in other, milder, economic downturns. The English economist John Maynard Keynes, who diagnosed this cause of economic slumps, also prescribed a remedy: government spending. When individuals do not buy enough, the government should step in to replace their missing purchases, and since the 1930s governments throughout the Western world have done just that during the periods of diminished economic activity that have come to be known as recessions.

The demand that fuels an economy ordinarily comes from within the country involved, but it can come, as well, from abroad. In the last third of the twentieth century, a number of

Asian countries pursued strategies of economic growth that placed heavy emphasis on exports, the largest share of which went to the United States.

In the second half of the 1990s, the American market took on a particularly important role in the international economy, especially for the Asian countries that already counted on selling to it. For a variety of reasons, demand stagnated almost everywhere else. Japan, bogged down in a decade-long slump, purchased fewer of its own products and reduced imports from other Asian countries. The prolonged Japanese recession came at a particularly bad time for the Asian countries that were struck by financial crises, for they needed to export in order to earn the money to pay off the loans with which they were burdened. At the same time, China depended on exports to sustain the double-digit annual growth rates to which it had become accustomed since the beginning of the 1980s. American purchasers of Japanese cars, Chinese-made clothing, and South Korean electronic appliances were not seeking to do favors for the people of these countries. No act is more self-interested than consumption. But the ongoing American spending spree performed an important economic service nonetheless.

All these Asian countries needed to export their products to sustain their economies, and with the other rich countries of the trilateral world—Western Europe as well as Japan—in sluggish economic condition, all relied heavily on the hearty appetites of American consumers for these products.[89] The United States thus did, in an international context, what governments, following Keynes, do for the countries they govern during economic slowdowns: It became the indispensable supplier of demand to the world.[90] To go along with its role, working through the IMF, as the world's lender of last resort, it acted as well as the global economy's "consumer of last resort."

In its capacity as the world's largest importer, and sometimes importer of last resort, the United States bought far more from other countries than it sold to them. It consistently ran a substantial trade deficit.[91] To balance its overall account it had to attract funds from abroad, and proved remarkably successful at doing so.[92] Foreigners had good reasons to put money in the United States: Its vast, vibrant economy offered attractive opportunities for direct investment, their money was safe from political upheavals there, and in the 1990s the American stock market rose rapidly.

Still, productive uses for capital were limited even in the United States, all the more so after the prices of American equities declined sharply after the turn of the new century. Under these circumstances, to balance the American current account in a world of flexible exchange rates the value of the dollar would normally be expected to decline, so that Americans would buy less from and sell more to the rest of the world.[93] Indeed, the dollar did decline against the euro through 2004 and beyond but held its value against the principal Asian currencies, particularly the Japanese yen and the Chinese yuan, because of the monetary policies adopted by the governments of those countries.

Asian governments bought dollars on a large scale, vastly expanding their own reserves, thereby propping up, by sustaining the demand for it, the American currency.[94] Japan and China did, in the first decade of the new millennium, what Germany and Japan had done in the 1960s: They absorbed dollars beyond the level that seemed economically sensible for them.[95] The two Asian countries lacked one of the motives behind the earlier episode: They did not depend on

American military forces to protect them from Soviet aggression. In another way, however, history did repeat itself. In both the earlier and the later cases, the governments in question wished to keep the value of their own currencies low in relation to the dollar in order to sustain high levels of exports to the United States.[96] In all four cases, exporting industries made substantial contributions to national economic growth, making export-led growth a political imperative. It was particularly important for the still-Communist government of China, whose promotion of rapid economic growth was a principal source of whatever claim it had on the loyalty of the Chinese people, among whom belief in the tenets of Marxism-Leninism and Maoism had died out.[97]

The arrangement that kept the engine of the global economy turning over at the beginning of the twenty-first century had an ironic element to it. The government of China took the savings of Chinese workers and peasants and used them in a less than economically optimal way—they would have brought higher returns elsewhere than they did invested in American treasury bills[98]—for the purpose of sustaining the far higher standard of living in the United States. By penalizing the poor to benefit the rich, this practice conforms to the Marxist definition of imperial exploitation, which the Communist Party of China that controlled the country's government and so carried out this policy, when it was founded in the early twentieth century, had ostensibly been organized to oppose.

It was perhaps no less ironic for the United States, a country whose foreign policy had had at its center for much of the twentieth century strenuous opposition to communism, to act as the mainstay of an economic relationship designed to perpetuate the political monopoly of the Communist Party of China. And it was certainly historically unusual for a country containing hundreds of millions of very poor people to be loaning money to one of the wealthiest countries, measured by per capita income, on the planet.

In the nineteenth century, when Britain was the world's leading financial power, London supplied capital to the less-developed parts of the world rather than vice versa.[99] Britain's status as a creditor enhanced its international position. The threat to withdraw its capital served as a source of leverage over others. America's standing as the world's largest debtor had the opposite potential to diminish its power, although the leverage on the United States available to its Asian creditors was limited by the fact that by withdrawing their loans they would inflict economic damage on themselves as well, in the spirit of the old saying that if a man owes a bank a hundred dollars he is in the bank's power, but if he owes the bank a million dollars the bank is in *his* power.[100]

That mutual vulnerability, however, illustrated the danger that the American role as the world's chief consumer posed, not only to the United States but to the international economy as a whole. The willingness of Japan, China, and other Asian countries to hold dollar obligations, while demonstrably large, was presumably not infinite. Eventually the saturation point would be reached and the process of reducing the American current account deficit would begin. Indeed, the sharp fall of the dollar, principally against the euro, in 2004 suggested that it had begun. The danger this portended was the same one as the shift away from the dependence on oil for much of the world's energy needs raised—the possibility that the change would not be smooth and gradual, affording time to adjust, but rather swift and sharp, inflicting serious economic damage on the United States and other countries.[101]

If foreign holders of dollars were to exchange them suddenly and on a large scale, the consequences might resemble the effects on the afflicted countries of the Asian financial crises of the 1990s. The value of the dollar would drop sharply, triggering inflation in the United States. To stem this inflation, and to attract the capital needed to balance the country's international account, American interest rates would rise, reducing the level of economic activity in the United States. Inflation and recession in the world's largest economy would inevitably inflict damage on other economies as well.[102] If the rest of the world concluded that the dollar was not safe to hold, moreover, this would undermine its status as the principal reserve currency.[103]

The depreciation of the dollar was not the only way in which the American current account deficit could be reduced. This could also be accomplished by greater savings in the American economy, in particular through the reduction of the federal budget deficit. The current account deficit would also decline if other countries saved less and consumed more. The first method proved politically difficult to carry out, however, requiring as it did lower federal spending, higher taxes, or both, while the economic policies of the governments of Asia and weak economic growth in Europe impeded the second, placing most of the burden of adjustment on the dollar, with the risks that that entailed.

Like the other global services that the United States provided, its role as the world's leading consumer served American interests as well as those of other countries. Unlike some of the other global services, other countries actually paid for this one, in the form of income forgone from more profitable uses for their capital than holding dollars. Even more than in the case of other services, the United States could not sustain this role by itself. Still, while the American role as global consumer differed in this respect from the other ways in which the United States functioned as the world's government, the difference was one of degree rather than of kind.

In providing other international economic public goods, and in its governmental roles in international security affairs, the United States depended, if not, as with consumption, on active cooperation from other countries, then at least on their passive acceptance of, and their deliberate avoidance of active opposition to, what it was doing. As the world's government, that is, the United States enjoyed, if only tacitly, a measure of what governments within sovereign states need in order to endure and to function effectively: legitimacy.

Chapter Four

INTERNATIONAL LEGITIMACY

It is the fate of great powers that provide order to do so against the background of a world that takes the protection while it bemoans the heavy hand of the protector.

FOUAD AJAMI, "IRAQ AND THE ARABS' FUTURE"[1]

Legitimacy

By reassuring, through its military presence in Europe and East Asia, countries in these regions that might otherwise regard each other as hostile, by taking responsibility for coping with the most oppressive and aggressive regimes of the international system, and by providing a currency, reserves, emergency loans, and the largest and most welcoming market for exports on the planet, the United States did for the world at the outset of the twenty-first century many of the things that the governments of sovereign states do for the societies in which they are constituted. How effectively, and for how long, can the United States function as the world's government?

The most effective and durable governments of sovereign

states have a particular standing in the eyes of those they govern: They are legitimate. The term comes from the Latin word for law, *lex, legis*, and means "lawful." Something is legitimate when it is "in accordance with established rules, principles and standards."[2] A government is legitimate when it is established according to the appropriate standards and operates in the proper way: Those who hold power have obtained it and use it in rightful fashion.

A legitimate government is like a ship with ballast that steadies it as it moves through the water. It is sturdier than one that lacks legitimacy because those it governs accept the fact of its rule without protest or rebellion and willingly obey its lawfully produced decrees. Legitimacy confers an additional source of strength upon a government. Those it governs not only passively tolerate it, they actively support it through the payment of taxes and, on occasion, by fighting to defend and preserve it.

In traditional societies, a legitimate ruler was someone who was descended from a previous legitimate ruler.[3] The ruling family, in turn, often owed its legitimacy to a putative association with the deity. The Chinese emperor was "the son of heaven." The Japanese emperor claimed direct descent from the sun itself. European monarchs ruled by "divine right."

As for the methods of rule, although traditional kings and emperors were not bound by the laws that govern most modern states, the elaborate rituals that surrounded the daily activities of hereditary monarchs served the same purpose. The costumes, the ceremonies, and the elaborate court etiquette demonstrated to the governed that their rulers were not acting arbitrarily but were following proper, divinely-mandated procedures.

In the twenty-first century, with few traditional regimes

remaining, the virtually universal principle of legitimacy has come to be democracy. A political system is legitimate if it comes into being with the consent of the people it governs. Particular governments must be popularly chosen—that is, democratically elected. Legitimacy requires that such governments conduct themselves in accordance with laws enacted by the people or by their elected representatives. The United States itself exemplifies both forms of democratic legitimacy. Its public life rests on a constitution ratified at the end of the eighteenth century and occasionally amended since then. It holds regular elections, and the elected officials make the laws by which, as long as they are in conformity with the constitution, the nation abides.

For the American role as the world's government as the twenty-first century began, by contrast, the basic features of democratic legitimacy seemed, by all appearances, to be missing. That role had not been democratically constituted: The world had never authorized the United States to carry out global functions on its behalf. Nor did American policies have to conform to rules enacted by other countries. To the contrary, American political leaders routinely insisted that they would never accord the power of veto over what the United States did beyond its borders to other governments.

The closest approximation of a globally-elected body to authorize international policies was the United Nations. Lacking the power to implement its decisions, the UN is not, and has no prospect of becoming, a world government. It does, however, have some of the features of a global parliament. It has universal membership: All sovereign states are represented. It has a founding document, the United Nations Charter, to which all members subscribe and that bears a resemblance to a constitution. (Unlike the American Constitution, however, the members of the UN do not all faithfully adhere to the provisions of the Charter. For many it is an expression of aspiration, for others, sheer hypocrisy.) Because it has some democratic features, the UN can bestow a kind of legitimacy on the policies of its members: Although a flawed vehicle for conferring formal international legitimacy, it is the only candidate for the task.[4]

The American-led wars in Korea in the 1950s and against the Iraqi occupation of Kuwait in 1991 had the support of the UN. Other American initiatives, however, did not receive the organization's blessing, notably the war to overthrow Saddam Hussein's regime in Iraq in 2003, which aroused opposition around the world. In the first decade of the twenty-first century, moreover, global discontent with American foreign policies went beyond its policies toward Iraq. Indeed, if one conspicuous feature of international affairs was the central role of the United States, another was, or seemed to be, deep and broad unhappiness with that role expressed in every part of the world. If the approval of those whom its policies affect is the test of a government's legitimacy, then the United States, in its capacity as the world's government, looked distinctly illegitimate. Specific policies, and the American international role in general, not only lacked a global mandate but also appeared to be affirmatively unpopular throughout the world.

Unlike the Persian Gulf War of 1991 to liberate Kuwait, the Iraq campaign of 2003 to topple Saddam Hussein failed to gain the approval of a majority of the members of the UN Security Council. Unlike in the earlier conflict, other countries did not make substantial contributions to paying the cost of the 2003 war. The later campaign provoked large antiwar and anti-American demonstrations in major cities in Europe and elsewhere.[5] Polls showed broad popular opposition to that war around the world, even in countries where the governments formally supported what the United States was doing.[6] The Iraq war was widely unpopular despite the fact that it deposed a corrupt, brutal dictator who had caused the deaths of hundreds of thousands of people and that it accomplished his removal with minimal loss of life. Polls showed, as well, anti-American sentiment the world over that both contributed to and was enhanced by, but did not arise exclusively from, unhappiness with the war in Iraq. The United States had been losing popularity, even in traditionally friendly countries, before the war was fought.[7] While disapproval was more pronounced in some places than in others, unfavorable opinions of the United States were to be found in every part of the planet. Especially in the wake of the war, in almost no country did those with a favorable view of American international activities outnumber those with an unfavorable one. In some places, the United States was seen as a threat to global peace on a par with the rogue state of North Korea.[8]

If the United States was, at the outset of the twenty-first century, supplying valuable services to other countries of the kind that governments provide to the citizens they govern, the inhabitants of these other countries showed few signs of appreciating what they were getting. To the contrary, the evidence suggested widespread disapproval of, and even hostility to, the American global role. This negative sentiment was both puzzling and ominous. It was puzzling that policies that had the effect of making people safer and richer should evoke the disapproval of those same people; and it did not augur well for those policies because, insofar as the durability and effectiveness of a government depends on its legitimacy in the eyes of those it governs, the prospects for an enduring and successful American role as the world's government seemed distinctly poor.

Why did the policies of the United States outside its own borders evoke such broad and noisy disapproval? And what effect was that disapproval likely to have on the nation's role as the world's government as the twenty-first century proceeded?

Resentment

An oil painting by the French artist André Fougeron entitled *Atlantic Civilization* that hangs in the Tate Modern Gallery in London captures the main elements of the negative view of the United States that so many non-Americans held in the wake of the Iraq war. At the center of the picture is a large gas-guzzling automobile carrying a soldier aiming his rifle. A portly, balding businessman, reminiscent of the grotesque capitalists of George Grosz's caricatures of Weimar Germany, doffs his hat and bows in the soldier's direction. Next to the car, another concentrates his gaze on a pornographic magazine. Above the car looms an electric chair. In the distance a factory spews pollution into the air. At the corner of the canvas, two women in traditional Middle Eastern attire cower beneath a piece of corrugated metal.

The picture represents the things that people the world over said they disliked about America and Americans in the first decade of the twenty-first century. As it happens, however, *Atlantic Civilization* was painted in 1953, a full fifty years before the United States attacked Iraq. The picture testifies to the fact that anti-American sentiment did not suddenly appear at the end of the Cold War, or at the beginning of the Iraq war. Nor did disharmony among the governments of the

Western democracies originate with the conflict over Iraq, as is demonstrated by the regular outbreaks of discord within the Atlantic Alliance during the Cold War and afterward, from the Suez crisis of 1956 to the recriminations over the American war in Indochina in the 1960s and 1970s to the dispute over how to punish the Soviet Union for the crackdown on the free Polish trade union Solidarity in the 1980s and the quarrels about how to respond to the conflicts in the Balkans in the 1990s. In the case of American policy toward Saddam Hussein's regime, as in the previous episodes, non-Americans and non-American governments emphatically disagreed with the policies that the government of the United States chose to carry out. But anti-American sentiment has been a feature of international life for so long, in so many different historical circumstances, in the face of so many twists and turns of American foreign policy and with those who embrace it objecting to so many different aspects of the American role in the world[9] because it stems not only from what the American government does but also from what the United States is.

What the United States is, first and foremost, is powerful, far more powerful after the Cold War than any other country. Like Goliath, who was neither the sentimental nor the theological favorite in his biblical clash with David, and for the same reasons, the United States, the Goliath of the international system, attracts little popular sympathy beyond its borders.

The powerful can be dangerous. They can bully, dominate, and, if they choose, crush those who are weaker. In a world in which all other countries are weak by comparison, beneath the dislike and disapproval of the United States that public demonstrations manifest and opinion polls record lies another, more potent feeling: fear.

In the modern world, individuals and groups everywhere not only fear Goliath, they also identify with David. The dominant political narrative, embraced by hundreds of millions of people as accurately portraying their own destinies, is that of the courageous triumph of the oppressed and the downtrodden over the mighty. Everyone now identifies with the underdog. This narrative first became politically prominent in the eighteenth century with the French Revolution and gained widespread currency in the twentieth through the successful overthrow of imperial rule the world over. The narrative has taken hold in the West as well. In films, the most popular form of entertainment for this narrative, heroic individuals—James Bond, Luke Skywalker, Indiana Jones—almost single-handedly defeat powerful, malevolent foes. By the new century it had become common for people and nations to see themselves as embattled victims of stronger forces. The United States symbolizes the powerful establishment with which, in both their national and personal myths, so many of the world's people believe they are at odds.

Important as the sheer magnitude of American power was as a source of hostility to the United States in the first decade of the twenty-first century, however, it was not the only one. The anti-American sentiment that manifested itself in official policies and public opinion the world over had its roots in the character not only of the United States but of the modern world itself.

It is a world that is more fluid and disorienting than the static environment in which people lived for millennia. Life in the traditional world tended to be short and subject to the vagaries of the weather and infectious diseases but was otherwise predictable. By contrast, in the twenty-first century, people everywhere found themselves buffeted by powerful, impersonal forces and the rapid and sweeping social changes set in motion by the Industrial Revolution.[10] These forces make life both distressing and confusing, thereby creating the need both for protection against the injuries they inflict and for explanations of their origins to replace the traditional religious ones that no longer command universal acceptance.

The accounts offered by the branch of systematic human inquiry that developed in response to these particular features of the modern world, social science, impressive though some of them are, have not fulfilled the psychological and emotional needs to which the upheavals of modern life have given rise. A less accurate but to some a more satisfying account is the conspiracy theory, which imputes what at first seems inexplicable to the deliberate machinations of a single, secret, and often malevolent intelligence.[11] In a similar spirit, it is both satisfying and plausible to assign to the United States responsibility for wars, revolutions, poverty, oppression, financial panics, inflation, economic slumps, and other misfortunes, and this counts as yet another source of anti-American sentiment.

It is satisfying because if the strings that manipulate events the world over lead back to Washington and New York, then the world may be seen as intelligible, coherent, and rational, if not benign. It is plausible because, as by far the most powerful member of the system of sovereign states, the United States surely does exercise considerable influence. Globalization—the spread around the world of cross-border economic transactions—is not an American invention, nor does the United States control the trade and investment that enriches some, harms others, and alters the daily routines of tens of millions; but American-based firms certainly do conduct a large part of the world's trade and investment, American economic policies do affect conditions in the rest of the world, and the system of global market relations within which these often disruptive transactions take places does rest on the military might and the economic strength of the international system's most powerful member.

Blaming the United States for disappointments and dislocations in other countries and the discontents that they provoke not only makes the world seem coherent, it also deflects the responsibility for these ills from the people who might well seem more appropriate targets for blame: the governments of the countries affected.[12] Those governments use the United States as a political lightning rod, drawing away from themselves the popular discontent that their shortcomings have helped to produce and that could, if directed against them, remove them from power. This was especially the case for a region that, by the evidence of opinion polls, harbored particularly intense anti-American feelings, the Arab Middle East.

The people of that region had good reason for anger at their own governments, which were, in varying degrees, corrupt, repressive, and incompetent. As a result, the societies they governed were poor and, with population increases outstripping economic growth in most of them, becoming poorer. The unhappy circumstances in which Arab peoples lived were particularly aggravating because of the superior conditions in other parts of the world, East Asia in particular, that had recently been as backward and weak as the Arab Middle East but had managed to pull themselves out of economic and political stagnation. The inglorious circumstances of the Arab world stood in stark contrast, as well, to periods of its own history, of which the Arabs' traditions and their religion constantly reminded them, during which their societies had led the world in military power and cultural sophistication.[13]

The result was a deep, regionwide sense of humiliation, leading to powerful feelings of anger. It was very much in the interests of the Arab rulers, who bore the principal responsibility for suppressing political freedom and failing to foster the conditions for economic well-being, to deflect this anger away from themselves. Their strategy for doing so relied heavily on blaming the United States for the troubles of the Arab world.[14]

The United States served a version of the same purpose, at the outset of the twenty-first century, for Europeans. Europe was, of course, a far more successful region than the Arab Middle East—more peaceful, more prosperous, and far better governed. Like the Arab world, however, Europe has a history of international primacy, indeed a longer, more recent, and, in shaping the modern world, a far more significant one. From the eighteenth to the middle of the twentieth century, Europe dominated the world. During the Cold War, the Europeans relied on the more powerful United States to protect them against the Soviet Union. With the end of that conflict, however, many Europeans—particularly in France, a country that saw itself as a cultural and political competitor of the United States even during the Cold War—expected to assume a more prominent global role. In the first post–Cold War decade this did not occur. The gap between the Europeans' aspirations and their achievements produced a measure of irritation—milder, to be sure, than the resentment of the Arabs—which fastened on the country that did play the leading role to which many of them aspired: the United States.[15]

Of all the regions of the world where anti-American sentiment was to be found, its presence in Europe was the most surprising to Americans, since America and Europe have a great deal in common: The United States is, after all, a European society implanted in North America. Of all the regional varieties of anti-Americanism, the European one was also the most disturbing to Americans, since the countries of the continent had been close allies of the United States for much of the twentieth century. Hostile attitudes to the global role of the United States were, finally, most consequential in Europe because the United States counted on European support and assistance in carrying out that role.

While the Europeans' disappointment at the modesty of the influence they were able to exert on global affairs contributed to their irritation at the United States, this was not its only cause, indeed not even the principal one. European disaffection came as well from the social, cultural, and political differences between Europe and the United States. Like negative attitudes toward the United States, those differences did not suddenly appear with the end of the Cold War or the dawn of the new century. In fact, they dated back to the founding of the American republic.

From its colonial origins, the United States lacked the entrenched social hierarchies of Europe. There was never an American monarchy or landed aristocracy that controlled the wealth and power of the new society. Americans lived as social equals, as the Frenchman Alexis de Tocqueville noticed when he visited in the 1830s—this equality was what he called "democracy" in America—in a way that Europeans did not. For this reason, political history in the United States took a course different from the one common in Europe.[16] America had no old regime against which to rebel in the eighteenth and nineteenth centuries. The pervasive equality of American life, combined with the economic opportunities that a vast, virtually unsettled continent afforded, discouraged the development of a self-conscious working class and so prevented socialist movements of the European style from taking root in America in the twentieth century.[17]

By the twenty-first century, these original differences had all but disappeared. Europe's hierarchies had crumbled: The monarchs that remained had lost effective power and the castles of the nobility had become hotels or museums. Tocqueville had predicted that Europe would eventually become as "democratic" as the United States, and by the beginning of the new century (and indeed well before then), his prediction had come true. At the same time, full-blooded socialism no longer commanded politically significant allegiance anywhere on the European continent.

Yet in comparison with Europe, the United States remained distinctive in three ways, each of which contributed to the unfavorable view of the American role in the world that many Europeans held: the importance of religious faith in daily life; attitudes toward violence within and outside the country's borders; and the prevailing view of the state and sovereignty. The differences that the Europeans found dismaying or offensive were most pronounced in the ranks of the Republican Party. Indeed, with its aversion to taxation, its support for an assertive American role in the world, and its embrace of a cluster of values—opposition to abortion being the most prominent—known as "social conservatism," the Republican Party had no real counterpart in any European country. The most conservative major political parties in Europe had more in common with the American Democrats.[18] This made the United States seem particularly alien in the first years of the new century, when a Republican president held office.

Americans take religion more seriously than do Europeans. More of them attend religious services regularly and say that the deity plays an important role in their lives.[19] One consequence of this is that American political discourse employs the moral categories of the language of religion more frequently than does the European variety.[20]

Religious observance is particularly pronounced among Republicans. The best predictor of whether a voter supported the Democratic or Republican candidate in the 2000 presidential election was whether he or she attended religious services regularly.[21] The "Christian right," composed of politically active and largely evangelical Protestants, had become, by the first decade of the twenty-first century, a large and influential constituency in the Republican Party.[22]

No doubt partly for that reason, Republican political leaders have been inclined to speak of international political issues in the language of political absolutes, which has disconcerted Europeans. One Republican president, Ronald Reagan, called the Soviet Union an "evil empire." Another, George W. Bush, referred to Iraq, Iran, and North Korea as the "axis of evil."

One reason that such language distressed Europeans was that it seemed to bespeak a greater inclination to go to war than they thought prudent: People are more likely to fight for political aims they regard as morally necessary than for goals they consider merely desirable or convenient.[23] Although not without the reservations about armed conflict that came to characterize all Western societies over the course of the second half of the twentieth century, Americans were, opinion surveys showed, more favorably disposed in principle to war than were Europeans. According to one poll, "only 41 percent of Europeans said that war could achieve just ends, compared with 82 percent of Americans."[24]

As well as the use of force abroad, Americans approve of legally sanctioned violence at home in greater numbers than Europeans do. Gun ownership is more widespread and far more fiercely defended in the United States than in Europe. And while Europeans generally regard capital punishment as barbarous and therefore unacceptable—no country in which it is permitted can join the European Union—a majority of Americans approves of it and the governments of a number of the fifty American states regularly conduct executions.

Here, too, the members of the political party that held the White House and so presided over the country's relations with the rest of the world at the beginning of the twenty-first century differed most sharply with the predominant European attitudes. Republicans were more likely to look favorably on war as an instrument of foreign policy[25] and to support gun ownership and capital punishment than Democrats.

Capital punishment is not the only governmental prerogative that Americans and Europeans assess differently. In general, Europeans feel less attached to the most basic prerogative of all—sovereignty, the capacity of the state to act independently. The unbridled exercise of sovereignty led, in the view of many Europeans, to the two disastrous world wars in the first half of the twentieth century. In the second half of that century, by contrast, the countries of Europe steadily surrendered sovereignty to what became the EU, with far happier results.

Americans place a higher value on their government's capacity to act independently, without restraints.[26] They have refused to follow the Europeans in committing themselves to limiting emissions of greenhouse gases under the terms of the Kyoto Protocol of 1997 and to abiding by the judgments of the International Criminal Court.

When it comes to the domestic activities of the state, however, the transatlantic positions are reversed. Europeans expect, and receive, more government services than do Americans and pay a higher proportion of their incomes in taxes for these services. The United States is the only developed country, for example, without a full government-supported health care system and the only Western democracy that does not provide child support to all families.[27] Here again, the Republican Party is home to those most committed to maximizing the American government's freedom of maneuver beyond the borders of the United States while minimizing its functions within them.[28] A Republican administration was therefore bound to strike Europeans as departing more sharply than a Democratic one from their own preferences and practices.[29]

These cultural and political differences between the Old World and the New were not born at the dawn of the twenty-first century. They had existed throughout the Cold War decades. But the American divergences from Europe became both more salient for, and more troubling to, Europeans then than they had been during the second half of the twentieth century, when the solidarity between the United States and Europe that the conflict with the Soviet Union imposed had rendered the dissimilarities between them both less noticeable and, when noticed, less disturbing.

After the Cold War, what was unattractive became more troubling as well because of the enormous power of the United States and the quasi-governmental role to which it gave rise. Europeans naturally preferred that American influence be exercised in ways congenial to them; and to the extent that American political ideas and social values differed from their own, this was less likely.[30]

In short, the United States aroused a range of negative sentiments in other countries both because of the way it conducted itself beyond its own borders and because of particular features of its society and its political culture—that is, both because of what it has done and what it is. Citizens and public officials in other countries disagreed with particular American policies, especially the invasion and occupation of Iraq, but they also feared American power, resented the singular independence the United States enjoyed in its international dealings, and were made uncomfortable by American beliefs, values, and customs that they did not share.

Individuals and groups that harbor such sentiments often take steps to change the circumstances that have created them, which in this case was the power of the United States. It would be in keeping with logic and with historical experience for other countries to put at the center of their public policies measures designed to reduce American power and to shield themselves from its effects. Yet in the early years of the twenty-first century this did not occur. In dealing with the United States, a gap, and not a small one, separated the world's words from its deeds. Mark Twain once said of the weather that everybody talks about it but nobody does anything about it. So it was with the rest of the world and the United States: Heated and widespread complaints about its international role were combined with an almost complete absence of concrete, effective measures to change or restrict it.

Criticism

The United States did not entirely lack for enemies in the wake of the Cold War. The al Qaeda terrorist network launched several attacks against American targets, including, of course, the most deadly terrorist assault in American history, against New York and Washington, D.C., on September 11, 2001. While al Qaeda certainly posed a threat to individual Americans, however, it did not threaten the American position in the world.[31]

Al Qaeda's principal target was not the United States. It sought to replace the existing governments of countries whose populations were predominantly Muslim with theocratic, fundamentalist rule presumably similar to the Taliban regime that had given it shelter in Afghanistan. It struck the United States to gain notoriety and admiration in the Islamic world and to weaken American support for the governments it hoped to dislodge. Al Qaeda's ultimate goal, if its declarations were to be believed, was to unite all forty-four Muslim-majority societies under a single government, thereby recreating the conditions of Islam's early history, when a caliphate held sway over all believers. That goal not only did not directly involve the United States, it was so ambitious as to be unachievable even if the United States did not exist. In pursuit of its goals, finally, al Qaeda lacked what had made Nazi Germany and the Soviet Union formidable contenders for international primacy. While it could enlist individuals in its cause, the terrorist network's ideology had poor prospects for attracting millions of dedicated followers to its ranks. As a formula for governance, that ideology had been tried in Afghanistan, Iran, and Saudi Arabia, and in none of them had it produced a society that people could be mobilized to fight and die on a large scale to reproduce.

Even more importantly, the totalitarian ideologies of the twentieth century, fascism and communism, captured control of powerful states—Germany and Russia—and this is what made them dangerous. Al Qaeda had no hope of taking over a country that could challenge the international position of the United States.

As for rogue states such as Iran and North Korea, whose governments resolutely opposed all things American and actively sought to obtain nuclear weapons, they certainly threatened American policies and American interests in their home regions; but neither had as a serious aim bringing to an end, or even substantially reducing, the global cultural, political, and economic presence of the United States.

Historically, sovereign states as mighty as the United States have encountered a particular kind of check to their power: Other countries have banded together to block them. France in the eighteenth and nineteenth centuries, Germany in the first half and the Soviet Union in the second half of the twentieth century all inspired the formation of a countervailing coalition that either fought or deterred and ultimately defeated them. The pattern has recurred so frequently that it almost seems a law of international relations.[32] It certainly conforms to the logic of relations among sovereign states, which seek, above all, to maintain their independence. Over-mighty countries threaten that independence. It is logical to take whatever steps are necessary to meet that threat. Countries that cannot effectively oppose powerful potential predators alone will be drawn to coalitions for this purpose.

In the first decade of the twenty-first century, the American margin of superiority in disposable power over the other members of the international system at least matched those of the great powers against which their neighbors and rivals had forged countervailing coalitions in the past. Yet an anti-American political and military combination showed no sign of being formed.

The countries of Europe, several of which had long histories as leading actors on the world stage, did not rouse themselves to enhance their military capabilities, nor did they
make any move to put the armed forces they did have to anti-
American uses. The French president Jacques Chirac spoke
of the desirability of a "multipolar world" in which the
United States would not be the only locus of effective
power,[33] but neither France nor its partners in the European
Union devoted themselves seriously to bringing such a world
into being. Active French opposition to the Anglo-American
war in Iraq was confined to sending its foreign minister to
Africa in the spring of 2003 to encourage governments there
not to support a UN Security Council resolution endorsing
the war. This modest diplomatic gesture hardly compared
with the great coalitions formed and the fierce wars waged
against Napoleon and Hitler.

China's size, surging economic growth, and deeply-rooted
sense of its own global significance seemed to make it a plausible candidate to play the role of America's rival for international primacy. But the still officially Communist government
of China assigned a low priority to equipping the country
with the tanks, aircraft, missiles, and naval forces necessary to
do so. The military hardware that China did accumulate was
designed to enforce its claim to the island of Taiwan, one
hundred miles from its coast, not to enhance its standing
around the world.

In general, when it came to allocating their resources, all
the countries of the world that might have challenged the
United States gave a higher priority to improving the well-
being of their citizens than to increasing their capacities to
thwart American initiatives or expanding the power they
could bring to bear on international events. Why was this so?

They certainly did not lack the wherewithal to arm themselves more heavily. All these countries were in fact considerably wealthier in the twenty-first century than they had been in the days when they had marshaled their resources to assert their own power or counterbalance that of others. Nor, it is safe to say, had the age-old group instinct for self-preservation that had given rise to so many violent conflicts somehow disappeared from the wealthy nation-states of the twenty-first century. Nor, as their vocal criticisms of American foreign policies demonstrated, were other countries so cowed and demoralized by its superior power that they dared not do anything to offend the United States. Rather, other countries did not pool their resources to confront the enormous power of the United States because, unlike the supremely powerful countries of the past, the United States did not threaten them.

Unlike the great powers against which broad coalitions were formed, it did not seek to conquer and occupy territory under the sovereign control of others. This was clear to the governments of all the other major countries despite the popular use of the term "empire" to describe America's global role. Such rhetoric notwithstanding, the rest of the world understood that the United States was not, and did not aspire to be, an imperial power.

In the decade and a half after the end of the Cold War, it did occupy several countries, but these episodes were exceptions that proved the rule. The American government undertook its nation-building missions in Somalia, Haiti, Bosnia, Kosovo, Afghanistan, and Iraq with reluctance. In each case the United States intervened for other reasons—to alleviate suffering or to depose a government it considered dangerous—and then found itself saddled with the unwanted responsibility of governing the country. In each case, and unlike the great empires of the past, the American goal was to build stable, effective structures of governance in order to be able to leave quickly rather than to stay comfortably. In each case, and again unlike the great empires of the past, the American government sought to share control of the occupied country with others rather than monopolize it.

Furthermore, the broad goals on behalf of which the United States sought to exercise its power in the world were widely shared in other countries.[34] By and large, people around the world believed democracy to be the most desirable and appropriate form of government, even—perhaps especially—in places that were undemocratically governed.[35] Also by large margins, people outside the United States endorsed the free market as the optimal method of economic organization and approved of the increasing connections, including the economic connections known as globalization, among different countries.[36] Other governments had no basis for mobilizing their citizens to overturn the global military, political, and economic arrangements that rested ultimately on American values because their citizens shared these values.

The global consensus in favor of those values was evident in the same opinion surveys that registered discontent with the United States. They showed that non-Americans routinely distinguished between the policies of the American government, which they often opposed, and the defining features of American society, which they generally admired.[37] They also distinguished between the policies of a particular American administration and the global role of the United States.[38] The United States continued to be a favored destination for students, immigrants, and tourists. A strikingly large proportion of people the world over considered it important to master the English language.[39]

While some of the things the United States did in the world attracted harsh criticism, moreover, other aspects of the American global role commanded widespread, if not necessarily loudly proclaimed, support. This was particularly the case for the American role in the international economy. Virtually every other country counted on access to the world's trade and financial systems, which depended heavily on the United States for their effective functioning, to enhance its own well-being. Virtually all countries used dollars for international transactions. Virtually all sold their products in the American market, and many invested in and received investment from the United States.[40] Many had needed, or anticipated needing, the emergency infusions of capital that the United States was crucial in supplying. Without the American role in providing a secure political framework for trade and investment, a currency for global transactions, a large market for foreign products, and loans for countries in acute financial distress, the economic prospects of other countries would suffer, and their governments knew this even if they did not often say so.[41]

On matters of international security as well, American policies commanded wider support than was often apparent. Europeans, for example, did not want rogue states to acquire nuclear weapons and the American emphasis on forceful measures to prevent them from so doing permitted European governments to adopt more conciliatory nonproliferation policies. The Europeans could proffer carrots, secure in the knowledge that the United States was at the same time wielding a stick. China could adopt a conciliatory policy, for similar reasons, toward North Korea. The Chinese could also approve of some of the consequences of the American military presence—dissuading Japan from enhancing its own military forces, for example—while opposing others, such as the protection the American Seventh Fleet afforded Taiwan.[42]

Because it did not threaten the vital interests of other countries, because its ultimate purpose was to promote values widely shared in the international system, and because many of its specific features in fact met with the approval of those with a direct stake in them, the American role as the world's government commanded wider international acceptance than the chorus of criticism and the visible anti-American sentiment that marked the early years of the twenty-first century suggested. To this source of strength was added another: Although the United States as the world's government lacked most of the formal properties of democratic legitimacy, it did have one of them. While people and governments outside the United States had no say in choosing the government of the United States, foreigners could and did have access to that government's decisionmaking process.

To a much greater extent in the American political system than in almost any other, authority is fragmented: There are many different centers of power. This can hinder the effective conduct of foreign policy. It is more difficult in the United States than elsewhere for the government to speak with a single voice and to act swiftly, coherently, and decisively.[43] The structure of the American government also, however, creates multiple points of access, which help to make the American global presence more acceptable than it would otherwise be.

Especially on the many issues that do not engage the attention of the American public as a whole, and on those matters on which no firm national consensus exists, an individual, a group, or a government seeking to affect American policy in a particular way can exert influence on one or more of the committees of the House of Representatives and the

Senate with jurisdiction over aspects of foreign policy and on one or more of the several departments of the executive branch of the federal government—State, Defense, Treasury, and Commerce—that conduct the nation's relations with other countries.

Those seeking to move the United States in one direction or another can present their views to American officials and the American public on radio and television and in magazines and newspapers. They can, and do, hire professional lobbyists to press their cases, primarily on economic matters but also on issues of security. Think tanks and pundits generate such a wide variety of proposals for American policies on all issues and toward every country that almost any approach is bound to have a champion somewhere.

The governments and people of other countries may resent the dimensions of American power, but they know that where that power affects them, they are not helpless. They can reason with and sometimes redirect the attention and energies of Goliath. They may not enjoy the formal representation in the American political system that is the hallmark of democratic legitimacy, but they can achieve what representation brings—influence over policy—which is yet another reason that the global role of the United States receives wider tolerance than what is said about it around the world would indicate.

Because the opportunities to be heard and heeded are so plentiful, it is often the case that countries with opposed aims each simultaneously attempts to persuade the American government to favor its cause. In this way international quarrels are played out within the American political system. This has sometimes led the United States to adopt a practice that governments within sovereign states frequently use, in particular in disputes between labor and management, and so counts as yet another governmental service the United States provides to the world: mediation.

The first notable instance of American international mediation took place in 1905, when President Theodore Roosevelt presided over a settlement of the Russo-Japanese War at Portsmouth, New Hampshire, an achievement for which he was awarded the Nobel Peace Prize. In the second half of the Cold War and in the post–Cold War period, the practice became increasingly common. American officials sought to resolve disputes between Arabs and Israelis, between India and Pakistan, and between Catholics and Protestants in Northern Ireland, as well as quarrels that received less international attention.[44] They did not fully succeed in every case, but the global standing of the United States made all parties to any international conflict anxious not to offend or alienate it, which provided it with diplomatic leverage. The propensity to act as a neutral third party and help to arrange mutually acceptable compromises between opposed—sometimes violently opposed—parties further served to render the enormous power of the United States internationally acceptable.

The gap between what the rest of the world said about the United States and what it did, or failed to do, about the American policies of which so many so loudly disapproved bespoke not hypocrisy (or not merely hypocrisy) but rather a tacit recognition that however unattractive one or another American policy might be, the overall American impact on the world was not so repugnant or dangerous as to warrant a serious effort to minimize it. A serious assault on American power would, for other countries, be tantamount to throwing out the baby with the bathwater. In this sense the world's relationship to the United States bore some resemblance to the critic's relationship to a play or film that he or she is assessing. Finding fault is normal, natural, even obligatory. The criticism is often well informed and cogent, almost always genuinely felt and sincerely expressed, and intended to improve what the actors, directors, writers, and producers do in the future. The critic does not, however, seek to displace the performers or take control of the performance. Nor do critics wish for such performances to cease entirely: That would deprive them of their livelihoods. An unspoken acceptance of a division of responsibilities underlies the work of the critic, as it did in the case of the world's response to the American performance as the world's government.[45]

In fact, the world's attitude toward the United States has some features in common with citizens' attitudes toward their governments in free societies. The public routinely directs harsh criticism against democratically constituted authorities. Far from suppressing political differences, after all, democracy is a political system the aim of which is to make it safe to express them openly so as to resolve them peacefully. The habitual criticisms in democracies of what governments do rests on two closely related and ordinarily unstated premises: first, that while particular policies may be undesirable, and indeed can be and often are changed, the political system from which they emerge is legitimate and so will endure and even be defended if need be; and second, that political disputes, however heated, will not spill over into violence.[46]

Other countries' attitudes toward the United States display a parallel to a particular feature of the American political system. Polls have consistently shown that Americans hold the institution of Congress in low regard. Yet individual members of the House of Representatives almost always win reelection. Just as Americans scorn Congress in general but approve of the individual member who represents them, so other countries often object to the global role of the United States in general but favor the American policies that have particular relevance to them.

The humorist Art Buchwald once wrote a tongue-in-cheek column about the quadrennial cycle of boom and bust in the Canadian home-building industry. During the American presidential election, Republican voters proclaim that the Democratic candidate is so unworthy of office that if he should be elected, they will move to Canada. Democrats say the same thing about the Republican candidate. Canadian developers rush to build homes to sell to the expected influx of immigrants. In the event, however, no matter which candidate wins, the partisans of the opposing party, despite their preelection threats, stay where they are. In the same spirit, other countries, despite their rhetoric, are not likely to take effective action to dislodge the United States from its position as the functional equivalent of the world's government.

This does not mean, however, that the country is destined to retain this status indefinitely. To the contrary, in the first decade of the twenty-first century, the American role in the world faced a serious challenge, but one that did not come from abroad. As the world's government the United States benefited from one of the consequences of formal legitimacy: the passive acceptance of its status by those its policies affected. It did not, however, enjoy the other benefit on which legitimate governments within sovereign states can count: active support. Other countries were by and large willing to allow the United States to carry out the global tasks it had undertaken without trying to obstruct them, but few displayed any inclination to offer significant assistance.

If the task of global governance qualified as a public good, countries other than the United States behaved as free riders, accepting the benefits without contributing to the costs. The governmental services the United States furnished to the world did cost something to provide, and it fell to the American people to pay those costs. The future of the American role as the world's government therefore depended on how much, and for how long, Americans would be willing to pay.

Leadership

Behind the American role as the world's government lie powerful forces, not the least of them the force of habit. By the beginning of the twenty-first century, American troops had been deployed around the world and the United States had been deeply engaged in the operation of the world's trade and financial systems for well over half a century. A global role for their country had come to be normal for Americans, fewer and fewer of whom had any adult memory of a more modest foreign policy.

By the time the new millennium began, that expansive approach to the world, with all the international tasks it entailed, had survived the disappearance of the circumstances that had given rise to it. The Cold War had ended, but the American foreign policies developed during that conflict for the most part persisted or were adapted to new international circumstances. Inertia, the property of continuing in the same position or along an existing path absent an interruption from the outside—which is a powerful force in political as well as in personal life—favors the continuation of the United States as the world's government.

That role has influential, articulate partisans within the

United States as well. Virtually all Americans with a serious interest in the country's relations with the rest of the world regard it favorably. It draws strength, as well, from a fundamental feature of American political culture.

The country's basic political principles have a particular significance in the United States because the country was founded on them. The American republic is not the political expression of a national group that has lived together in the same place for many generations, as are most of the countries of Europe. It is instead a political community largely populated by people who arrived, or whose forbears arrived, from beyond North America and became Americans by embracing its founding principles. All powerful states have some tendency to want to export what they value most about themselves. Because of its singular history, that tendency is particularly pronounced in the United States.

Still, because the country is a freewheeling democracy, the scope and direction of foreign policy in the United States is destined to be permanently contested. Whether the country continues to function as the world's government will depend on how the American public assesses the policies that constitute their country's global role. That assessment, in turn, will emerge from the two-tiered structure of American public opinion concerning foreign policy.

Where the role of the United States in the world is concerned, American society is divided between a relatively small foreign policy elite, which is knowledgeable about and often active in matters of foreign policy, and the public as a whole, whose interest is episodic.[47] The division is a common one in contemporary democracies, in which most citizens lack the time and interest to acquire detailed knowledge of what are often technically complicated matters and public policy is set not directly by all citizens but by their elected representatives.[48]

The elite, which includes the government officials who conduct foreign policy as well as people in the private sector engaged in international trade and finance and those who study and comment on these issues for a living, manages America's relations with other countries. It sets the general course of foreign policy. Matters that do not affect American society as a whole—relations with dozens of countries and on many different issues—are usually decided by members of the elite with little or no input from the wider public. It is on such issues, and they are the majority in foreign policy, that other countries can hope to exert influence. Although the members of the foreign policy elite are often at odds with one another over particular issues, such as the wisdom of the war in Iraq, almost all of those who pay close attention to America's relations with other countries believe that the United States should play a major role in the world.[49]

Although largely detached from the day-to-day conduct of America's relations with the rest of the world, the wider public does not lack influence over them. The public establishes the limits within which foreign policy is conducted. It sets the boundaries beyond which the elite must not steer the country. While it does not direct it, the public does constrain foreign policy.[50] It does so through its power to elect the officials responsible for that conduct. If the policies that elected officials carry out do not win public approval—and, to be sure, these officials, especially the president, have considerable leeway to shape the public's view of the actions they take—the officials are voted out of office. In the second half of the twentieth century, actual elections ceased to be necessary to force changes of policy. Opinion polls taken between elections registered public sentiment on foreign policy and other issues, to which officials accommodated themselves.

If the foreign policy elite functions, for the conduct of the international relations of the United States, like the professional management of a commercial enterprise, the wider public may be compared to the firm's board of directors, which may not choose to intervene often but has the final say over its direction. The wider public lacks the elite's overriding and principled commitment to the expansive international role that the United States assumed during the Cold War and that has carried over into the post–Cold War era. But most Americans do not oppose such a role in principle.[51] Instead, they tend to judge foreign policies on a case-by-case basis, according to two practical criteria: the direct effect on the United States, and the cost.

The American public is willing to lend active support to foreign policies—to contribute money and even American lives to carrying them out—to the extent that these policies directly affect America and Americans. As between protecting American interests and promoting American values, the nation's interests have priority. As between themselves and others, Americans favor investing their blood and treasure in projects that affect themselves. It is more important to them to assure the safety and the prosperity of the United States than to promote the safety and prosperity of other countries. They do not oppose the spread of democracy and free markets beyond the borders of the United States or rescuing distressed peoples whose fates do not directly affect them, and they are even willing to lend modest support to efforts to achieve these goals; but they balk at substantial military or economic outlays in pursuing them. The budget for the Department of Defense is many times that of the agency charged with promoting American values abroad, the National Endowment for Democracy. This moral and political calculus does not bespeak unusual financial stinginess or moral callousness: Americans approach the world much as other peoples do.[52]

Sometimes the protection of interests goes hand in hand with the promotion of values. In World War II and the Cold War, the United States sought both to protect itself and to secure the freedom of other countries. In each conflict, however, the protection of the United States had priority. Germany and Japan attacked and conquered a number of countries before December 1941, but the United States did not enter the war until it was itself attacked. During the wars in Korea and Vietnam, polls showed that most Americans believed that the principal reason for fighting was to resist communism and so safeguard the United States rather than to defend South Korea or South Vietnam.[53]

For the American public, foreign policy, like charity, begins at home. Although more willing to support policies that affect them directly than those that do not, even to the more highly valued initiatives Americans apply a cost-benefit calculation. The greater the effects of a particular policy on the safety and well-being of the United States—the larger, that is, the stakes for Americans—the higher the price the public will pay to see it through to a successful conclusion.

Americans have been willing to pay whatever seemed necessary to cope with threats to their security. Nazi Germany and imperial Japan posed mortal threats, and in response the United States waged total war against them, mobilizing virtually all of the resources of American society to win World War II. The two major conflicts of the Cold War era, the Korean and Vietnam wars, also cost the country a good deal. But because they judged the stakes to be lower than in World War II, the American people placed limits on the efforts they were willing to underwrite. As American casualties mounted, public opinion turned against the wars. The presidents responsible for them, Harry Truman and Lyndon Johnson, each saw his popularity plummet and decided not to run for reelection. In each case his successor brought the conflict to a conclusion without achieving all of the goals for which it had been fought.[54]

During the Cold War the proportion of its national income that the United States spent on foreign and security policies varied. It rose during the Korean and Vietnam wars and in the wake of international events—the Soviet Union's launch of Sputnik, the first Earth-orbiting satellite, in 1957 and the Soviet invasion of Afghanistan in 1979—that made the world appear suddenly more dangerous. But in the more than four decades of that conflict, it never approached the roughly 40 percent of its income that the country spent at the height of World War II.[55] In the wake of the Cold War, defense spending fell almost by half, from between 5 and 6 to 3 percent of the gross domestic product.[56]

The nation's willingness to expend its most precious resource, the lives of its soldiers, also decreased. For the military interventions of the 1990s, in Haiti, Bosnia, and Kosovo, which were undertaken to relieve suffering rather than to protect the United States, the maximum politically allowable number of American casualties turned out to be zero.

Americans were willing and able to pay, along with their British and Soviet allies, enough to win World War II. They and their allies paid enough to win the Cold War. In the first post–Cold War decade, they paid enough to sustain the American role as the world's government. A central question for twenty-first-century international relations is whether the American public will continue to pay to provide the world with the governmental services on which other countries have come, in many cases without acknowledging it, to rely. The answer to that question will depend less on the legitimacy others accord that role than on the benefits Americans believe they derive from it.

Costs

In theory the American public ought to endorse without hesitation the global economic tasks for which their country had responsibility in the first decade of the twenty-first century, since for the most part these confer economic benefits on the United States. In practice, however, matters are not so simple.

The use of the dollar as the world's currency and as the most widely held reserve brings some financial advantage, but to retain that status, especially when the euro is available for the same purpose, may well require policies that reassure the rest of the world that the dollar will maintain its value and so is safe to hold. The required policies, however, may be, or be thought to be, inconsistent with the domestic economic goals of the United States. They may, that is, be unacceptable to the American public because they entail a greater measure of austerity than Americans will tolerate.

In the past, the American government has chosen to print more dollars than the world would have preferred to hold. This practice helped to precipitate the 1971 collapse of the system of monetary rules devised at Bretton Woods, New Hampshire, in 1944. In the future, the government may need to borrow more money than others are prepared to lend, and difficulties in borrowing may persuade the citizens and governments of other countries that holding dollars is financially risky.[57]

The American role as the world's lender of last resort, like the dollar's role as the world's vehicle currency and reserve, costs the American taxpayer very little. The loans come from the IMF, to whose resources the United States contributes only a modest fraction (and over which the American government exercises influence out of proportion to its actual contribution), and these loans are usually repaid with interest. Yet support in the United States for this particular international economic service is far from robust. The part that the American government played in the 1990s in arranging rescue packages for financially distressed countries in Latin America and East Asia came under criticism from both within the foreign policy elite and from the wider public. The elite criticism charged the IMF with having created a moral hazard problem by relieving public authorities and private firms of some of the consequences of their own mismanagement and misjudgment. From the broader public came resentment at transferring funds to foreigners who had only themselves to blame for their misfortunes, a sentiment that seemed to be based in part on the mistaken belief that these funds, like domestic welfare payments, came directly out of the pockets of American taxpayers and would never be repaid.

A national commitment to free trade also ought—again in theory—to command broad support in the United States. Trade rewards all parties to it, after all, and from the point of view of the professional economist the purpose of trade is to receive imports—products that are either otherwise unavailable or cheaper to purchase than comparable goods made domestically. Imports enhance the welfare of the recipient country. The politics of trade, however, works against a welcoming attitude to imports, with the losers from free trade better organized and thus politically more formidable than the more numerous winners. The losers from trade, moreover, command public sympathy. Polls show broad support for the goal of protecting American jobs.[58]

Furthermore, it is easy to imagine two economic conditions that tend to increase protectionist sentiment becoming more pronounced. One is a strong dollar, the result of high interest rates needed to attract foreign capital to finance the current account deficit. A strong dollar makes exports from the United States expensive and imports to the country cheap, harming both individuals and firms that rely on selling abroad and that therefore compete with imports.[59] This occurred in the 1980s and generated political pressure to restrict imports.

The other condition is the growing tendency for American firms to have clerical and administrative tasks performed in other countries. As the twenty-first century began, the migration of factories to countries with lower wage levels had been underway for half a century, but the outsourcing of white collar jobs had become economical only recently, as technology made possible cheap and instantaneous transoceanic communication on a large scale. The number of white-collar jobs transferred from the United States to India and other countries was not large.[60] But the fact that it had become feasible to carry out abroad the tasks once performed exclusively in the United States by Americans had the effect of making large numbers of Americans feel that their employment was precarious, which added to the pool of potential active supporters of protectionist trade policies.

The end of the Cold War also deprived American proponents of free trade of an historically effective argument, namely that maintaining economic interdependence with

Western Europe, Japan, and other trading partners reinforced the military alliances with those countries on which success in the global competition with communism depended.[61]

If the economic aspects of the global governance that the United States supplies, which do not, on the whole, require contributions from American taxpayers or American troops, are not certain of continued public support, the prospects for the policies that make the world a more secure, less dangerous place, which do sometimes require significant contributions of American blood and treasure, must be counted at least as uncertain, if not more so.

The Cold War did even more to encourage the United States to undertake tasks enhancing international security than it did to promote policies that strengthened the international economy. In that conflict, the Soviet Union and international communism threatened the United States. To cope with that threat, the American public supported policies that made other countries safer as well. In this area of international relations, the attacks of September 11 seemed, at first, to provide a replacement for the Cold War.

Their immediate effects resembled those that the Japanese attack on Pearl Harbor, the launch of Sputnik, and the invasion of Afghanistan had had: They expanded the international military, political, and economic efforts of the United States.[62] Once again the world suddenly seemed to Americans a more dangerous place. To meet the heightened danger, the American government adopted new foreign policies, in the case of September 11 the declaration of a war against terrorism and military operations to remove hostile governments in Afghanistan and Iraq.

In pursuit of victory in World War II and the Cold War, the United States deployed troops in, and involved itself in the internal affairs of, many countries around the world. The first conflict made America a global power; the second sustained this status. The war against terrorism also expanded the horizons of American security policy. The United States found itself taking an interest, for example, in the largely Muslim former Soviet countries of Central Asia, in which American involvement had previously been negligible but where terrorist organizations were suspected of recruiting and training cadres.

The potential for even further expansion was vast; virtually any country can serve as a sanctuary for individuals or groups seeking to harm America and Americans. Countries in which the government does not exercise effective control over the territory—"failed states"—offer particularly hospitable environments for terrorists. This gives the United States an incentive to try to create effective structures of governance in each place—to engage, that is, in "nation-building"—which is what happened in Afghanistan and Iraq.[63] Yet the September 11 attacks were unlikely to have, in the end, anything like as powerful an impact on America's relations with the rest of the world as did World War II and the Cold War.

Terrorists cannot hope to conquer, occupy, and govern the United States. Unlike Nazi Germany, imperial Japan, and Soviet Russia, they had not, in the early years of the twenty-first century, demonstrated the capacity to conquer, occupy, and govern successfully any country at all. Fighting terrorism required not assembling large armies and developing powerful weapons, let alone using them (or being prepared to use them) against comparably armed enemies, as in World War II and the Cold War, but rather engaging in patient international police work that relies heavily on the painstaking collection of intelligence.

As for nation-building, the American experience in Afghanistan and Iraq did not increase the national appetite for the task. The pacification of Iraq, especially, proved more difficult and costly—in soldiers' lives as well as taxpayers' money—than had been initially anticipated. The number of troops the United States deployed there proved inadequate to keep order, but even those deployments—on the order of 150,000 American troops—severely strained the American military. A majority of Americans came to consider the decision to intervene there to have been a mistake. Like the Vietnam War a generation earlier, the Iraq conflict seemed likely to make the United States wary of, rather than well disposed to, further, similar ventures.

Even without the Cold War, however, and even if the threat of terrorism could not, by itself, underpin a security policy as expansive as that of the Cold War, two tasks continued to justify in American eyes the deployment, and perhaps even the use, of the armed forces of the United States: reassurance, which provides insurance against the kind of major conflict that Americans made considerable sacrifices to fight and to prevent in the twentieth century; and nuclear nonproliferation, a goal that polls consistently showed Americans to be willing to pay to pursue.[64]

Reassuring the countries of Europe and East Asia that the distribution of power in their regions will not change in such a way as to require changes in their own security policies and that, in any case, the United States will remain on hand to deter a neighboring country if it adopts an aggressive foreign policy, requires some American military deployments in these parts of the world. While no formula exists for determining just what forces are needed to convey reassurance, it stands to reason that the less nervous countries are about their neighbors to begin with, the more confidence they will have that their neighborhoods will remain peaceful, and the smaller the American military contingent needed to promote reassurance will therefore have to be. In Europe, if not in East Asia, it was easy to envision, in the opening years of the twenty-first century, the American military presence being reduced to very low levels without adverse consequences; and indeed the Defense Department did plan to draw down the garrisons that it had maintained in Western Europe for the better part of six decades.[65] In August 2004, the Pentagon announced the withdrawal of 70,000 troops from overseas bases, in Asia, including Korea, as well as from Europe. According to the secretary of defense, Donald Rumsfeld, "We've decided that it's time to shift our posture in Europe and Asia and around the world and move from static defense, which does not make much sense today, to a more deployable and usable set of capabilities."[66]

Nonproliferation tends to be a more taxing mission than reassurance, especially when it requires the actual use of military force, as American officials believed it did in the case of Iraq. Ironically, the failure to prevent the spread of nuclear weapons could actually lighten the burden of the American role in providing international security. If a rogue state were actually to acquire nuclear weapons, the United States would be reluctant to go to war against it. (This is, of course, a principal reason that countries seek these weapons.) In that case, the United States would probably shift to a policy of deterrence, in order to check the political aims on behalf of which the newly nuclear-equipped regime might be tempted to employ its military forces.[67] As the principal purpose of its military deployments during the Cold War, deterrence is a familiar policy to the United States and one that, in the confrontation with the Soviet Union, the American government found ways to carry out at relatively modest cost.

In the absence of major nation-building missions beyond Afghanistan and Iraq, with the costs of providing reassurance dropping, at least in Europe, and the price of resisting the spread of nuclear weapons or coping with the consequences of failing to resist it at least not rising sharply—none of which is certain but all of which are at least plausible—the overall cost that the American public would have to authorize to sustain the role that the United States has played since the end of the Cold War in making the world secure would be a relatively modest one, at least by the standards of the second half of the twentieth century. Even in that case, however, the continuation of the major post–Cold War American security policies would not be assured. The American role as the world's government will face a particular and formidable challenge as the twenty-first century proceeds, however benign the world turns out to be, because that challenge will come not from outside but from within the United States.

The American public will decide whether to support measures the foreign policy elite initiates in the twenty-first century, as it did in the twentieth, largely on the basis of their costs. The willingness to pay will depend not only on the absolute costs of providing reassurance, nonproliferation, a global currency, and emergency loans to the rest of the world. It will depend as well on the magnitude of competing demands on the nation's resources, and these will be unprecedentedly heavy.

The government of the United States is committed to providing pensions and health care, through the Social Security and Medicare programs, to Americans in their mid-sixties and older. These commitments, embodied in law, are considered binding: Indeed, they are commonly called "entitlements," denoting something owed a person simply by virtue of his or her citizenship. In the first half of the twenty-first century, the costs of these entitlement programs will rise sharply for demographic reasons, putting pressure on all other outlets for public expenditure, including foreign policy.[68]

Western governments began to assume responsibility for providing old-age pensions and health care, as well as other services to the needy, in the twentieth century, and in the course of that century the obligation to provide for the welfare of their citizens steadily expanded in scope and cost. So, therefore, did the fraction of a society's output appropriated by the state in taxes and redistributed in the form of welfare benefits of various kinds. The resources that the government takes through taxation and devotes to welfare cannot, of course, be used either for private purposes by the people who pay the taxes or for the historic governmental goals of protecting the country from external enemies and projecting its power abroad. The rise of the welfare state established a potential conflict between international and domestic expenditures—between guns and butter.

In the second half of the twentieth century, the United States managed to have both without undue difficulty. The costs of the Cold War were relatively modest, at least when compared with the costs of World War II and with the proportion of the national output that the Soviet Union, America's less economically efficient rival, had to devote to waging it. The cost of welfare increased steadily, but not so rapidly as to convince Americans that they could afford either guns or butter but not both. In the twenty-first century, however, social welfare costs will rise sharply enough to put in doubt the public's willingness to pay for both social welfare and global governance.

Underlying the explosion in entitlement costs is the changing age distribution of the American population. The two principal programs, Social Security and Medicare, operate on a "pay as you go" basis. Benefits come out of current revenues: People in the workforce pay, through their taxes, for the benefits given to those who are already retired. The age structure of virtually all societies throughout history has been shaped like a pyramid, with the young at the bottom outnumbering their elders at the top. The less sharply the pyramid tapers upward and the more rectangular it therefore becomes—that is, the higher the ratio of retirees to workers—the greater will be the economic strain of supporting the elderly. In the twenty-first century, that ratio will rise sharply, as the largest age cohort in American history, the "baby boom" generation born between 1946 and 1964, reaches retirement age and has to be supported by the less numerous generations that follow it.[69]

The burden will be all the heavier because Americans are living longer than ever before, increasing the number of entitlement recipients at any one time. The burden of entitlements on American society and the American economy will be further increased by the all but certain growth in the costs of health care, the result of the new medicines and new treatments that the medical community will surely provide.[70] The foreseeable costs of fulfilling the commitments made to American citizens already born is staggering and goes far beyond the amount of money the government can expect to collect in taxes at current rates. Estimates of these "unfunded mandates" range from 45 to 75 *trillion* dollars.[71]

The huge bill for entitlements as the twenty-first century proceeds will compel either a very steep rise in the taxes younger Americans pay or a sharp reduction in the benefits older Americans receive, or, what is most likely, both. Neither will be popular. The mark of this unpopularity is the fact that although the fiscal problems the aging of the baby boomers will pose have long been well known, candidates for political office, who have the ultimate responsibility for coping with these problems, have virtually ignored them.[72] The required tax increases and cuts in benefits are likely to be substantial enough to affect the context in which public policy is made. The entitlements explosion, especially in conjunction with rising energy costs but even without these, will create a new political climate in the United States, and in this new climate the international services that the country came to provide during and after the Cold War are not necessarily destined to flourish.

Democracies favor butter over guns.[73] The ultimate responsibility for the society's resources rests with the people themselves, and most people see to their own immediate well-being before concerning themselves with events beyond their borders.[74] The founding document of the American republic, the Declaration of Independence of 1776, announced that all persons have certain fundamental rights, which the independent country the signers proposed to build would guarantee, namely "life, liberty, and the pursuit of happiness"—presumably individual happiness. The document did not mention international stability or global prosperity as goals to which the new country would devote itself.

As the provision of welfare becomes more expensive and therefore more controversial, other public programs, especially those involving other countries and not clearly connected to the physical safety of Americans, may well lose political support. Under these circumstances it will become increasingly difficult for the foreign policy elite to persuade the wider public to support the kinds of policies that, collectively, make up the American role as the world's government. Foreign policy will be relegated to the back burner, regarded as less worthy of concern and attention than the government's financial obligations to its own citizens.

This may well occur even if the costs to the United States of its role as the functional equivalent of the world's government remain relatively modest, indeed even if those costs should decline. History's great powers often relinquished their positions of international prominence when the costs of retaining those positions exceeded what they were willing or able to pay. The greatest threat to the American international position in the twenty-first century seems more likely to come from the competing costs of social welfare programs within the United States, which threaten to reduce public support for any and every other public purpose. Such a development is likely to be gradual, not sudden, like the growth of a cataract that gradually obscures a person's vision rather than an immediately life-changing heart attack.

The reduction of domestic support for the tasks of global governance is not certain to take place. The course of world history, and of the history of the foreign policy of a particular country, cannot be precisely foreseen. What the United States does in the world in the twenty-first century will depend in no small part on events that, like the September 11 attacks on New York and Washington, cannot be reliably predicted. Still, the certain increase in the costs of social welfare programs, and the strong political bias for giving them priority over the tasks the United States carried out in, with, and on behalf of other countries, means that in the course of the new century the world may have to do without some, or even most, of the global governance the United States was supplying when the century began.

Chapter Five

THE FUTURE

Always keep a-hold of nurse,
For fear of finding something worse.

HILAIRE BELLOC, *Cautionary Verses*

A World Without America

If public pressure within the United States were to compel the American government to withdraw most or all of the military forces stationed beyond North America and to do far less than it had become accustomed to doing to discourage the spread of nuclear weapons, to cope with the consequences of fiscal crises outside its borders, and to help keep global markets open to trade, what impact would this have on the rest of the world?

The last occasion on which the United States placed itself on the periphery rather than at the center of international affairs, the period between the two world wars, was not a happy one. Indeed, the antecedents of the American twenty-first-century role as the world's government lie in the fear, after World War II, that in the absence of an expansive American international presence the world would experience repetitions of the two global disasters of the 1930s and the 1940s—the Great Depression and World War II. It was to prevent a recurrence of these economic and political calamities that the United States assumed the responsibilities it bore during the Cold War, which, modified and extended, comprise its post–Cold War role as the world's government. Although the history of the interwar era will not precisely repeat itself even if the United States takes a far less active part in international affairs, a substantial contraction of the American global role would risk making the world a less secure and less prosperous place.

In the interwar period, Germany and Japan came to be governed by people committed to the precepts of aggressive ideologies and determined to expand by force their countries' spheres of imperial control. The Western democracies at first hoped that German and Japanese aspirations could be satisfied peacefully in ways consistent with their own safety. When this proved to be impossible, the result was the bloodiest and most destructive war in human history.

No early twenty-first-century version of imperial Japan and Nazi Germany is likely to appear: The twentieth-century ideologies of conquest—fascism and communism—have been discredited and no comparable set of ideas, whose adherents could seize control of a powerful state and thus menace the world, are in circulation. The militant Islam of the early twenty-first century does bear a resemblance to the twentieth century's totalitarian ideologies[1] but does not pose a threat of the same kind or of the same magnitude as fascism and communism did. The Islamist ideology lacks appeal in the world's most powerful countries and has had little success in gaining control of even less powerful, predominantly Muslim countries.

Still, the twenty-first century is not necessarily destined to be free of conflict involving the strongest members of the international system. At the start of the century, China loomed as a potential disturber of the peace by virtue of its size, its surging economic growth, and its long premodern history of cultural and political primacy in East Asia. Together, these national characteristics could fuel a drive for enhanced power and status.

China will no doubt increase its international influence as the twenty-first century proceeds, and one issue in particular has the potential to set off a major war in East Asia—Beijing's claim to rule the effectively independent and, unlike the mainland, democratically governed island of Taiwan. The China of the initial decade of the twenty-first century lacked, however, the rapacious ideology that had inspired Nazi Germany and imperial Japan. The communism in the name of which Mao Zedong ruled the country in the third quarter of the twentieth century had lost credibility and support among the Chinese. If China does provoke international conflict, its motives will not arise from the kinds of political convictions that produced the two world wars and the Cold War. As the new millennium began, the Chinese people and the Chinese government seemed far more interested in enriching themselves through peaceful participation in the global economy than in embarking on campaigns of conquest, even against Taiwan.

The greatest threat to their security that the members of the international system did face in the new century, one that the United States had devoted considerable resources and political capital to containing and that a serious reduction in the American global rule would certainly aggravate, was the spread of nuclear weapons. Nuclear proliferation poses three related dangers.

The first is that, in the absence of an American nuclear guarantee, major countries in Europe and Asia will feel the need to acquire their own nuclear armaments. If the United States withdrew from Europe and East Asia, Germany might come to consider it imprudent to deal with a nuclear-armed Russia, and Japan with a nuclear-armed China, without nuclear arms of their own. They would seek these weapons in order to avoid an imbalance in power that might work to their disadvantage. The acquisition of nuclear weapons by such affluent, democratic, peaceful countries would not, by itself, trigger a war. It could, however, trigger arms races similar to the one between the United States and the Soviet Union during the Cold War. It would surely make Europe and East Asia less comfortable places, and relations among the countries of these regions more suspicious, than was the case at the outset of the twenty-first century.

The spread of nuclear weapons poses a second danger, which the United States exerted itself to thwart to the extent of threatening a war in North Korea and actually waging one in Iraq and that the recession of American power would increase: the possession of nuclear armaments by "rogue" states, countries governed by regimes at odds with their neighbors and hostile to prevailing international norms. A nuclear-armed Iraq, an unlikely development after the overthrow of Saddam Hussein's regime, or a nuclear-armed Iran, a far more plausible prospect, would make the international relations of the Persian Gulf far more dangerous. That in turn would threaten virtually every country in the world because so much of the oil on which they all depend comes from that region.[2] A nuclear-armed North Korea would similarly change the international relations of East Asia for the worse. Especially if the United States withdrew from the region, South Korea and Japan, and perhaps ultimately Taiwan, might well decide to equip themselves with nuclear weapons of their own.

A North Korean nuclear arsenal would pose yet a third threat: nuclear weapons in the hands of a terrorist group such as al Qaeda. Lacking the infrastructure of a sovereign state, a terrorist organization probably could not construct a nuclear weapon itself. But it could purchase either a full-fledged nuclear explosive or nuclear material that could form the basis for a device that, while not actually exploding, could spew poisonous radiation over populated areas, killing or infecting many thousands of people.[3] Nuclear materials are potentially available for purchase not only in North Korea but elsewhere as well.

In the first decade of the twenty-first century, a large quantity of dangerous nuclear material, much of it protected by flimsy safeguards or by no safeguards at all, was located in the territory of what had been, during the Cold War, one of the world's two great nuclear powers, the Soviet Union. The impresario of Pakistan's nuclear weapons program, A. Q. Khan, was discovered in 2004 to have transferred bomb-relevant technology to other countries, presumably in order to enrich himself.[4] The destitute totalitarian regime of North Korea would have no scruples about, indeed a substantial interest in, trafficking in nuclear weapons and weapons-related material for financial gain.

In the wake of September 11, a terrorist group in possession of a nuclear weapon that could not be deterred from launching an attack, as the Soviet Union had been deterred during the Cold War, loomed as the gravest threat to the safety of the United States in the eyes of American officials. No task had a higher priority for American foreign policy than preventing such groups from obtaining such weapons. A terrorist attack using nuclear materials almost anywhere would dwarf the events of September 11 in damage inflicted. Such a terrible event would have an impact on international relations difficult to predict but, especially if it occurred in the United States, Europe, or Japan, probably more sweeping than the 2001 assaults on the World Trade Center and the Pentagon in reducing global economic output, restricting the cross-border flows of goods, money, and people, and increasing spending on arms, armies, espionage, and police.

Although the spread of nuclear weapons to powerful countries had the potential, should they wage war using them, to cause far more damage, the possession of such armaments by terrorists posed the most urgent global threat because such groups were apparently actively attempting to acquire them and would surely use them if they succeeded. To the extent that American foreign policies reduced the likelihood that such an attack would take place, the United States was performing a service of unsurpassed importance for the rest of the world.

Although the spread of nuclear weapons, with the corresponding increase in the likelihood that a nuclear shot would be fired in anger somewhere in the world, counted as the most serious potential consequence of the abandonment by the United States of its role as the world's government, it was not the only one. In the previous period of American international reticence, the 1920s and 1930s, the global economy suffered serious damage that a more active American role might have mitigated. A twenty-first-century American retreat could have similarly adverse international economic consequences.

The economic collapse of the 1930s caused extensive hardship throughout the world and led indirectly to World War II by paving the way for the people who started it to gain power in Germany and Japan. In retrospect, the Great Depression is widely believed to have been caused by a series of errors in public policy that made an economic downturn far worse than it would have been had governments responded to it in appropriate fashion. Since the 1930s, acting on the lessons drawn from that experience by professional economists, governments have taken steps that have helped to prevent a recurrence of the disasters of that decade.[5]

In the face of reduced demand, for example, governments have increased rather than cut spending. Fiscal and monetary crises have evoked rescue efforts rather than a studied indifference based on the assumption that market forces will readily reestablish a desirable economic equilibrium. In contrast to the widespread practice of the 1930s, political authorities now understand that putting up barriers to imports in an attempt to revive domestic production will in fact worsen economic conditions everywhere.

Still, a serious, prolonged failure of the international economy, inflicting the kind of hardship the world experienced in the 1930s (which some Asian countries also suffered as a result of their fiscal crises in the 1990s) does not lie beyond the realm of possibility. Market economies remain subject to cyclical downturns, which public policy can limit but has not found a way to eliminate entirely. Markets also have an inherent tendency to form bubbles, excessive values for particular assets, whether seventeenth century Dutch tulips or twentieth century Japanese real estate and Thai currency, that cause economic harm when the bubble bursts and prices plunge. In responding to these events, governments can make errors. They can act too slowly, or fail to implement the proper policies, or implement improper ones.

Moreover, the global economy and the national economies that comprise it, like a living organism, change constantly and sometimes rapidly: Capital flows across sovereign borders, for instance, far more rapidly and in much greater volume in the early twenty-first century than ever before. This means that measures that successfully address economic malfunctions at one time may have less effect at another, just as medical science must cope with the appearance of new strains of influenza against which existing vaccines are not effective. Most importantly, since the Great Depression, an active American international economic role has been crucial both in fortifying the conditions for global economic well-being and in coping with the problems that have occurred, especially periodic recessions and currency crises, by applying the lessons of the past. The absence of such a role could weaken those conditions and aggravate those problems.

The overall American role in the world since World War II therefore has something in common with the theme of the Frank Capra film *It's a Wonderful Life*, in which the angel Clarence, played by Henry Travers, shows James Stewart, playing the bank clerk George Bailey, who believes his existence to have been worthless, how life in his small town of Bedford Falls would have unfolded had he never been born. George Bailey learns that people he knows and loves turn out to be far worse off without him. So it is with the United States and its role as the world's government. Without that role, the world very likely would have been in the past, and would become in the future, a less secure and less prosperous place.

The abdication by the United States of some or all of the responsibilities for international security that it had come to bear in the first decade of the twenty-first century would deprive the international system of one of its principal safety features, which keeps countries from smashing into each other, as they are historically prone to do. In this sense, a world without America would be the equivalent of a freeway full of cars without brakes. Similarly, should the American government abandon some or all of the ways in which it had, at the dawn of the new century, come to support global economic activity, the world economy would function less effectively and might even suffer a severe and costly breakdown. A world without the United States would in this way resemble a fleet of cars without gasoline.

Their awareness, sometimes dim and almost never explicitly spelled out, of the political, military, and economic dangers that would come with the retreat of American power causes other countries to refrain from combining to try to displace the United States from its place at the center of the international system. Virtually all of them harbor some grievance or other against the twenty-first-century international order, but none would welcome the absence of any order at all, which is what the collapse of American power might well bring. Grudgingly, tacitly, silently, other countries support the American role as the world's government out of the well-grounded fear that while the conduct of the United States may be clumsy, overbearing, and even occasionally insufferable, the alternative would be even worse, perhaps much worse.

If America should, for whatever combination of reasons, cease to function as the world's government, some replacement would be needed to avoid the costs and dangers that would otherwise ensue. What could take the place of American power? The logical substitute is something that has occasionally been proposed but never actually created: a proper world government.

World Government

Because the United States does for the world some of the things that governments do for and within the countries they govern, it follows that a formally constituted supranational authority with the power over the international system that governments exercise within its member states would do these things as well, if not better. This logic has not been lost on observers of international relations. The idea of a genuine world government recurs in commentary on world politics over the centuries.[6] Just as it has been said of the always tantalizing but never realized economic prospects for Latin America's largest state that Brazil is the country of the future and always will be, so world government has always been an idea whose time has not yet come—and probably never will.

The idea achieved its greatest prominence in the twentieth century. In the wake of two devastating world wars, international organizations were established—the League of Nations after the first, the United Nations following the second—that some of their champions hoped would turn into full-fledged international governments.[7] Two of the problems with which the United States, in its capacity as the provider of governmental services to the world, has had to cope—the spread of nuclear weapons and the outbreak of monetary crises—have seemed serious enough to warrant proposals for the establishment of agencies with supranational powers to deal with them. In 1946, at the dawn of the atomic age, the

United States devised the Baruch Plan, a scheme for putting all the steps of the bomb-making process, from the mining of uranium to the fabrication of explosives, under an international authority.[8] In the late 1990s, after the Asian crises, the idea was floated of establishing a genuine global bank, one with the power, previously reserved for sovereign states, to issue money.[9]

Neither proposal was adopted. As for the postwar international organizations, the League of Nations, while it lasted, did not assume, and the United Nations, since its founding, has not even come close to assuming sovereign power over the international system. For a genuine global government to come into being, the world's independent countries would have to cede their sovereign prerogatives to it. This they have never been willing to do. The United States refused to join the League of Nations because the United States Senate feared abdicating to that body the sovereign right to decide on going to war. Partly as a result, the UN was designed to reassure its member states that they would not surrender their sovereign prerogatives by joining.

To be sure, sovereignty has seldom been absolute: Few governments have exercised complete and unchallenged power within their borders.[10] In the twentieth century, moreover, formidable forces, in particular the spreading conviction that the international community is justified in intruding on the internal affairs of independent countries in order to protect its citizens from persecution by their governments,[11] challenged governments' freedom of action within their own borders. Still, no government seriously contemplated the ultimate formal surrender of sovereignty for the purpose of creating a world government. Indeed, the prevailing international trend ran in the opposite direction. The twentieth century saw the multiplication, rather than the consolidation, of sovereignty, as the large multinational empires that had dominated the planet for most of modern history dissolved into many individual nation-states.

Reversing this trend to form a universal government, should the world's almost 200 countries somehow be tempted to try, would risk creating a global Leviathan powerful enough to suppress the liberties that the citizens of so many of them have come to enjoy.[12] The danger to liberty aside, the construction and operation of a genuine government on a global scale would pose huge practical problems: The twenty-first-century governments of the world's sovereign states, even the smallest of them, have not invariably been, after all, models of efficiency and probity.

The services that the United States provides to the world, which a formal world government could also furnish, involve preventing developments that could damage all other members of the international system, including the wealthiest and most powerful of them. The United States sought to reassure the major powers of Europe and East Asia, to forestall nuclear proliferation, to support the transborder flows of goods and money and to contain financial crises for fear that the failure to do so would open the way to serious harm to the interests, and the citizens, of the United States itself. In the first decade of the twenty-first century, the leading causes of actual suffering and misery were not, however, these potential dangers but rather two different, ongoing problems: civil wars and global poverty. The effects of these events and conditions were felt locally but not, on the whole, globally,[13] and so the American government did relatively little to address them. A world government, if such a thing were established, could contribute to solving these problems, but at the cost of thrusting upon the United States and other Western countries the responsibility for them—and the places where they fester—that the Western powers were at pains to avoid.

After the Cold War, most of the violence serious enough to qualify as war took place within the same country rather than, as had been true in the twentieth century, between and among sovereign states. A number of these conflicts arose from the efforts of one group to escape the jurisdiction in which it had been placed and form its own independent country,[14] an issue that would lose much of its salience if national sovereignties were abolished. The formation of an effective global Leviathan would also help to put an end to the other common post–Cold War cause of large-scale violence, the collapse of effective government. Within "failed states," in which the government has lost the capacity to keep order, and in a number of the conflicts triggered by efforts at secession as well, the violence has more closely resembled criminal activity than organized warfare—although these cases were not necessarily less destructive than more formally organized conflicts.[15] The prevention of such violence requires the establishment of authority.[16]

A world government would, by definition, have responsibility for establishing order everywhere, and so would have to go about the task of supplying authority in the chaotic corners of the world. It would fall to the wealthiest and most capable members of the international system to furnish the necessary resources, and this they could certainly do: A large infusion of Western peacekeepers and Western resources would undoubtedly make Africa more peaceful, for example. But the wealthy and powerful countries, including the United States, have shown themselves unwilling to devote serious attention and resources to uplifting the unstable and weak ones,[17] and their reluctance counts as yet another reason that they are unlikely to take part in the creation of a genuine world government.

A similar political logic applies to the other great ongoing source of distress on the planet: the poverty in which, at the outset of the twenty-first century, so many of its inhabitants lived. The poor, according to scripture, will always be with us, and throughout history most human beings have lived in conditions of scarcity and hardship. The world of the twenty-first century does not lack for such conditions. More than 1 billion people live on less than $1 per day, while another 1 to 2 billion live on less than $2 per day.[18]

What is new in the contemporary international system is not poverty but affluence, made possible by the great and distinguishing feature of the modern world: economic growth. The economic well-being that hundreds of millions of fortunate people enjoy makes the deprivation and misery in which billions of others live seem intolerable.[19] In the twentieth century, the affluence of the West made the poverty elsewhere seem not only intolerable but unnecessary—a problem to be solved rather than, as it had been seen for millennia, a condition to be endured. For much of the second half of the past century, those most concerned with alleviating global poverty believed that this required a change in the policies of the rich countries themselves toward the poor—either less exploitation or greater generosity, depending on political taste.

By the twenty-first century, the consensus on the subject had shifted to an emphasis on the responsibility of the poor countries themselves for taking the steps necessary to lift themselves out of poverty through the promotion of economic growth.[20] Such growth is the product of a familiar combination of policies: a stable currency, less-than-stifling levels of taxation, the protection of property rights, working systems of transportation and communication, and adequate provision for public health and education.

The countries that are able to put such policies in place are those with institutions capable of carrying them out, above all honest, efficient government and an effective financial system. A world government could impose such institutions.[21] The European great powers did so in the age of empire, and in some parts of the world this led to better economic results than were subsequently achieved under the independent indigenous regimes that replaced imperial rule.[22] As with ending large-scale violence, however, fostering the conditions necessary for economic progress in the poorest parts of the world would involve the wealthy and powerful countries far more deeply in the affairs of the destitute than they have thought necessary for their own well-being. The fact that greater responsibility on the part of the rich and powerful of the planet for the conditions in which the poor and weak live would be an important consequence of the formation of a world government is yet another reason that the most influential members of the international system will not seriously entertain the idea of creating one.

The establishment of a world government is therefore no more likely to occur in the twenty-first century, even if the United States lowers its international profile considerably, than in the centuries preceding. Still, a substantial retraction of American power without the advent of a global authority to replace it would not necessarily plunge the world into deadly and costly disorder because government, whether formally constituted or supplied de facto by the United States, is not the only source of order in the international system.

International Society

Government is not the essence of social life. In human affairs it is secondary, emerging from, and playing a supporting role for, what is primary: the social relations and the norms they embody that make up society.[23] So it is in international affairs. There is an international society, consisting of the many economic, political, legal, cultural, and personal ties between and among sovereign states and their inhabitants. International society has existed for millennia, since humans first began regular exchanges between separate communities, and the connections that comprise it have multiplied over the years. The web of international society has become progressively thicker as governments have done more business of all kinds with one another and more and more people from all parts of the world have come to travel, trade, and organize themselves for various purposes across sovereign borders.

Within a community, the expansion of society has a contradictory effect on its government. On the one hand, the more numerous and intensive social relations become, the greater will be the need for government to protect and supplement them. On the other, the denser the thicket of social relations, the more likely the society in question will be to produce nongovernmental networks, associations, and institutions that stand apart from the government but do some of the work that it does. These are the components of the rich civic life that Tocqueville found and admired in early nineteenth century America. They have come to be known, col-lectively, as civil society.

Civil society exists in the international system as well as within the societies of independent countries. Associations of all kinds operate across, as well as within, sovereign borders. Private firms seeking profits, nongovernmental organizations concerned with health, human rights, the environment, and other matters, and governments and their specialized depart-ments and agencies all interact regularly across these borders.

As within most countries, so in the international system as a whole civil society has expanded dramatically. The world's international organizations—those, that is, involving govern-ments, which make up only a fraction of international civil society—form an ever-thickening alphabet soup, the ingredi-ents of which have become staples of newspaper headlines: the UN and NATO are the most familiar to Western readers, but the global assortment also includes APEC (Asia-Pacific Eco-nomic Cooperation), the IAEA (International Atomic Energy Agency), OPEC (Organization of Petroleum Exporting Countries), SARCC (South Asia Regional Coordinating Council), and many others. Private economic transactions across borders and the firms conducting them have expanded enormously in number. As for nongovernmental associations, their number was estimated to be, at the end of the twentieth century, 200 times greater than had been the case at the begin-ning. Of the approximately 50,000 nongovernmental, not-for-profit organizations with some international dimension, an estimated 90 percent had been established since 1970.[24]

Of all the regions of the world, the one where interna-tional civil society was thickest in the early years of the twenty-first century—where cross-border networks were most numerous, active, and effective—was Europe. The twenty-five-member European Union, while not itself a state, had a number of governmental features, including a parliament, a central bank, a court, and a large body of laws and regulations to which all its members voluntarily conformed. Europe had less need than other parts of the world for the governmental services the United States furnished because European civil society generated so many of them itself. To the extent that the world comes to resemble Europe, therefore, the need for the United States to function as the world's government will diminish and the contraction of American power, should this occur, will be less consequential.

The rest of the world may indeed become progressively like Europe. This is, after all, one of the principal themes of modern history. The political forms that dominated the planet in the twenty-first century had their origins on the European continent: the nation-state, democracy, and capitalism. These forms spread beyond Europe because they provided what people everywhere wanted: security, power, and wealth. The EU is the latest political innovation to appear in Europe and it, too, offers a powerfully attractive model. As it has taken root and expanded both its geographic scope and its political and economic functions, Europe has become an ever more firmly peaceful place and Europeans have enjoyed rising levels of economic well-being.

The politics and economics to which Europe is committed lend themselves particularly well to the growth of civil society. By limiting the purview of the state, democracy marks out social space in which nongovernmental organizations can flourish. The essence of a market economy is voluntary cooperation among independent agents, which is how the networks of civil society work. It is therefore not fanciful to imagine that by the end of the twenty-first century other regions will look as Europe did at its beginning: crosshatched with nongovernmental networks, voluntary associations, and international organizations that will support the kinds of governmental tasks that the United States has come to carry out.

It is far-fetched, however, to suppose that such a development will occur soon, in the early part of the current century. For in the century's first decade, it was the differences between Europe and the rest of the world—the features that lent themselves to the formation and growth of the EU that other regions did not share—that stood out.

The countries of Europe have a long and rich history of interaction with one another. Not all of these interactions were peaceful, of course, but the people of European societies share a sense of familiarity lacking in other parts of the world that helped make the EU possible. They have a number of other features in common. For all the many differences it contains, Europe is, compared with other regions, a relatively homogeneous place, and this, too, facilitated the broad, deep, institutionalized cooperation of the early twenty-first century. The range of geographic and population sizes across the continent is not, on the whole, particularly great. All the European countries are, by the world's standards, affluent, especially Western Europe, the EU's center of gravity, without the extreme differences in per capita income found in other parts of the world.

Europeans also share a Roman and Christian heritage, giving them more in common than neighboring countries in other parts of the world have with each other. The democratic politics and free market economics on which the EU rests, moreover, are more widely and firmly established in Europe than in Asia, Africa, or Latin America—and better and longer established in the western than in the eastern part of Europe itself.

Asia is destined to rise in importance in the course of the twenty-first century as Asian countries, especially the largest of them, China and India, become wealthier and more powerful. Yet the prospects for the kinds of international institutions found in Europe, and the cooperation that these institutions foster, are distant at best. Asia is a far more heterogeneous region: Its countries vary greatly in size; the distances between and among them are greater. Their economic circumstances vary widely: The differences in per capita income between, for example, Singapore and Japan, on the one hand, and Bangladesh and Burma, on the other, far exceed any such disparities found in Europe. The countries of Asia have more diverse cultural backgrounds than those of Europe, with Confucian, Buddhist, Hindu, and Muslim traditions represented in the region. Moreover, all members of the European Union are democracies, whereas Asian governments range from the similarly free political systems of India and Japan to the military dictatorships of Pakistan and Burma to Communist-ruled countries, notably China and Vietnam. Although an Asian version of the European Union would be desirable, therefore, the many and deep differences that mark the countries of the region make a close economic and political association among them unlikely.

Nor is Asia likely to establish, in the early years of the twenty-first century, a security community comparable to Europe's North Atlantic Treaty Organization. NATO rests on firmly peaceful relations among all its members, none of which has any reason even to contemplate war against any of the others. This is not the case in Asia, where China reserves the right to use force to gain control of Taiwan, the Communist regime of North Korea poses a standing threat to its neighbors, and India and Pakistan are deeply at odds over the status of the Indian province of Kashmir.

The remaking of Asia, or indeed other parts of the world, in Europe's image does not, therefore, offer a promising way, in the short term, to replace the governmental services of the United States, should these cease to be available. Europe's distinctive array of political and economic strengths do, however, make the EU itself a plausible candidate to assume some of the responsibilities of global governance.

Europe

With 450 million people, an economic output larger than that of any other political unit, and members with glorious histories of scientific discovery, cultural achievement, and global power, the EU has reason to expect to play a leading role in the world of the twenty-first century. The movement toward ever-closer European integration that began after World War II and continued in the new millennium stemmed in part from the desire to recapture some of the global influence the nation-states of Europe exercised from the sixteenth through the nineteenth centuries but lost in the twentieth.

Many Europeans, especially those whose native language is French, hope to wield the increased influence to which they aspire independently of and, where they deem it appropriate, in opposition to the United States.[25] Jacques Chirac, the president of the French republic in the early years of the twenty-first century, deemed desirable the creation of a "multipolar world," by which he meant a world of more than one center of power—a world, that is, with a Europe capable of standing up to, and blocking, the United States.[26]

A powerful, assertive Europe could also collaborate with its Cold War North American ally, with which, after all, it shares fundamental values and basic political and economic institutions. In so doing, Europe would complement, if not replace, the United States in its role as the functional equivalent of the world's government. Like the vision of Europe as a counterweight to the United States, a future in which a vigorous and internationally active EU serves as a make-weight, augmenting the American global role, has European support.[27] Unlike the multipolar world touted by President Chirac, this alternative use of enhanced European power has American champions as well.[28]

At least in the early years of the twenty-first century, however, Europe was likely to follow neither path. In important ways the EU has had, and will continue to have, powerful effects on other countries. But as a source of governmental services to the international system, Europe seems destined, in the short term, to be neither a counterweight nor a make-weight but instead a lightweight.[29]

Europe will be able to play a larger role in the world to the extent that the members of the EU can act in unison, as a single political entity. Europe has made remarkable strides toward unity since the end of World War II and in international economic matters does approximate a single powerful actor on the world stage. In international trade negotiations, there is a single European negotiator and a single European position. In monetary affairs, the single European currency, the euro, gives the EU the basis for dealing with the United States and the dollar as an equal.

In international relations more generally, the EU's member countries have committed themselves, on paper, to devising a common foreign and security policy, a commitment prominent enough to have acquired its own acronym—CFSP—and a designated high representative for it.[30] In the early years of the twenty-first century, however, the EU had made little progress in adopting such a policy, and the French and Dutch rejection of a proposed EU constitution in 2005 made the goal even more distant. In noneconomic issues Europe did not speak with one voice. The different countries retained the right to decide policy for themselves, and as the number of EU members grew, the task of merging their varying preferences into a single approach to major problems was bound to become more difficult. In the 1970s, the then American secretary of state Henry Kissinger is said to have asked rhetorically, "If I want to speak to Europe, what number do I call?" The designation of a high representative for common foreign and security policy supplied such a number. But the person taking the call did not have the power to speak on behalf of, let alone implement, a single European foreign policy.

This was particularly the case for policies involving the use of force, as was demonstrated by the sharp divisions within Europe over the 2003 war in Iraq.[31] That war, and the widespread unhappiness with it even in countries in which the government supported the American effort, illustrated another cardinal feature of twenty-first-century Europe, one that works against a wider international role, either in concert with or in opposition to the United States, for the EU: its pronounced unwillingness, leading to a vanishingly small capacity, to go to war.

The sentiment of warlessness, the principled aversion to armed conflict, which took root in all the Western democracies in the second half of the twentieth century,[32] had, at the outset of the twenty-first century, established a particularly powerful presence in Europe. The Europeans' dismay at the Iraq war, while a response to the particular circumstances surrounding it, reflected as well this broadly shared feeling. Asked in 2003 whether, in some circumstances, war is necessary to obtain justice, only 12 percent of the European respondents answered strongly in the affirmative. The figure for Americans was 55 percent.[33]

This attitude to war stemmed from more than a reflexive revulsion at the death and destruction modern war can inflict, which Europe had experienced at first hand twice in the first half of the twentieth century. It was based as well on the conviction, which emerged from the continent's experience in the second half of that century, that the political goals for which democracies fight wars—to defend and expand their own values and institutions, above all peace, democracy, and free markets—can be more effectively (not to mention more cheaply and safely) achieved by other means. Europeans had come to believe in the power of example and of co-optation (both wielded by Europe itself) to accomplish these ends.[34]

The peace that reigned in Europe after 1945, the liberty that flourished there, and the remarkable prosperity the countries of the western part of the continent achieved, together make for a powerful advertisement for adopting the political and economic institutions and the foreign policies that produced these results. An added incentive is the prospect for European countries of joining the EU itself, for which constitutional politics and a market economy are requirements, and thereby gaining access to the benefits, above all economic ones, that EU membership bestows. For countries beyond Europe, the comparable incentive for good government and good international behavior is the promise of trade and investment, yielding similar, if more modest, benefits.

There is much to be said for this point of view. Imitation is not only the sincerest form of flattery; it is, over the long term, the most reliable way to implant Western values and practices. Individuals more readily change their patterns of conduct by observing, admiring, and adopting the behavior of others than they do in response to hectoring or coercion. So it is with groups of individuals, including entire societies and sovereign states.[35] In this sense, the force of example and the prospect of inclusion do have more power than warfare, and they can claim some impressive post-1945 achievements.

The transformation of Germany and Japan during the Cold War into peace-loving democracies owed a great deal to the model offered by Western societies and to German and Japanese membership in Western security and economic organizations. Similarly, the example of, and the lure of membership in, the EU undoubtedly hastened and smoothed the post–Cold War transition of the countries of Central Europe from Communist rule and command economies to democracy and free markets. Perhaps most importantly and certainly most dramatically, the Cold War itself was won more by the force of example than the force of arms—a point often more fully appreciated by Europeans than by Americans.[36]

Whereas most people become, with the proper socialization, law-abiding and peaceful citizens, however, some do not, which is why all societies have police forces, courts, and jails. Similarly, the Europeans' peaceful, conciliatory, incentive-offering method for dealing with potential sources of international conflict is the best possible approach—except where it isn't. On some governments and some leaders—the Baath regime of Iraq and Saddam Hussein, for example—the power of the European example and the prospect of economic ties that could enrich the societies they govern do not have the desired effect. With others, the economic incentives the Europeans prefer to offer for good behavior will not work without a credible threat to apply force if the bad behavior persists. In dealing with some countries, that is, the use of force or the credible threat to use it is unhappily necessary, and here the EU had, in the first decade of the twenty-first century, little to contribute.

The military forces of its member countries, most of them deployed under the auspices of the Western alliance, NATO, were not impressive. The Europeans had come to see their global mission as embodying civilization, not defending it.[37]

Although the non-American members of NATO had 1.25 million people under arms and 1 million more in reserve, only 55,000 of them were judged to be readily deployable.[38] The Europeans lacked both the means to transport the troops that could fight rapidly beyond Europe's borders and the advanced equipment, notably precision-guided munitions, that the American military used to devastating effect in the post–Cold War conflicts that it waged. No European country, not even the best armed and militarily most proficient of them, Britain and France, was capable of waging war on an appreciable scale by itself.[39] The European opposition to American unilateralism in the use of force, loudly proclaimed in objection to the Iraq war, thus amounted to a demand for a voice in, and perhaps a veto over, the decision to go to war without a credible promise to bear any appreciable share of the fighting when such a decision is made. The Europeans sought a kind of representation without taxation.[40]

Europe's armed forces did engage in peacekeeping, patrolling troubled places to keep fighting from breaking out again once it had stopped. Over the course of the year 2003, an average of approximately 70,000 European peacekeepers were deployed outside their home countries.[41] In December 2004, the European Union assumed responsibility for peace-keeping in Bosnia. Even in peacekeeping, a less arduous mission than war fighting, however, the Europeans' efforts had strict limits. They sent fewer troops to Afghanistan to support the fragile, pro-Western elected government there than they had promised, and fewer than were needed to secure the country.[42]

In the years following the end of the Cold War, European governments regularly announced plans to enhance and integrate their armed forces, but the goals were invariably modest.[43] Moreover, while the plans were announced by prime ministers, foreign ministers, and defense ministers, no finance minister ever stepped forward with a program of tax increases and reductions in social programs to raise the money required to pay for significantly expanded military efforts. In no country in the EU was the political will present to spend appreciably more than it was already doing on defense; during the first post–Cold War decade, Europe's military spending declined markedly in comparison with that of the United States.[44] In a survey of Europeans, majorities in most countries agreed that Europe should become a super-power, but when asked whether they favored spending more money on the military to achieve this goal, half these people said that they did not.[45] The absence of public support for larger and more capable military forces had, in addition to the sentiment of warlessness and a belief in the power of example and co-optation, two other powerful underlying causes, one of them found in the United States as well, the other unique to Europe.

As in the United States, the changing age distribution of the European population, with more older and fewer younger people, made the delivery of the benefits that the governments had promised their citizens after retirement an increasingly expensive proposition, leaving little appetite for new spending for other public programs.[46] Indeed, because of lower birthrates, fewer immigrants, and more generous benefits, the burdens the members of the European Union would have to try to sustain in the twenty-first century were proportionately even heavier than those of the United States.[47]

The second reason for the European disinterest in strong military forces is, at root, geographic. While the United States operates all over the world, and therefore in some turbulent and dangerous places, the relevant arena for the Europeans is Europe itself, the most peaceful, placid region of the planet. Societies muster military forces to respond to threats. At the beginning of the twenty-first century, because of their focus on their own region, Europeans did not, on the whole, feel threatened. Although they had suffered terrorist attacks for years, no single attack killed as many people, and none therefore had the psychological and political impact, as the September 11 assaults did in the United States. Whereas Americans saw the struggle against terrorism as a war to be fought and won by military means, the Europeans regarded the threat of terrorism as a problem to be managed, using political measures and police work.

Consequently, despite the aspirations for (and sometimes the presumption of) global influence about which its leaders routinely spoke, the EU did relatively little beyond Europe's borders. It directed its energy and attention inward.[48] In the early years of the twenty-first century, its official rhetoric to the contrary notwithstanding, Europe maintained a parochial outlook on the world.

Parochialism did not mean the absence of significant influence. If Europeans concerned themselves almost exclusively with their own neighborhood, that neighborhood was a large and important one. To have replaced the interstate rivalries that were normal on the continent for so long— rivalries that periodically erupted into wars that in the twentieth century spread all over the world—with a peace so widely accepted that by the early twenty-first century it was all but taken for granted was a monumental achievement and a great benefit not only to the Europeans themselves but also to all other inhabitants of the planet. The model the EU offered, of a cooperative, peaceful, prosperous community of sovereign states, had a powerful demonstration effect in the last third of the twentieth century on countries to the south—Spain, Portugal, and Greece—and to the east—Poland, Hungary, and the Czech Republic—of its Western European core.

The European model carried the promise of exerting comparably benign influence on two politically, economically, and culturally significant neighbors of the expanded twenty-five-member EU: Russia, by territory the world's largest country and for that reason and because of its history as one of the two chief protagonists of the Cold War, an important member of the international system; and Turkey, a predominantly Muslim country and therefore one whose future could set a precedent for the rest of the Islamic world. To the extent that the European example enhances the commitments of Russia and Turkey to democratic politics, free market economics, and peaceful relations with their neighbors, this would validate the Europeans' belief that the EU provides a valuable service as an example to the world simply by existing.

Outside the European continent, however, where active efforts were required, and even where the use of force was not involved, Europe, despite its pretensions, did little to provide the kinds of services that governments furnish within sovereign states and that the United States supplied to the international system. The EU fell short of its potential, for example, in keeping the global economy operating at a comfortable rate by generating demand for goods and services. The features of its economies that distinguished them from the American version, and that Europeans prized—the generous social services and the high taxes to pay for them, and the extensive regulations, especially governing labor—worked to inhibit economic growth in the larger countries of the EU.[49] As a result, the global economy relied heavily on demand from the United States for its own growth, with the economically dangerous consequence of a chronic American current account deficit.

On the problem of global poverty, which European governments touted as demanding the serious attention of the rich countries, the European performance did not match its rhetoric. Europeans were fond of noting that their governments devoted higher proportions of their total national outputs to economic assistance to poor countries than did the United States.[50] To the alleviation of poverty in countries with very low average incomes, however, the most valuable contribution the wealthy countries can make is not to donate a tiny fraction of their gross domestic products in the form of aid[51] but rather to open their home markets to the things that poor countries produce. On this score the European record was no better than the American one, and in some respects worse.[52] The principal exports of the poorest countries are agricultural commodities: the European Union's Common Agricultural Policy obstructs agricultural imports. The United States engaged in agricultural protectionism as well, but not on quite the same scale as the EU or Japan.[53]

Even to the prevention of global warming, a textbook example of an international public good and one that Europe had taken the lead in hammering out an international agreement—the Kyoto Protocol—to achieve, Europe made a very modest, limited contribution. To be sure, in the production of the greenhouse gases that threaten to raise the planet's temperature, the United States was, by some distance, the world's worst offender. If the American per capita consumption of carbon-based fuels were to fall to the European level, the problem of global warming (and other international problems as well) would become less serious. Even the implementation of the reductions in greenhouse gas emissions mandated by Kyoto would not, however, lower their accumulation in the Earth's atmosphere sufficiently to guarantee that the planet's temperature would not rise significantly.[54] Kyoto's national quotas for emission reductions seem to have been set as much to make it easy for the countries of Europe to fulfill them as to guard against a potentially dangerous and costly rise in temperature.[55] Even so, not all European countries were, in the first decade of the twenty-first century, on the way to achieving the reductions in emissions that, by signing the protocol, they had agreed to accomplish.[56]

In providing to the world as a whole the kinds of services that governments within countries supply to the people they govern, the EU, for all its virtues, has remained largely on the sidelines. In this way Europe has lived up to its nineteenth-century designation as, in contrast to North America, the Old

World. It resembles a retired person: still possessed of a lively mind, full of opinions based on long and rich experience, and ready, on the basis of that experience, to offer advice, much of it sound, on how the world should be organized and managed—but not available actually to do the work of organization and management.

For better or for worse, therefore, the world has, in the first decade of the twenty-first century, no substitute for the United States as the provider of governmental services to the international system. Rather than being home alone, the United States is, in this sense, abroad alone. Insofar as American foreign policy is unilateral, this is by default as well as by choice. The American government and the American public can, and will, decide whether, how far, and for how long to sustain the policies that amount, collectively, to bearing the burden of global governance. They will not have the option that, all other things being equal, they might well prefer: sharing that burden with others.

"Victor Hugo, Alas"

No good deed, an old saying has it, goes unpunished. The American role as the functional equivalent of the world's government qualifies as a good deed of sorts. True, the various policies that make up that role are not inspired by disinterested motives. The United States intends what it does in the world to further its own interests, above all the overriding interest in remaining secure. But other countries do derive benefits from those policies that come, in effect, as gifts because these countries neither request nor pay for them.

For those gifts the United States does not exactly suffer punishment—although there are people around the world seeking to kill Americans out of hatred of its global role as well as the values it embodies. But these services do go largely unrecognized and unappreciated. The Nobel Peace Prize is regularly awarded to individuals or groups for mediating international conflicts or working on behalf of noble causes, but no one has suggested giving it to the American public for supporting the policies of reassurance, nuclear nonproliferation, and economic stabilization that have done far more to avoid war and mitigate other causes of human suffering than any Nobel laureate has managed.

One reason others do not recognize the contribution the policies of the United States make to their own well-being is undoubtedly the familiar human tendency to take favorable circumstances for granted, even when they are of relatively recent provenance. One generation of Europeans suffered the horrors of World War II. The next generation, mindful of these horrors, struggled to build a Europe in which they would not recur. The third generation, only dimly aware of the sacrifices required to create it, takes the historical miracle of a peaceful, prosperous continent for granted.[57] Few Americans, to give a different example, concern themselves with the conditions of their houses' foundations until termites appear. The United States has acted as the world's pest-control service and has been doing so long enough that many of the gains to the rest of the world from the American international role go virtually unnoticed.

Another reason for the lack of international public acknowledgment of what the United States does in the world is that to recognize the American role would be tantamount to bestowing formal approval on it and conceding a unique global status to the United States. Other countries resist this for both valid reasons—disagreements with the United States on important issues of international policy—and less than wholly admirable ones—concern that this would diminish their own international standing.

Perhaps the most important reason for other countries' failure explicitly to acknowledge and appreciate that the United States furnishes valuable services to the international system is that to do so would risk raising the question of why those who take advantage of these services do not pay more of the costs of supplying them. It would risk, that is, other countries' capacities to continue as free riders.

To be a free rider is to get something for nothing, an arrangement no person or government will lightly abandon. The matter of nuclear proliferation, the most serious challenge to international security in the twenty-first century, illustrates the powerful attraction of avoiding paying the cost of an international public good, even where the failure to obtain it can have direct and adverse consequences for the country avoiding payment. Virtually every country in the world, including the most important ones, has endorsed the general policy of stopping the spread of nuclear weapons: the Nuclear Nonproliferation Treaty (NPT) commands almost universal acceptance. Yet when regimes seek to flout the NPT and the international norms it embodies, most countries do considerably less than they could to prevent this, even when they themselves would be threatened if the quest for nuclear weapons were to succeed. They have resisted full commitment to the cause of nonproliferation because they have had other interests to pursue and because they have felt confident that the United States would assume the burden of

denying nuclear weapons to the countries in question (or protecting them from the consequences of proliferation), regard-
less of what they did or failed to do.

If Saddam Hussein had acquired nuclear weapons, for
instance, he could have used them to bully and dominate
other Middle Eastern countries. Yet with a few exceptions—
Saudi Arabia played host to an American military contingent
whose mission was to keep Saddam in check—the governments of the region contributed little or nothing to the effort
to deny him such armaments that culminated in the 2003 war
that removed him from power. They preferred instead to
burnish their nationalist credentials by keeping their distance.

Similarly, Iranian nuclear weapons, coupled with the ballistic missiles the Iranian government seemed bent on building, would jeopardize the security of both the EU and Russia.
Yet the European and Russian governments balked at refer-
ring Iran's nuclear weapons program to the United Nations
Security Council and at threatening Iran with a full economic
embargo if it did not give up its efforts to fabricate a bomb, a
threat that would have maximized the chances of bringing
about the desired result. Among their reasons was a reluctance to risk a rupture in their commercial relations with
Iran.[58]

To restrict and ultimately end the nuclear weapons program of the third dangerous rogue state of the early twenty-
first century, North Korea, the threat of an economic
embargo also offered the best hope of success without resort-
ing to force. The two neighboring countries whose participation was necessary to make such a measure effective, South
Korea and China, both declined to include such a threat in
their negotiating strategies. Neither wanted to live next to a
nuclear-armed North Korea but both had other, competing

priorities as well. Both were wary, for example—although for different reasons—of triggering a collapse of the North Korean regime. With North Korea, as with Iran, other countries did not contribute as much as they could have, and as much as was needed to optimize the chances for success, to the nonproliferation efforts led by the United States.

The approach other countries took to American foreign policies went beyond the disinclination to share its costs to include harshly negative assessments of those policies as well. To accept benefits that are available without paying for them is free riding: to accept benefits without paying for them and simultaneously to complain about the way they are being provided shades over into hypocrisy. The sharp criticism of heavy-handedness and misjudgments in the conduct of American foreign policy that emanated regularly from other capitals, while certainly not always unjustified, was reminiscent of the scene in the 1941 film *Casablanca*, in which Claude Rains as the French police chief Captain Renault, looking for an excuse to close temporarily Rick's, a night club and casino whose roulette tables he regularly patronizes, blows his whistle, orders it shut, and declares, "I am shocked, shocked to discover that gambling is going on here." Immediately thereafter, a croupier hands him a large wad of cash with the words, "Your winnings, sir," to which Rains mutters under his breath, "Thank you very much."

Such thanks as the United States receives for its role as the world's government are similarly conveyed discreetly; but the absence of global public acknowledgment of America's global role does not mean that other countries, or at least the officials of other countries charged with monitoring international affairs and conducting foreign policy, are entirely unaware of the advantages it brings them. They may not like the fact of America's centrality in world affairs, and they certainly disagree with specific American policies, but if asked to designate the necessary conditions for a tolerable international order in the early twenty-first century, many would surely include the continuation of the American international role, albeit in the same spirit of rueful irony in which, when asked to name his country's greatest nineteenth-century writer, a French literary critic replied, "Victor Hugo, alas."

If a global plebiscite on the role of the United States in the world were held by secret ballot many, perhaps most, of the foreign policy officials in other countries would vote in favor of continuing it. Their American counterparts would make the same judgment. Both groups find the case for Goliath a persuasive one. It might not, however, persuade the American public, which might well reject the proposition that it should pay for providing the world with governmental services. American citizens see their country's foreign policy as a series of discrete measures designed to safeguard the interests, above all the supreme interest of physical security, of the United States itself. They have never been asked to ratify their country's status as the principal supplier of international public goods, and if they were asked explicitly to do so, they would undoubtedly ask in turn whether the United States ought to contribute as much to providing them, and other countries as little, as was the case in the first decade of the twenty-first century. To make sacrifices largely for the benefit of others counts as charity, and for Americans, as for other people, charity begins at home.

The film comedian of the 1930s and 1940s W. C. Fields began his career in vaudeville as a juggler, a skill he had acquired as a boy. One day he read a book that explained the technique of juggling and found himself unable to do it. He had to forget what he had read in order to be able to resume his performances. Similarly, the American role in the world may depend in part on Americans not scrutinizing it too closely.

If closer scrutiny does turn the public against the American role as the world's government—if mounting domestic obligations or a major, traumatic event or series of events such as the collapse of the dollar or a terrorist attack even more deadly than those of September 11 should cause the United States to decrease dramatically the scope of its international activities—the world would become a messier, more dangerous, and less prosperous place.

At best, an American withdrawal would bring with it some of the political anxiety typical during the Cold War and a measure of the economic uncertainty that characterized the years before World War II. At worst, the retreat of American power could lead to a repetition of the great global economic failure and the bloody international conflicts the world experienced in the 1930s and 1940s. Indeed, the potential for economic calamity and wartime destruction is greater at the outset of the new century than it was in the first half of the preceding one because of the greater extent of international economic interdependence and the higher levels of prosperity—there is more to lose now than there was then—and because of the presence, in large numbers, of nuclear weapons.

In the worst case, the world would ultimately face the same problem that it confronted in 1945: how to organize itself to prevent a recurrence of the catastrophes through which it had just passed. In such circumstances, international governance might become available from new sources, and be provided in new ways. The countries of the world might, for the first time, be willing to vest substantial economic and military power in an international organization such as the United Nations, or some reformed or entirely new version of it.

Europe might find ways to act effectively beyond its borders both militarily and economically. In Asia, far more effective mechanisms of cooperation might be established, out of the perception of an urgent necessity for them. In the wake of disaster, that is, novel and previously unthinkable mechanisms of cooperation might become possible. But the kind of global disaster, or string of disasters, that could give rise to these mechanisms would be a very high price to pay for finding a substitute for the global role of the United States.

The American role as the functional equivalent of the world's government raises two final questions. The first of them is whether that role is good or bad for the world. This is a matter of judgment, not fact; and a proper judgment depends ultimately not on whether this or that American foreign policy could be improved—many undoubtedly could—but rather on whether that role is preferable to the plausible alternative. The plausible alternative is not considerably better global governance but considerably less of it, and the consequences of less governance are not likely to be pleasant. For that reason, the verdict of other governments is, on the whole, in favor of the American role. Although they sometimes speak as if they would prefer that the United States shrink its global presence dramatically, they do not act as if that is what they really want.

The second question is whether, or rather for how long, that role will endure. Its persistence depends on the willingness of the American public to support it. That will depend, in turn, on the costs of the country's global activities and Americans' disposition, given the other demands on the public purse, to pay for them, which cannot be forecast with any confidence. About other countries' approach to the American role as the world's government, however, whatever its life span, three things can be safely predicted: They will not pay for it; they will continue to criticize it; and they will miss it when it is gone.

Notes

Chapter 1: The World's Government

1. "The United States' role in the world is today almost routinely characterized as that of an empire." Timothy Garton Ash, *Free World: America, Europe, and the Surprising Future of the West* (New York: Random House, 2004), p. 132.

2. Among the books with this as their theme were Andrew J. Bacevich, *American Empire: The Realities and Consequences of U.S. Diplomacy* (Cambridge, Mass.: Harvard University Press, 2003); John Newhouse, *Imperial America: The Bush Assault on the World Order* (New York: Knopf, 2003); Chalmers Johnson, *The Sorrows of Empire: Militarism, Secrecy, and the End of the Republic* (New York: Metropolitan Books/Henry Holt, 2004); and William Odom and Robert Dujarric, *America's Inadvertent Empire* (New Haven: Yale University Press, 2004). Among the even more numerous articles devoted to this subject were James Kurth, "Migration and the Dynamics of Empire," *The National Interest* 71 (Spring 2003); Peter Bender, "America: The New Roman Empire?" *Orbis* (Winter 2003); Julie Kosterlitz, "The Empire Strikes Back," *National Journal*, December 14, 2002; Richard Reeves, "The Great Debate Over American Empire," http://www.uexpress.com/Richard Reeves, May 14, 2003; and Trudy Rubin, "United States is an empire in denial," *The Philadelphia Inquirer*, May 2, 2003. A complete list of books and articles devoted to the theme of the United States as a twenty-first-century empire would be considerably longer.

3. See Warren Zimmerman, *First Great Triumph: How Five Americans Made Their Country a World Power* (New York: Farrar, Straus and

Giroux, 2003), pp. 264, 322–323. The United States had, of
course, expanded across North America during the nineteenth
century, but the inhabitants of the territory so acquired ultimately
became full citizens, which was not true of the European empires.
Furthermore, on several occasions the American government
declined to try to incorporate new territories because it did not
wish to confer citizenship on their populations. Ibid., pp. 21,
291–292.

4. "Nothing has ever existed like this disparity of power; nothing ...
    The Pax Britannica was run on the cheap, Britain's army was
    much smaller than European armies, and even the Royal Navy
    was equal only to the next two navies—right now all the other
    navies in the world combined could not dent American maritime
    supremacy. Charlemagne's empire was merely western-European
    in its reach. The Roman Empire stretched farther afield, but there
    was another great empire in Persia and a larger one in China.
    There is, therefore, no comparison." Paul Kennedy, "The Colos-
    sus with an Achilles' Heel," *New Perspectives Quarterly* (Fall 2001),
    http://www.digitalnpq.org/archive/2001_fall/colossus.html, cited
    in Thomas Donnelly, "The Underpinnings of the Bush Doc-
    trine," Washington, D.C.: The American Enterprise Institute for
    Public Policy Research, February 2003, p. 2.

5. "In 1960, the United States' share of world output was thirty per
    cent; by 1980 it had dropped to twenty-three per cent; today it is
    twenty-nine per cent. The American economy is now larger than
    the next three largest economies—those of Japan, Germany, and
    Great Britain—combined." Fareed Zakaria, "Our Way," *The New
    Yorker*, October 14 & 21, 2002, pp. 74–75. "According to these
    authors, nothing achieved by the United Kingdom—not even in
    the first flush of the Industrial Revolution—ever compared with the
    United States' recent economic predominance." Niall Ferguson,
    "Hegemony or Empire?" *Foreign Affairs* 82 (15) (September–
    October 2003). "U.S. research and development spending accounts
    for more than 40 percent of the global total, and in the area of med-
    ical and biotechnology research, the United States spends more
    than the rest of the world combined." Clyde Prestowitz, *Rogue
    Nation: American Unilateralism and the Failure of Good Intentions*
    (New York: Basic Books, 2003), p. 27.

6. Zakaria, op. cit., p. 74.

7. By way of historical comparison, when Great Britain had the world's mightiest navy, in the late nineteenth and early twentieth centuries, the British government sought to maintain a "two-power standard," keeping its naval forces stronger than the combined strength of the next two most powerful navies.

8. "American military personnel now operate in three-quarters of the world's 192 countries." Christopher M. Gray, "The Costs of Empire," *Orbis* (Spring 2003), p. 359. "Long before Afghanistan made them famous, teams of special forces were discreetly operating in 125 countries." Dana Priest, *The Mission: Waging War and Keeping Peace with America's Military* (New York: W. W. Norton, 2003), p. 17.

9. "It is everywhere. Some 380m people speak it as their first language and perhaps two-thirds as many again as their second. A billion are learning it, about a third of the world's population are in some sense exposed to it and by 2050, it is predicted, half the world will be more or less proficient." "A world empire by other means," *The Economist*, December 22, 2001, p. 65.

10. Priest, op. cit., p. 30.

11. This was not always an accurate description of what the adherents to these ideologies did when they held power. The Soviet Union, for example, while asserting the contrary, was in fact as much an empire as its Romanov predecessor.

12. Michael Doyle, *Empires* (Ithaca: Cornell University Press, 1986), p. 19.

13. Empire does not, however, consist of any and every form of international inequality. Such a definition would strip the term of most of its content, since it would have nothing to do with the behavior of the more powerful party.

14. In the immediate aftermath of World War I, for example, Britain moved to take control of the former Ottoman territory of Transjordan expressly to prevent the French from claiming it, even though France has been Britain's close ally in the mortal struggle with Germany that had just concluded and the British had no particular enthusiasm for governing the territory. See Ephraim Karsh and Inari Karsh, *Empires of the Sand: The Struggle for Mastery in the Middle East, 1789–1923* (Cambridge, Mass.: Harvard University Press, 2001), p. 316.

15. S. E. Finer, *The History of Government from the Earliest Times. Vol-*

ume I: Ancient Monarchies and Empires (Oxford: Oxford University Press, 1997), pp. 2–3.

16. "The tendency for public goods to be underproduced is serious enough within a nation bound by some sort of social contract, and directed in public matters by a government with the power to impose and collect taxes. It is ... a more serious problem in international political and economic relations in the absence of international government." Charles P. Kindleberger, "International Public Goods Without International Government," *American Economic Review* 76 (1) (March 1986), p. 2.

17. Mancur Olson, *The Logic of Collective Action: Public Goods and the Theory of Groups* (Cambridge, Mass.: Harvard University Press, 1982. First published 1965), pp. 22, 28, 34.

18. Government ordinarily consists of three functions: the executive, the legislative, and the judicial. It is the executive that supplies public goods. The United States therefore functions as the world's *executive*.

19. "In small groups with common interests there is accordingly *a surprising tendency for the 'exploitation' of the great by the small.*" Olson, op. cit., p. 35.

20. This was the case with the British, the French, and the Soviet empires. The Habsburg, Romanov, and Ottoman empires collapsed because they were defeated in war.

21. On two occasions the United States conspicuously did *not* mobilize its resources for international purposes. Between the end of the American Civil War and World War I its economic output came to surpass that of any other country, but its international influence remained modest. Between the two world wars the United States also chose not to take as large a part in the political and economic affairs of the world as its power would have made possible.

    On the first of those occasions, see Fareed Zakaria, *From Wealth to Power: The Unusual History of America's World Role* (Princeton: Princeton University Press, 1998). On the second episode, see Charles P. Kindleberger, *The World in Depression, 1929–1939* (Berkeley: University of California Press, 1973), and Martin Wolf, *Why Globalization Works* (New Haven: Yale University Press, 2004), pp. 128–129.

22. "... the raising and maintaining of military forces, particularly

standing military forces, is the overwhelmingly most important reason for the emergence of the civil bureaucracy." Finer, op. cit., p. 16.

23. Steven R. Weisman, *The Great Tax Wars: Lincoln to Wilson—The Fierce Battles over Money and Power That Transformed the Nation* (New York: Simon and Schuster, 2002), pp. 93, 308.

24. On this general point, see Ernest R. May, *"Lessons" of the Past* (New York: Oxford University Press, 1976 paperback).

25. The triumph of liberal economic ideas and practices is the theme of Michael Mandelbaum, *The Ideas That Conquered the World: Peace, Democracy, and Free Markets in the Twenty-first Century* (New York: PublicAffairs, 2002), Part III.

26. In the early part of the Cold War, American diplomacy emphasized the conclusion of defense pacts with friendly governments all over the world. In 1956, the United States had such pacts with forty-two other countries, although it did not deploy troops in all of them. Derek Leebaert, *The Fifty-Year Wound: How America's Cold War Victory Shapes Our World* (Boston: Little Brown/Back Bay Books, 2003), p. 198.

27. Ten months after the end of World War II, "out of 12.1 million men in service when Japan surrendered, some 9 million had been granted outright discharges, with Congress soon deciding to authorize an army of only 669,000." Ibid., p. 27.

28. Mandelbaum, op. cit., pp. 52–53.

29. "By the end of the 1990s, the United States was devoting less than 3 percent of its gross national product to defense, the lowest proportion since the eve of World War II." Bacevich, op. cit., p. 155.

30. This is a principal theme of Mandelbaum, op. cit. See especially Chapter 1.

31. Ibid., p. 38.

32. "Today, none of us expect our soldiers to fight a war on our own territory. The immediate threat is not conflict between the world's most powerful nations."

"And why? Because we all have too much to lose. Because technology, communication, trade and travel are bringing us ever closer together. Because in the last 50 years, countries like yours and mine have tripled their growth and standard of living. Because even those powers like Russia or China or India can see the horizon, the future wealth, clearly and know they are on a steady road toward it. And because all nations that are free value that freedom, will defend it absolutely, but have no wish to trample on the freedom of others." Blair, op. cit.

33. Paul Kennedy, *The Rise and Fall of the Great Powers* (New York: Random House, 1988).

Chapter 2: International Security

1. On the rise of "warlessness" in the West, see Michael Mandelbaum, *The Ideas That Conquered the World: Peace, Democracy and Free Markets in the Twenty-first Century* (New York: PublicAffairs, 2002), pp. 121–128, and John Mueller, *The Remnants of War* (Ithaca: Cornell University Press, 2004), p. 40.

2. In August 2004, the United States had 116,400 military personnel assigned to its European Command, roughly two-thirds of them in Germany. Philip Carter, "We Have *How* Many Troops in Europe?" http://www.slate.com, August 18, 2004. The number was scheduled to drop to 72,000 over ten years. "Moving On," *The Economist*, August 21, 2004, p. 25.

3. Michael Mandelbaum, *The Dawn of Peace in Europe* (New York: The Twentieth Century Fund, 1996), p. 20.

4. It was for this reason that the last leader of the Soviet Union, Mikhail Gorbachev, agreed that a reunified Germany could be a member of NATO. Ibid., p. 18.

5. Another way to distinguish between the two is that the purpose of reassurance is to impart the confidence that explicit deterrence will not be necessary.

6. Because deterrence in East Asia was tacit, not explicit, it differed from Cold War deterrence in Europe. Then the United States had proclaimed that it would fight if the Soviet Union attacked its allies. In East Asia after the Cold War, the American government did not follow this pattern in the case of China and Taiwan. Instead, the United States practiced deterrence not by attempting to make China certain that it would defend Taiwan but rather by seeking to induce a measure of uncertainty that it would *not* do so.

7. Mandelbaum, *The Ideas*, p. 171.

8. It was not only the American military presence in the region that

kept China from attacking Taiwan. Should it attempt to conquer the island, it would by no means be assured of success even if the United States did not intervene. Moreover, a Chinese attack would certainly lead to restrictions on, if not the elimination of, the country's expansive economic intercourse with the rest of the world, upon which the rapid growth of the Chinese economy, and so the legitimacy of Communist rule, had come to depend heavily in the early years of the twenty-first century.

9. For a more dire view of the consequences of an American military withdrawal, see Zbigniew Brzezinski, *The Choice: Global Domination or Global Leadership* (New York: Basic Books, 2003), pp. 91–96.

10. This view is set out in Robert Cooper, *The Breaking of Nations: Order and Chaos in the Twenty-first Century* (New York: Atlantic Monthly Press, 2003), pp. 63–64.

11. In addition, Article III of the NPT commits the nuclear-armed signatories to work toward the abolition of all nuclear weapons, a goal that none of them has made a high priority.

12. The case of France illustrates the point. The French acquired nuclear weapons in 1964, ostensibly on the grounds that these armaments were necessary for France's security, but also—and perhaps principally—to enhance France's international standing. The logic that underpinned the French nuclear program applied equally to Germany, but the French were unyielding in their opposition to the idea that their neighbor and partner in the European Community should have the same military forces as they.

13. The same sort of taboo attaches to chemical and biological weapons, which helps to account for the practice of grouping them together with the far more destructive nuclear armaments as "weapons of mass destruction." See Michael Mandelbaum, *The Nuclear Revolution: International Politics Before and After Hiroshima* (New York: Cambridge University Press, 1981), Chapter 2.

14. This may have occurred in the case of India. By formally testing a nuclear weapon in 1998, it triggered a comparable step by Pakistan. When both countries had nuclear weapons, India's margin of military superiority over Pakistan was probably somewhat smaller than it had been when neither had declared nuclear arsenals.

15. "... history is full of examples where U.S. intelligence successfully

alerted policy makers to cases and trends in proliferation. For years, the United States raised concerns (dismissed by many states in Europe and Russia) over Iran's nuclear ambitions that have proven to be true. U.S. intelligence concluded in 2002 that North Korea had a secret uranium program, which Pakistan has now admitted to assisting." Jon Wolfsthal, "The Key Proliferation Questions," Washington, D.C.: Carnegie Endowment for International Peace, Carnegie Issue Brief, vol. 7, no. 6, March 24, 2004, p. 1.

16.   Would-be proliferators can also buy equipment that members of the Nuclear Suppliers Group will not sell them from countries that do not belong to that organization. Another potential source of weapons-related material is the territory on which the Soviet Union once stood. Although the successor governments there have not formally offered the bombs, equipment, and expertise within their borders for sale, collectively they harbor considerable amounts of all three, much of which was not carefully safeguarded even a decade and a half after the Soviet collapse.

17.   Walter Russell Mead, *Power, Terror, Peace, and War: America's Grand Strategy in a World at Risk* (New York: Knopf, 2004), pp. 60–61.

18.   In the "National Security Strategy of the United States" white paper issued under President Bush's name on September 17, 2002, rogue states are described as those whose regimes "brutalize their own people and squander their natural resources ... display no regard for international law ... are determined to acquire weapons of mass destruction ... sponsor terrorism around the globe and reject basic human values and hate the United States and everything for which it stands." "National Security Strategy of the United States," http://www.whitehouse.gov/nsc/print/nssall.html, p. 10.

19.   For speculation on the disruptive uses to which Saddam Hussein might have put nuclear weapons had he managed to obtain them, see Kenneth Pollack, *The Threatening Storm: The Case for Invading Iraq* (New York: Random House, 2002), Chapter 8.

20.   "Theater" missile defenses, deployed outside the United States, would, if they worked (or were believed by an adversary to work), protect American armed forces stationed abroad and so strengthen the United States against regional adversaries, including rogue states.

21. As of February 2004, sixteen countries were participating in this initiative. Graham Allison, *Nuclear Terrorism: The Ultimate Preventable Catastrophe* (New York: Times Books, 2004), pp. 160, 242.

22. Don Oberdorfer, *The Two Koreas: A Contemporary History* (Reading, Mass.: Addison-Wesley, 1997), Chapters 13 and 14.

23. Passengers in the fourth airplane overpowered the hijackers, whose intended target may have been the Capitol in Washington, D.C., and it crashed in a field in Pennsylvania, killing all forty-five people aboard.

24. Walter Laqueur, *The New Terrorism: Fanaticism and the Arms of Mass Destruction* (New York: Oxford University Press, 1999), pp. 43, 79.

25. For al Qaeda, "attacking America and its allies is merely a tactic, intended to provoke a backlash strong enough to alert Muslims to the supposed truth of their predicament, and so rally them to purge the faith of all that is alien to its essence." Max Rodenbeck, "Islam Confronts Its Demons," *The New York Review of Books*, April 29, 2004, p. 16.

26. For the contrary argument, that twenty-first-century terrorism is likely to prove to be a manageable problem, see John Mueller, "Harbinger or Aberration: A 9/11 Provocation," *The National Interest* (Fall 2002).

27. By one estimate, al Qaeda was active in as many as fifty countries. Mark Huband and John Willman, "Holy war on the world," *Financial Times*, November 28, 2001, p. 6.

28. Until September 11, and by some measures even including the events of that day, terrorism had not posed a particularly grave threat to Americans. "Even with the September 11 attacks included in the count, the number of Americans killed by international terrorism since the late 1960s (which is when the State Department began its accounting) is about the same as the number killed over the same period by lightning—or by accident-causing deer or by severe allergic reaction to peanuts. In almost all years the total number of people worldwide who die at the hands of international terrorists is not much more than the number who drown in bathtubs in the United States." John Mueller, "Laboring Under a False Sense of Insecurity," Columbus, Ohio: The Mershon Center, January 27, 2004, p. 1.

29. Terrorists affiliated with or sympathetic to al Qaeda were also

thought to be operating in Iraq during the American occupation of that country.

30. "September 11 seems to have had a particularly dramatic effect on the vice president [Dick Cheney]: he immediately started to speculate how much worse it would have been if weapons of mass destruction had been used." John Micklethwait and Adrian Wooldridge, *The Right Nation: Conservative Power in America* (New York: The Penguin Press, 2004), p. 211. On the possibility of terrorists acquiring weapons of mass destruction, see Allison, op. cit.

31. Bush, op. cit., p. 1.

32. On some historical antecedents of this doctrine, see John Lewis Gaddis, *Surprise, Security, and the American Experience* (Cambridge, Mass.: Harvard University Press, 2004), pp. 16, 61–62.

33. "The President's State of the Union Address, January 29, 2002," http://www.whitehouse.gov/news/releases/2002/01/20020129–11. html.

34. Bush, "National Security Strategy of the United States," p. 11. In this way the new doctrine went beyond the classic American statement of the conditions that justify a preemptive attack, which were set down by then Secretary of State Daniel Webster in 1837: when the necessity of self-defense is "instant, overwhelming, and leaving no choice of means and no moment for deliberation." David Sanger, "Beating Them To the Prewar," *The New York Times*, September 28, 2002, p. A19. It was, however, in keeping with the formula of a later Secretary of State, Elihu Root, who proclaimed "the right of every sovereign state to protect itself by preventing a condition of affairs in which it will be too late to protect itself." "Six Degrees of Preemption," *The Washington Post*, September 29, 2002, p. B2.

35. According to Secretary of Defense Donald Rumsfeld, "The coalition did not act in Iraq because we had discovered dramatic new evidence of Iraq's pursuit of WMD [weapons of mass destruction]; we acted because we saw the existing evidence in a new light—through the prism of our experience on 9/11." Quoted in Melvyn P. Leffler, "Bush's Foreign Policy," *Foreign Policy*, September–October, 2004, p. 26.

36. David Hannay, "Before and after," *Times Literary Supplement*, February 13, 2004, p. 6.

37. Peter D. Feaver, "The Fog of WMD," *The Washington Post*, January 28, 2004, p. A21.

38. British prime minister Tony Blair drew the same lesson. "After such a catastrophe [as September 11], to stand by and watch Iraq rebuild its chemical and biological arsenal, perhaps a nuclear weapon, 'would be to grossly ignore the lesson of September 11 and we will not do it,' Mr. Blair said." Patrick E. Tyler, "Leaders Sought a Threat; Spies Get the Blame," *The New York Times*, February 1, 2004, News of the Week in Review, p. 1.

39. "If the Iraqi regime is able to produce, buy or steal an amount of highly enriched uranium a little larger than a single softball, he could have a nuclear weapon in less than a year. And if we allow that to happen a terrible line would be crossed. Saddam Hussein would be in a position to blackmail anyone who opposes his aggression. He would be in a position to dominate the Middle East. He would be in a position to threaten America. And Saddam Hussein would be in a position to pass nuclear technology to terrorists." George W. Bush, Address in Cincinnati, October 7, 2002, reprinted in *The Washington Post*, October 8, 2002, p. A20.

40. In 1994, American military officials estimated that a war on the Korean peninsula "would cost 52,000 U.S. military casualties, killed or wounded, and 490,000 South Korean military casualties in the first ninety days, plus an enormous number of North Korean and civilian lives, at a financial outlay exceeding $61 billion, very little of which could be recouped from U.S. allies." Oberdorfer, op. cit., p. 315.

41. Although dislodging the North Korean and Iranian governments would have posed far greater military difficulties, the political and economic tasks following their overthrow might have placed a lighter burden on the United States than did the post-Saddam occupation of Iraq. While in Iraq the United States had to assume full responsibility for administering the country, South Korea would have inherited responsibility for a post-Communist North Korea (which was one reason the South Koreans were reluctant to see the Pyongyang regime, odious though it was, deposed altogether) and the opposition in Iran was probably sophisticated and coherent enough to govern the country without outside assistance.

42. This did not mean that Saddam had abandoned his interest in such weapons. According to the onetime head of the United Nations inspection team, the "combination of researchers, engineers, know-how, precursors, batch production techniques and testing is what constituted Iraq's chemical threat—its chemical

weapon. The rather bizarre political focus on the search for rusting drums and pieces of munitions containing low-quality chemicals has tended to distort the important question of WMD in Iraq and exposed the American and British administrations to unjustified criticism." Rolf Ekeus, "Iraq's Real Weapons Threat," *The Washington Post*, June 29, 2003, p. B7.

A government report issued in the fall of 2004 concluded that Saddam Hussein clearly intended to produce chemical, biological, and nuclear weapons if and when the United Nations sanctions against Iraq were lifted, but at the time of the war, Iraq did not have large-scale programs for weapons production. See Douglas Jehl, "Iraq Study Finds Desire for Arms, But Not Capacity," *The New York Times*, September 17, 2004, p. A1; Christopher Hitchens, "The Buried Truth," http://www.slate.com, October 8, 2004; David Brooks, "The Report That Nails Saddam," *The New York Times*, October 9, 2004, p. A31.

43. At the outset of the war, the president made an indirect reference to the events of September 11 and depicted Saddam as a direct threat to the United States: "We will meet that threat now, with our Army, Air Force, Navy, Coast Guard, and Marines, so that we do not have to meet it later with armies of firefighters and police and doctors on the streets of our own cities." Quoted in *AEI Newsletter*, Washington, D.C.: The American Enterprise Institute, September 2003, p. 2.

44. "Remarks by the President on Iraq," Cincinnati, Ohio, October 7, 2002, http://www.whitehouse.gov/news/release/2002/10/2002100 7-8.html

45. Allison, op. cit., p. 137.

46. Niall Ferguson, *Colossus: The Price of America's Empire* (New York: The Penguin Press, 2004), pp. 159–160.

47. For an interesting discussion of the actual but not necessarily explicitly expressed reasons for war, see Mead, op. cit., pp. 116–120.

48. "Mr Bush conjured up a link between Iraq, al-Qaeda and September 11th that probably did not exist. He created an impression of a threat to the American homeland that the intelligence does not seem to justify. And when tabloid newspapers read Britain's dossier to mean that Britons themselves could come under chemical attack within 45 minutes, Mr Blair did not trouble to put them

right." "Saddam Hussein's weapons mirage," *The Economist*, January 31, 2004, p. 13.

49. Thucydides, *The Peloponnesian War*, translated by Rex Warner (Harmondsworth, England: Penguin Books, 1972), p. 402.

50. A 1999 report concluded that "since the end of the Cold War, the United States has embarked upon nearly four dozen military interventions ... as opposed to only 16 during the entire period of the Cold War." *New World Coming: The United States Commission on National Security/21st Century*, Washington, D.C.: U.S. Commission on National Security/21st Century, 1999, p. 128.

51. That protection, in the form of an American- and British-patrolled "no fly zone" over the Kurdish territories that kept Saddam's military forces south of them, continued until Saddam was unseated by the Anglo-American invasion of March and April 2003.

52. One reason for the humanitarian intervention in northern Iraq was to make it possible for Kurdish refugees to leave Turkey, a NATO ally of the United States.

53. The names given to several of these interventions denoted the motives underlying them. The one in Iraq was "Operation Provide Comfort," in Somalia it was "Restore Hope."

54. The deaths of eighteen American servicemen in Somalia caused the Clinton administration to withdraw the American troops there. Some observers concluded that the television pictures of suffering people far away created a groundswell of public pressure on policymakers to act to end that suffering. Some of these policymakers shared this view, but the evidence available from public opinion polls did not support it. See Johanna Neuman, *Lights, Camera, War* (New York: St. Martin's Press, 1996), p. 14, and John Mueller, "The Common Sense," *The National Interest* 47 (Spring 1997).

55. One difference is that the doctrine of preventive war was formally announced and elaborately justified in a way that humanitarian intervention was not. The fullest statement of the case for the second policy came from British prime minister Tony Blair, who said, in 1998—and in Chicago, rather than in his own country: "We have to enter the new millennium making it known to dictatorships that ethnic cleansing will not be approved. And if we fight, it is not for territorial imperatives but for values. For a new interna-

tionalism where the brutal repression of ethnic groups will not be tolerated. For a world where those responsible for crimes will have nowhere to hide." Quoted in Cooper, op. cit., pp. 59–60.

Bill Clinton, the patron of humanitarian intervention, never offered a full-scale account of it as a doctrine of American foreign policy. He did say, in a university commencement speech (also in Chicago) in 1999: "We intervened militarily in Kosovo because I believe that when ethnic hatred and fighting turns into the mass slaughter and uprooting of totally innocent civilians, if we have the power to stop it, we ought to." "Remarks by the President at University of Chicago Convocation Ceremonies," June 12, 1999.

56. The first two episodes of humanitarian intervention, in Iraq and Somalia, occurred during the presidency of the first George Bush, like his son, a Republican.

57. Samantha Power, *"A Problem from Hell": America and the Age of Genocide* (New York: HarperCollins Perennial, 2003), pp. 278, 483.

58. For this and other reasons, even in the 1990s the United States did not send troops to rescue every beleaguered group, eschewing involvement in some of the bloodiest repressions around the world, notably the 1994 massacres in Rwanda.

59. By the last month of 2004, in response to the question of whether the Iraq war had been worth fighting, 56 percent of the respondents in the United States answered in the negative. John F. Harris and Christopher Muste, "56 Percent in Survey Say Iraq War Was a Mistake," *The Washington Post*, December 21, 2004, p. A4.

60. To be sure, nation-creation and state-building can be closely connected. Indeed, the second can cause the first. When different groups are put into the same political jurisdiction, governmental policies, in particular the imposition of a common language, can create sentiments of social and political solidarity where none had existed. While in the modern era the state is supposed to be the expression of the previously formed nation—hence the term "nation-state"—it is also the case that the state can help to form the nation. See, for example, Ernest Gellner, *Nations and Nationalism* (Oxford, England: Blackwell, 1983).

61. For all its success, neither the United States nor any other country recognized the Kurdish enclave as a state. All agreed that it prop-

erly belonged to Iraq—albeit, in the American view, an Iraq not ruled by Saddam Hussein.

62. Quoted in Julia Preston, "U.N. Establishes Force for Somalia: All but 9,000 U.S. Troops to Leave by May," *The Washington Post*, March 26, 1993, p. A13.

63. Dana Priest, *The Mission: Waging War and Keeping Peace with America's Military* (New York: W. W. Norton, 2003), Chapter 14; Nicholas Wood, "NATO Expanding Kosovo Forces to Combat Violence," *The New York Times*, March 19, 2004, p. A3.

64. Priest, op. cit., pp. 56, 390.

65. The desire not to belong to a particular state caused a number of the wars of the post–Cold War period: "... in multi-ethnic societies where one group forms an absolute majority, the risk of war is 50% higher than in societies where this is not the case." "The global menace of local strife," *The Economist*, May 24, 2003, p. 24.

66. Compounding the difficulty of promoting democracy is the fact that in some undemocratically ruled countries, the United States has other goals that may conflict with democracy. In Saudi Arabia, for example, a more open political sytem might bring to power Islamic fundamentalists, who might then interfere with the world's access to its reserves of oil.

67. The study of the social bases of political and economic institutions has a long history, the seminal figures of which were Montesquieu in the eighteenth century, Tocqueville in the nineteenth, and Max Weber in the twentieth. A contemporary example, one among many that could be cited, is Lawrence E. Harrison and Samuel P. Huntington, editors, *Culture Matters: How Values Shape Human Progress* (New York: Basic Books, 2000).

68. See, for example, the reference by National Security Adviser Condoleezza Rice at the Twenty-Eighth Annual Convention of the National Association of Black Journalists, The White House, Washington, D.C., May 1, 2003, http://www.whitehouse.gov/news/releases/2003/08/20030807–1.html.

69. On the differences between Germany and Japan, on the one hand, and the objects of post–Cold War American state-building, on the other, see Martin Wolf, "Supremacy is not enough to remake the world order," *Financial Times*, July 9, 2003, p. 13.

70. "... deliberate, purposive societal change of any importance is difficult to achieve ... the record of major deliberate efforts by public

authorities to change societies significantly is one of failure or massive underachievement." Amitai Etzioni, "A self-restrained approach to nation-building by foreign powers," *International Affairs* 80 (1) (January 2004), p. 4.

71. This was the diagnosis of the administration of the second George Bush, which committed the United States to working "with those in the Middle East who seek progress toward greater democracy, tolerance, prosperity and freedom." Condoleezza Rice, "Transforming the Middle East," *The Washington Post*, August 7, 2003, p. A21. See also Natan Sharansky with Ron Dermer, *The Case for Democracy: The Power of Freedom to Overcome Tyranny and Terror* (New York: PublicAffairs, 2004).

72. Mueller, op. cit., pp. 176–179. On the reasons that the end of the Cold War produced instability in the poorest countries, see Mandelbaum, *The Ideas*, pp. 183–190.

73. On the Clinton administration, see, for example, Gaddis, op. cit., p. 76. On the Bush administration, see the 2002 National Security Strategy, Part VII.

74. For an overview of what is and is not known about constructing functioning governments, see Francis Fukuyama, *State-Building* (Ithaca: Cornell University Press, 2004).

75. "[The United States] failed to build effective state institutions in a long list of countries: Cuba, the Philippines, Haiti, the Dominican Republic, Mexico, Panama, Nicaragua, and South Vietnam." Martin Wolf, "Why a president's greatest challenge is state building," *Financial Times*, November 3, 2004, p. 17.

76. The ascendancy of liberal politics and economics is the principal theme of Mandelbaum, *The Ideas*.

77. Ibid., pp. 268–270. For this reason the United States used what leverage and influence it had to promote free market economies in post-Communist Russia and in China, a country that, in the twenty-first century, while still governed by a Communist Party had otherwise abandoned Marxism-Leninism.

Chapter 3: The Global Economy

1. Lawrence H. Summers, "America Overdrawn," *Foreign Policy* (July–August 2004), p. 47.

2. Among sovereign states, great wealth has historically provided the material basis for great military power, and in wars among the strongest states, victory has usually gone to the wealthiest and most productive of them, the ones "with the longest purse." The relationship between wealth and power and the decisive role of wealth in major wars are principal themes of John Mearsheimer, *The Tragedy of Great Power Politics* (New York: W. W. Norton, 2001), and Paul Kennedy, *The Rise and Fall of the Great Powers* (New York: Random House, 1988).

3. Martin Wolf, *Why Globalization Works* (New Haven: Yale University Press, 2004), pp. 25–33.

4. "Law does not say to man, Work and I will reward you but it says: Labour, and by stopping the hand that would take them from you, I will ensure to you the fruits of your labour ... If industry creates, it is law which preserves ... " Jeremy Bentham, *Principles of the Civil Code*, cited in Ian Shapiro, *The Moral Foundations of Politics* (New Haven: Yale University Press, 2003), p. 21. See also Wolf, op. cit., p. 61.

5. This is a theme of Niall Ferguson, *Colossus: The Price of America's Empire* (New York: The Penguin Press, 2004). See, for example, pp. 186, 191, 193, 197. See also Niall Ferguson, *Empire: The Rise and Demise of the British World Order and the Lessons for Global Power* (New York: Basic Books, 2003), pp. xxiv, 361.

6. In the first period of globalization, the proportion of international transactions, especially investment, between rich and poor societies was higher. "In 1913, close to half of all direct investment and portfolio equity flows went to countries whose incomes per head were less than 40 per cent of the US level. Today, the share of the cross-border flows of direct and equity investment that go to such relatively poor countries is little over 10 per cent, even though a bigger fraction of the world's population is located in such countries." Martin Wolf, "Location, location, location equals the wealth of nations," *Financial Times*, September 25, 2002, p. 15. One of the reasons for the difference is that in the earlier period the rich exercised imperial control over many of the poor.

7. According to one survey, 38 percent of global primary energy came from oil alone in 2001, and 62 percent came from oil and gas together. Martin Wolf, "Stable oil supplies are worth defending from Iraqi aggression," *Financial Times*, February 26, 2003, p. 15. Ground transportation by road using automobiles and trucks

depends almost entirely on gasoline refined from crude oil.

8. In the first decade of the twenty-first century, for example, vessels from both the American Navy and the American Coast Guard were deployed to the Persian Gulf. Chip Cummins, "As Threats to Oil Facilities Rise, U.S. Military Becomes Protector," *The Wall Street Journal*, June 30, 2004, p. A1.

9. Not coincidentally, few of those regimes governed in democratic fashion. The possession of oil encourages the centralization and perpetual retention of political power for the purpose of controlling the resources that the sale of oil brings.

10. In 2004, these countries accounted for 30 percent of all oil exports, a figure that was expected to rise to between 54 and 67 percent by the year 2020. Andrew Higgins, "In Quest for Energy Security, U.S. Makes New Bet: on Democracy," *The Wall Street Journal*, February 4, 2004, p. A6.

11. Quoted in John Cassidy, "Pump Dreams," *The New Yorker*, October 11, 2004, p. 45.

12. Paul Roberts, *The End of Oil: On the Edge of a Perilous New World* (Boston: Houghton Mifflin, 2004), pp. 96–97, 100.

13. Low prices also hurt American oil producers. Thus, in 1987 then vice president George H.W. Bush persuaded the Saudis to cut back their production in order to boost the price consumers would pay for all oil, including the oil produced within the United States. Ibid, p. 104.

14. Higgins, op. cit., p. A6.

15. "[I]f Kuwait had produced carrots rather than oil, it is most unlikely that a great coalition would have been assembled to reverse Iraqi aggression." Robert Cooper, *The Breaking of Nations: Order and Chaos in the Twenty-first Century* (New York: Atlantic Monthly Press, 2004), p. 58.

16. The attacks had their origins in two events in 1979, a pivotal year for the contemporary Middle East, and the Saudi responses to them. One was the Iranian revolution, which posed an ideological threat to the Saudi regime, which rested its power on the claim that its Wahhabi-inspired rule conformed to the authentic precepts of Islam. Iran's clerics disputed this claim and denounced the al-Saud dynasty as un-Islamic. Their denunciations inspired rioting in the holy city of Mecca and the seizure by radicals of the Grand Mosque there during the annual pilgrimage to Mecca in that year.

The Saudi government responded by enforcing an even harsher and more repressive form of religion on the society it ruled and by using part of the flood of new revenues made available by the two oil shocks of the 1970s to spread its intolerant, aggressive variety of religion throughout the Muslim world. (The Iranian revolution also triggered the Iran-Iraq war, which, because it left Saddam Hussein's treasury depleted, then led to the Iraqi raid on Kuwait for the sake of plunder and so to the 1991 Gulf War.)

The second seminal event of 1979 was the Soviet invasion of Afghanistan. The Saudis encouraged and paid Arabs and other Muslims, many inspired by Wahhabi ideas, to travel to Afghanistan to fight the Soviet troops there. Veterans of the Afghan war formed the core of al Qaeda, and they recruited the organization's members from the ranks of young men who had been indoctrinated in Saudi-funded religious schools.

17. On this ideology, see Daniel Pipes, *Militant Islam Reaches America* (New York: W. W. Norton, 2002), Part I.

18. The regime also compiled an extraordinarily poor record of economic management, which contributed to the local discontent with it. Because the real price of oil had declined from its post-oil-shocks peak in the early 1980s, because the kingdom had no other sources of income, and because the population grew rapidly, per capita income declined precipitously—by about 60 percent—in the last two decades of the twentieth century. Martin Wolf, "The building pressures that threaten the world's oil well," *Financial Times*, December 4, 2002, p. 13.

19. See Simon Henderson, *The New Pillar: Conservative Arab Gulf States and U.S. Strategy* (Washington, D.C.: The Washington Institute for Near East Policy, Policy Paper no. 58, 2004).

20. Irwin M. Stelzer, "Can We Do Without Saudi Oil? Alas, no." *The Weekly Standard*, November 19, 2001.

21. An al Qaeda takeover of Saudi Arabia would create pressure on the United States to assure the adequacy of the world's supply of oil by seizing the Saudi oil fields. As in the case of Iraq in 2003, the seizure might well prove a straightforward military operation, but the subsequent occupation would likely be fraught with difficulties.

22. Michael Mandelbaum, *The Ideas That Conquered the World: Peace, Democracy and Free Markets in the Twenty-first Century* (New York: PublicAffairs, 2002), Chapter 8.

23. Francis Fukuyama, *State-Building* (Ithaca: Cornell University Press, 2004), Chapter 2.

24. Daniel Pipes and Adam Garfinkle, editors, *Friendly Tyrants: An American Dilemma* (New York: St. Martin's Press, 1991).

25. On the controversy over how much usable oil remains, see Jeffrey Ball, "As Price Soars, Doomsayers Provoke Debate on Oil's Future," *The Wall Street Journal*, September 21, 2004, p. A1.

26. J. R. McNeill and William McNeill, *The Human Web: A Bird's-Eye View of World History* (New York: W. W. Norton, 2003), pp. 230–231.

27. These are discussed in Roberts, op. cit. Hydropower makes a sizable contribution to the world's supply of electricity, but few if any major rivers remain unexploited for this purpose.

28. Ibid., pp. 133, 265.

29. Scott Barrett, *Environment and Statecraft: The Strategy of Environmental Treaty-Making* (New York: Oxford University Press, 2003), pp. 393–395. Government participation will likely also be necessary to build new energy infrastructure, for instance, long pipelines for transporting natural gas, just as governments have built dams for generating hydroelectric power. Roberts, op. cit., p. 249.

30. David Goodstein, *Out of Gas: The End of the Age of Oil* (New York: W. W. Norton, 2004), pp. 17, 27, 45, 122; Roberts, op. cit., pp. 46, 48–49, 60.

31. Roberts, op. cit., pp. 7, 146.

32. The external costs—economists call them "externalities"—are public "bads," and coping with them is therefore a public good—something that is desirable but that will only be done if the government does it.

33. Roberts, op. cit., p. 275.

34. Ibid., pp. 60–61. National oil companies owned by governments tightly control foreign participation, which means that "the international oil industry is the only business in the world in which global capital cannot invest in the lowest-cost, most efficient production." J. Robinson West, "Paying the Pumper," *The Washington Post*, July 23, 2004, p. A29.

35. Roberts, op. cit., p. 46.

36. "Already there are visible tensions among east Asian nations over competition for oil and gas, and between the US and Asian gov-

ernments over the political credentials of Iran (suspected of plans to build nuclear weapons) as a source of additional oil." Victor Mallet, "Power hungry: Asia's surging energy demand reverberates around the world," *Financial Times*, May 12, 2004, p. 13.

37. This is what happened throughout the industrialized world in the 1970s in response to the two oil shocks of that decade. Roberts, op. cit., pp. 151, 218.

38. "To create the equivalent of $1 of GDP, Europeans use only about two-thirds as much energy as the Americans." Clyde Prestowitz, *Rogue Nation: American Unilateralism and the Failure of Good Intentions* (New York: Basic Books, 2003), p. 83.

39. The United States is to the consumption of oil what Saudi Arabia is to its production, a country whose share of the world's total is so large that its own policies can affect the world price.

40. "...economic downturns have occurred after each oil price jump of the last three decades." Wolf, "Stable oil supplies," p. 15. A gasoline tax would differ from the price increases occasioned by the two oil shocks in that the additional revenue would stay within the consuming country and could, in theory, be recycled by the government to sustain a high level of economic activity.

41. Another reason for the energy policy perpetuating heavy reliance on oil is that powerful interests, including oil companies, favor this and lobby to retain it. No major industry is built around using less energy, so conservation lacks powerful champions. Roberts, op. cit., pp. 283, 286, 294.

42. Ibid., p. 153.

43. The potential also exists to extract a considerable amount of oil from shale and tar sands, albeit by methods more expensive than the processes by which it is presently obtained. Peter Huber and Mark Mills, "Oil, oil everywhere ... ," *The Wall Street Journal*, January 27, 2005, p. A13.

44. "...any meaningful climate policy is, by definition, one that is anticoal." Roberts, op. cit., p. 269.

45. Goodstein, op. cit., pp. 72–76.

46. A widely cited estimate, by the United Nations Intergovernmental Panel on Climate Change, foresees that without a significant reduction in greenhouse gas emissions, global temperatures will increase by as much as seven degrees Fahrenheit by 2050 and by as much as ten degrees by 2100. Roberts, op. cit., p. 120.

47.   Because it requires giving up all fossil fuels, and not only oil, addressing the problem of global warming would cost even more. By one reckoning the expense of slowing carbon dioxide emissions could cost a full percentage point of the American gross domestic product each year for the next century. Ibid., p. 118.

48.   Andrew C. Revkin, "U.S. Report, in Shift, Turns Focus to Greenhouse Gases," *The New York Times*, August 26, 2004, p. A16; Naomi Oreskes, "Undeniable Global Warming," *The Washington Post*, December 26, 2004, p. B7.

49.   A commonly cited danger point is 450 parts per million (ppm). Roberts, op. cit., p. 125.

50.   "Climage-change science is based on computer models. Like financial forecasts, they try to predict the future by analysing the past. They run on the biggest computers ever devised, but they attempt to describe a system of mind-defying complexity ... Models can never tell us with abolute certainty what is happening to our climate." Fiona Harvey, "In knots over the unknowns of climate change," *Financial Times*, December 18/December 19, 2004, p. 7.

51.   On the flaws of the Kyoto Protocol, see Thomas C. Schelling, "What Makes Greenhouse Sense?" *Foreign Affairs* (May–June 2002). Schelling argues that the appropriate response to global warming is not to take extraordinary measures to reduce emissions, since they would reduce economic growth, but rather to use some of the economic growth that avoiding those measures would make possible to cope with the effects of global warming when they appear.

52.   Barrett, op. cit., pp. 393–395.

53.   Gold was not always literally transferred from one country to another. Great Britain managed the system, using its own banks and discount rates (along with those of other countries) to keep countries in balance. An account of the working of the gold standard may be found in Barry Eichengreen, *Golden Fetters: The Gold Standard and the Great Depression* (New York: Oxford University Press, 1992).

54.   The dollar also offered an advantage to countries that held it as a reserve. They could earn interest on their dollar holdings, as they could not on their gold stocks.

55.   Robert Gilpin, *The Political Economy of International Relations*

(Princeton: Princeton University Press, 1987), pp. 136–137. According to de Gaulle in 1965, the role of the dollar in the Bretton Woods system "has enabled the United States to be indebted to foreign countries free of charge. Indeed what they owe those countries they pay … in dollars that they themselves can issue as they wish … This unilateral facility attributed to America has helped spread the idea that the dollar is an impartial international [means] of exchange, whereas it is a means of credit appropriated to one state." Quoted in Niall Ferguson, "Euro Trashing," *The New Republic,* June 21, 2004, p. 17.

56. Robert Gilpin, *The Challenge of Global Capitalism: The World Economy in the Twenty-first Century* (Princeton: Princeton University Press, 2000), p. 61.

57. Gilpin, *Political Economy*, p. 140.

58. Ibid., pp. 135–136.

59. Gilpin, *The Challenge*, p. 121; Kenneth W. Dam, *The Rules of the Global Game: A New Look at U.S. International Economic Policymaking* (Chicago: University of Chicago Press, 2004 paperback), p. 201.

60. Gilpin, *The Challenge*, pp. 207–209.

61. The actual monetary gains to the United States from the privileged position of the dollar, called "seignorage," "have surely been relatively small measured against the size of the U.S. and world economies." Dam, op. cit., p. 202.

62. They are called panics because they often stem from contagious and ultimately self-fulfilling fears that a bank will run out of money. This puts a premium on speedy action to claim funds that have been deposited with the bank. Bubbles, in which the value of an asset is bid up and then crashes as investors rush to withdraw their money, occurred well before the modern era: the Dutch tulip craze of the seventeenth century and the British South Sea bubble of the eighteenth are examples. See Edward Chancellor, *Devil Take the Hindmost: A History of Financial Speculation* (New York: Farrar, Straus and Giroux, 1999).

63. To forestall panics, governments also regulate banks and insure deposits up to a certain amount.

64. Gilpin, *Political Economy*, pp. 79–80.

65. "Per capita incomes tumbled to almost one-third their 1996 level in Indonesia, with the other crisis-stricken Asian countries show-

ing declines ranging from a quarter to nearly half of the 1996 levels." Jagdish Bhagwati, *In Defense of Globalization* (New York:
Oxford University Press, 2004), p. 199.

66.   "By 1999, Asian economies were growing again: South Korea's
growth was 10.9 percent, Thailand's 4.4 percent. (Indonesia was
an exception.)" Robert Samuelson, "What the Boom Forgot," *The
New Republic*, May 3, 2004, p. 32.

67.   Nor could it seize their assets when the countries failed to repay
their loans, which was not an unknown occurrence. A onetime
chief economist of the organization said in 2004, "We have a
problem of serial default—with Brazil defaulting seven times,
Argentina five, Venezuela nine and Turkey six ... " Christopher
Swann, "Sixty years on, and still contentious," *Financial Times*,
May 29/30, 2004, p. 4.

68.   The United States controls 17.6 percent of the votes. The next
largest shareholder in what is, in effect, an international credit
union, is Japan, with 6.6 percent.

69.   The American role in the financial crises is described in Paul
Blustein, *The Chastening: Inside the Crisis That Rocked the Global
Financial System and Humbled the IMF* (New York: PublicAffairs,
2001). See, for example, pp. 141–144, 168, and 172.

70.   Some of the reforms the IMF demanded involved opening
national financial systems to foreign participation, which would
benefit the American firms that dominated the global financial
services industry.

71.   Adam Smith, *The Wealth of Nations* (New York: The Modern
Library, 1994, first published 1776), p. 14.

72.   "In a regime of Free Trade and free economic intercourse it
would be of little consequence that iron lay on one side of a political frontier and labour, coal, and blast furnaces on the other. But
as it is, men have devised ways to impoverish themselves and one
another; and prefer collective animosities to individual happiness." John Maynard Keynes, *The Economic Consequences of the
Peace* (New York: Penguin Books, 1988, first published 1920), p.
99.

73.   The challenges are described in Douglas Irwin, *Against the Tide*
(Princeton: Princeton University Press, 1996).

74.   Wolf, *Why Globalization Works*, pp. 107–108; Bhagwati, op. cit. pp.
53–54, 64. It is a particularly important cause of economic growth

for small countries with meager endowments of natural resources. Trade therefore offers special benefits to the weak and, in mineral wealth, the poor.

75. Before the twentieth century, tariffs on imports also served for many governments as their most reliable source of revenue.

76. Wolf, *Why Globalization Works*, p. 90.

77. According to one study, American trade barriers cost Americans $170,000 for each job they saved, a sum considerably exceeding the average salary for the protected jobs. Gilpin, *The Challenge*, p. 91.

78. The contribution that trade makes to economic hardship tends to be overestimated. Studies show that American workers are more often displaced by technological advances than by competition from abroad. But it is easier to oppose foreigners than to stand athwart the march of progress at home. "Globalisation and its critics: A survey of globalisation," *The Economist*, September 29, 2001, p. 9. Nor, contrary to widespread belief, is it true that trade with poor countries depresses wages in rich ones. Bhagwati, op. cit., pp. 123–127.

79. Dam, op. cit., pp. 62–65.

80. Mandelbaum, op. cit., pp. 341–342.

81. The strong dollar of the 1980s also contributed to protectionist sentiment in the United States by making imports relatively cheap and exports expensive.

82. The provisions were justified by their proponents as conforming to rather than departing from the spirit of free trade by encouraging openness to imports by other countries. The United States also began to practice protection by administrative rather than legislative means, by implementing, for example, "anti-dumping" regulations. Dam, op. cit., pp. 151–161.

83. On the drawbacks of such agreements see Martin Wolf, "America and Europe share the responsibility for world trade," *Financial Times*, April 23, 2003, p. 13, and Jagdish Bhagwati and Arvind Panagariya, "Bilateral trade treaties are a sham," *Financial Times*, July 14, 2003, p. 15. One motive for NAFTA, it should be noted, was to put pressure on Europe and Japan to conclude the global trade negotiations, the Uruguay Round, then under way. Dam, op. cit., p. 134.

84. At the World Trade Organization meeting in Seattle in Novem-

ber 1999, the American president, Bill Clinton, gave the impression that he personally favored including labor and environmental provisions in trade agreements.

85. Dam, op. cit., Chapter 13.

86. On the trends that strengthened the political forces favoring free trade see Wolf, *Why Globalization Works*, pp. 311–312.

87. Bhagwati, op. cit., p. 89.

88. In 1994, Congress denied the president "fast track" authority—the power to submit for Congressional ratification a trade agreement for an up-or-down vote without the opportunity to add amendments to it—which in the previous twenty years had greatly assisted the passage of such agreements. This was a sign of weakened support for expanding trade. In 2001, however, the Bush administration succeeded in securing fast-track authority.

89. "Even a modest reduction in the growth of American consumer demand in the years ahead would have serious consequences for the rest of the global economy, given that nearly 60 percent of the total growth in world output since 1995 has come from the United States." Ferguson, *Colossus*, p. 291.

90. "The world economy has a classic Keynesian problem: excessive desired savings. It has found a Keynesian solution: a spender of last resort . . . the US public and private sectors have spent the excess desired savings generated elsewhere. John Maynard Keynes would have approved." Martin Wolf, "Big spenders are keeping the global economy moving," *Financial Times*, April 28, 2004, p. 15.

91. The underlying cause of the American trade deficit, as with all trade deficits, was the excess of investment over savings within the United States: ". . . the real cause of America's growing taste for imports, of course, is not unfairly cheap production in China—usually named as the culprit—but its low saving, the result of rampant household borrowing and a huge federal budget deficit." "The not-so-mighty dollar," *The Economist*, December 6, 2003, p. 9.

92. "In the early 1990s, about 20 percent of all capital from countries with a current account surplus (countries that export more goods and services than they import) made its way to U.S. capital markets. By the end of the decade, that figure had risen to almost 70 percent." Charles A. Kupchan, *The End of the American Era: U.S. Foreign Policy and the Geopolitics of the Twenty-first Century* (New

York: Knopf, 2002), p. 93. The United States could have filled the gap in another way: "An individual living beyond his or her means can either borrow or sell something to make up the difference between income and consumption. A country has a third option, which is to print money. No one wants the inflation that that would cause, and the Federal Reserve is very unlikely to accommodate such a strategy." Stephen Cecchetti, "A harsh lesson on why the US deficit matters," *Financial Times*, February 3, 2004, p. 15.

93. Dam, op. cit., pp. 202–203.

94. Martin Wolf, "The Fund is not equal to the job it was meant to do," *Financial Times*, March 10, 2004, p. 13. "...the financial authorities of Japan, China, Korea, and other Asian countries have been pursuing what used to be called a 'mercantilist' policy. They have been intervening heavily and persistently in the currency markets to limit, or in the case of China, to halt altogether any tendency for their currencies to appreciate. They have collectively acquired dollar assets, mainly U.S. Treasury obligations, sufficient to finance almost the entire U.S. current-account deficit over the past year—as well as the U.S. government's budget deficit." Roger Kubarych, "Trade adjustment: A hint that the weak dollar is working," New York: The Council on Foreign Relations, January 14, 2004, p. 1.

95. They were able to do this because of their high savings rates. "Behind these surpluses lie astonishingly high savings rates. Between 1997 and 2001 the gross national savings rate of the developing countries in the east Asian region was 37 per cent of GDP ... Japan has the highest savings rate among the high-income countries, at 30 per cent of GDP. At the opposite end, US savings averaged less than 18 per cent of GDP." Martin Wolf, "Why Europe was the past, the US is the present and a China-dominated Asia the future of the global economy," *Financial Times*, September 22, 2003, p. 13. On the similarities between global trade patterns and monetary flows in the first decade of the twenty-first century, on the one hand, and the trade and monetary patterns of the 1950s and 1960s, on the other, see Pam Woodall, "The dragon and the eagle: A survey of the world economy," *The Economist*, October 2, 2004, pp. 4–5, and Martin Wolf, "The

underrated dangers of the dollar's orderly decline," *Financial Times*, December 17, 2003, p. 19.

96. Martin Wolf, "A paper victory over the currency protectionists," *Financial Times*, February 11, 2004, p. 13.

97. China had an additional motive for accumulating dollars: the lesson of the financial crises that had struck other Asian countries that a very large supply of reserves may be necessary for economic security. Wolf, "Why Europe was the past," and Wolf, "A Paper Victory."

98. "For the region itself, the approach represents a waste of money ... The central banks [of Asia] are not holding dollars because they are a good investment." Alan Beattie, "Storing up trouble: Asia's policy of accumulating reserves becomes a source of friction with an indebted US," *Financial Times*, September 24, 2003, p. 11.

99. "In the decades before the First World War, Britain ran current account surpluses averaging about 4 per cent of gross domestic product. Last year, however, its successor as world power ran a deficit of close to 5 per cent of GDP and had net external liabilities of 25 per cent." Martin Wolf, "The rake's progress of the dollar comes under threat," *Financial Times*, January 8, 2003, p. 13.

100. Ferguson, *Colossus*, p. 282.

101. Peter G. Peterson, *Running on Empty: How the Democratic and Republican Parties Are Bankrupting Our Future and What Americans Can Do About It* (New York: Farrar, Straus and Giroux, 2004), pp. 92–93. See also Fred Bergsten, "The Risks Ahead For The World Economy," *The Economist*, September 11, 2004, p. 64. For the case that high American current account deficits will prove to be sustainable, see Richard Cooper, "How big is the hole in the economy?" *Financial Times*, November 1, 2004, p. 15. On this point, see also David H. Levey and Stuart S. Brown, "The Overstretch Myth," *Foreign Affairs*, March–April 2005.

102. Even more drastic consequences can be imagined. See, for example, Harold James, "Lessons to learn from the decline and fall of empire," *Financial Times*, December 30, 2002, p. 11.

103. On the risks to the dollar's status as the world's principal reserve, see "The passing of the buck?" *The Economist*, December 4, 2004, pp. 71–73. For the case that this status is secure for the foreseeable future, see Henry Kaufman, "Why there can be no alternative to the US dollar," *Financial Times*, December 9, 2004, p. 13.

Chapter 4: International Legitimacy

1. Fouad Ajami, "Iraq and the Arabs' Future," *Foreign Affairs* 82 (1) (January–February 2003), p. 18.

2. *Random House Dictionary, Second Edition Unabridged* (New York: Random House, 1987), p. 1099.

3. Thus, a common usage of the "legitimate" refers to the acknowledged offspring of legally married parents.

4. Robert Cooper, *The Breaking of Nations: Order and Chaos in the Twenty-first Century* (New York: Atlantic Monthly Press, 2003), p. 167. In the 2003 confrontation with Iraq, British prime minister Tony Blair believed that UN approval was necessary to secure domestic support in Great Britain for forceful action. Philip H. Gordon and Jeremy Shapiro, *Allies at War: America, Europe, and the Crisis over Iraq* (New York: McGraw Hill, 2004), p. 106.

5. Gordon and Shapiro, op. cit., p. 144.

6. John Micklethwait and Adrian Woolridge, *The Right Nation: Conservative Power in America* (New York: The Penguin Press, 2004), p. 390.

7. Clyde Prestowitz, *Rogue Nation: American Unilateralism and the Failure of Good Intentions* (New York: Basic Books, 2003), p. 45.

8. Micklethwait and Woolridge, op. cit., p. 222.

9. "To the Europeans ... the United States is unduly religious, almost embarrassingly so, its culture suffused with sacred symbolism. In the Islamic world, the burden is precisely the opposite: There, the United States scandalizes the devout, its message represents nothing short of an affront to the pious and a temptation to the gullible and the impressionable young." Fouad Ajami, "The Falseness of Anti-Americanism," *Foreign Policy* (September–October, 2003), p. 58.

10. "Large majorities in 42 of 44 countries believe that their traditional way of life is getting lost and most people feel that their way of life has to be protected against foreign influence." The Pew Global Attitudes Project, *Views of a Changing World, June 2003* (Washington, D.C.: The Pew Research Center for the People & The Press, 2003), p. 11.

11. A very useful account of the origins and varieties of conspiracy theories is Daniel Pipes, *Conspiracy: How the Paranoid Style Flourishes and Where It Comes From* (New York: The Free Press, 1997).

12. Barry Rubin and Judith Colp Rubin, *Hating America: A History* (New York: Oxford University Press, 2004), p. 85.

13. This is a major theme of Bernard Lewis, *What Went Wrong? Western Impact and Middle Eastern Response* (New York: Oxford University Press, 2002).

14. Rubin and Rubin, op. cit., pp. 158–160. Arab regimes also relied for their survival on blaming the misfortunes of their societies on Israel, whose ability to survive in the face of decades-long hostility and periodic military assaults from the Arab world and whose social cohesion and economic success under these extraordinarily challenging circumstances served as a standing reproach to the Arabs and a painful reminder of their own failures. "In Egypt, for instance, the only permitted political topic is Israel's flaws. Arab sentiment is being misdirected toward an exclusive focus on the Israeli-Palestinian topic in order to distract people from thinking about changing their own governments." Jeffrey Goldberg in "Political Islam: A Conversation with Gilles Kepel and Jeffrey Goldberg," *Center Conversations* 22, Washington, D.C.: The Ethics and Public Policy Center, July 2003, p. 5.

15. "If [American power] was already irksome to some people during the cold war, it has become intolerable to many in its aftermath. Europeans are beginning to feel their impotence." Ian Buruma, "Ties that loosen," *Financial Times*, January 10/11, 2004, p. W4. European resentment of the United States emerged during the 2002 World Cup, the global soccer championship. The American team performed better than several of the major European teams, including that of France, the defending champion, despite the fact that the game has far less importance in North America than in Europe. The European reaction was, according to one observer, "all about threat, but the threat has nothing to do with the world of soccer. It has to do with 20th-century history, with the American century, with the sense of cultural superiority." Stefan Fatsis, "A New World Order," *The Wall Street Journal*, June 21, 2002, p. W4. On European resentment of American power, see also Josef Joffe, "The Demons of Europe," *Commentary* (January 2004).

16. This is the thesis of Louis Hartz, *The Liberal Tradition in America* (New York: Harcourt Brace and World, 1955).

17. Seymour Martin Lipset, *American Exceptionalism: A Double-Edged Sword* (New York: W. W. Norton, 1997 paperback), p. 87.

18. Micklethwait and Woolridge, op. cit., p. 338.

19. Ibid., pp. 150, 310, 313.

20. "Protestant-inspired moralism not only has affected opposition to wars, it has determined the American style in foreign relations generally ... Support for a war is as moralistic as resistance to it." Lipset, op. cit., p. 20.

21. Micklethwait and Woolridge, op. cit., p. 12. "This year's Pew survey finds a wider gap in strong religious commitment between Republicans and Democrats than at any time over the 16-year period that the Pew Research Center has measured basic political, social and economic attitudes." *Evenly Divided and Increasingly Polarized: 2004 Political Landscape* (Washington, D.C.: The Pew Research Center for the People and the Press, November 2003), p. 3.

22. Micklethwait and Woolridge, op. cit., p. 85.

23. Another reason was that before the twentieth century, religion's extensive intrusion into political life in Europe often produced persecution and conflict. It had this effect even at the end of the twentieth century. Michael Elliott, "How Europe Gets Bush Wrong," *Time*, December 1, 2003, p. 40.

24. Daniel Dombey, "Americans are from Mars, Europeans from Venus, says survey on world views," *Financial Times*, September 9, 2004, p. 4. By the findings of a different survey, "55 percent of Americans 'strongly agree' that war is sometimes necessary to obtain justice; the figure in Europe is just 18 percent." Micklethwait and Woolridge, op. cit., p. 298.

25. The war in Iraq produced a substantial partisan split (*Evenly Divided and Increasingly Polarized*, pp. 6–7). Part of that difference was no doubt caused by partisanship: The fact that a Republican president was conducting it made Republicans more and Democrats less likely to support it. The differences also reflected, however, underlying differences in attitudes toward war in general.

26. Pew Global Attitudes Project, *Views of a Changing World*, p. 101.

27. Micklethwait and Woolridge, op. cit., pp. 7, 303. As a consequence, income inequality is more pronounced in the United States than in Europe, another feature of American society that many Europeans find unattractive.

28. Ibid., p. 196. The differences between Republicans and Democrats on issues of sovereignty are matters of degree. Although a

Democratic administration signed the Kyoto Protocol and the pact establishing the International Criminal Court, it did nothing to implement either one, declining to submit both to the Senate for ratification. The Democrats' approach gained greater sympathy among Europeans because it stressed practical objections to both international agreements, whereas the Republicans opposed them on principle. Fred Hiatt, "Obstinate Orthodoxy," *The Washington Post*, March 31, 2003, p. A13.

29. Accordingly, substantial majorities in other countries favored the Democratic candidate in the 2004 presidential election. Joanna Chung and Daniel Dombey, "Global poll favours Kerry over Bush," *Financial Times*, September 9, 2004, p. 1.

30. People of other countries also believed that the United States failed to take their interests into account in making and carrying out its foreign policies. Pew Global Attitudes Project, *Views of a Changing World*, p. 29.

31. If anything, al Qaeda's activities served to buttress the American global position by persuading the American public to support a more assertive foreign policy than it would otherwise have been willing to do.

32. In the eighteenth century, the Anglo-Irish statesman Edmund Burke said of his own country, "I dread our own power and our own ambition; I dread our being too much dreaded ... We may say that we shall not abuse this astonishing and hitherto unheard-of power. But every other nation will think we shall abuse it. It is impossible but that, sooner or later, this state of things must produce a combination against us which may end in our ruin." Quoted in Robert W. Tucker, "Alone or with Others: The Temptations of Post–Cold War Power," *Foreign Affairs* (November–December 1999), p. 16.

33. Gordon and Shapiro, op. cit., p. 152.

34. "... the broader *Pew Global Attitudes* survey shows wide support for the fundamental economic and political values that the U.S. has long promoted. Globalization, the free market model and democratic ideals are accepted in all corners of the world." Pew Global Attitudes Project, *Views of a Changing World*, p. 1. See also *A Year of Contention at Home and Abroad: 2003 Year-End Report* (Washington, D.C.: The Pew Research Center for the People and the Press, 2004), p. 9.

35. Pew Global Attitudes Project, *Views of a Changing World*, pp. 33, 37, 66.
36. Ibid., pp. 75, 99.
37. Rubin and Rubin, op. cit., p. 182.
38. "People who have unfavorable views of the United States for the most part base those opinions on their feelings about President Bush, not the United States." Pew Global Attitudes Project, *Views of a Changing World*, p. 22.
39. "Three-quarters of those interviewed in almost every country think children need to learn English to succeed in the world today." Ibid., p. 10. See also p. 78.
40. "In 2000 American firms had some $3,000,000,000,000 worth of assets in Europe, and European firms had some $3,300,000,000,000 worth of assets in America." Timothy Garton Ash, *Free World: America, Europe, and the Surprising Future of the West* (New York: Random House, 2004), p. 122.
41. Gordon and Shapiro, op. cit., p. 12.
42. In a conference on Sino-American relations held in Beijing, "in response to a U.S. participant's question as to whether China wants the United States to remove its troops from the region, a Chinese delegate stated the following: 'If the United States needed $5 to support all U.S. troops in Asia and asked China to cover the costs, China would have to break the money into five parts and evaluate how each dollar is spent.' He said that China would pay the first dollar for Japan, as Japan must be restrained militarily. China would also pay the second dollar for Korea, as China does not want to be responsible for the Korean peninsula. The third dollar, however, is for the protection of Taiwan, and for that the Chinese would not pay. China would not pay the fourth dollar either, as it would be for the South China Sea, which China views as an internal or bilateral matter. Finally, the fifth dollar is for the Middle East, which China would most likely pay because it is necessary for stability in that region." Summary Report, Conference on U.S.-China Relations and Geopolitical Trends, sponsored by the John F. Kennedy School of Government, Harvard University, March 26–28, 1997, Beijing, China, p. 6.
43. According to a 1946 briefing paper by the British Foreign Office: "The Americans are a mercurial people, unduly swayed by sentiment and prejudice ... Their Government is handicapped by an

archaic constitution, sometimes to the point of impotence ... "
Quoted in R. W. Johnson, "Every Club in the Bag," *London
Review of Books*, August 8, 2002, p. 15.

44. Charles A. Kupchan, *The End of the American Era: U.S. Foreign
Policy and the Geopolitics of the Twenty-first Century* (New York:
Alfred A. Knopf, 2002), p. 15.

45. Although precise figures are probably impossible to obtain, it did
seem, in the early years of the twenty-first century, that critics
offer praise to the dramas they review somewhat more often than
citizens and governments of other countries express admiration
and appreciation for the foreign policies of the United States.

46. On the community of interests and values encompassing Europe
and the United States, see Tod Lindberg, "We," in Lindberg, editor, *Beyond Paradise and Power: Europe, America, and the Future of a
Troubled Partnership* (New York: Routledge, 2004).

47. Richard Sobel, *The Impact of Public Opinion on U.S. Foreign Policy
Since Vietnam* (New York: Oxford University Press, 2001), pp.
12–13. "In the last seventy years ... only a few events have notably
caused the public to divert its attention from domestic matters,
and at no time between the Tet offensive in the Vietnam War in
early 1968 and the terrorist bombings of September 11, 2001, did
foreign policy issues outweigh domestic ones when the public was
asked to designate the country's most important problem." John
Mueller, *The Remnants of War* (Ithaca: Cornell University Press,
2004), p. 150. An early study of public opinion and foreign policy
divides the public into three rather than two categories. See
Gabriel Almond, *The American People and Foreign Policy* (New
York: Frederick A. Praeger, 1960, first published, 1950), p. 138.

48. Martin Wolf, *Why Globalization Works* (New Haven: Yale University Press, 2004), pp. 68–69.

49. The imperative of an assertive American role in the world is a staple of the rhetoric of leaders of both political parties. In his
farewell address as president, the Democrat Bill Clinton said,
"America's security and prosperity require us to lead the world."
The *New York Times*, January 19, 2001, p. A16. The vice president
in the Republican administration that succeeded Clinton's, Dick
Cheney, said of the war against terrorism, "America has friends
and allies in this cause but only we can lead it. Only we can rally
the world in a task of this complexity, against an enemy so elusive

and so resourceful. The United States, and only the United States, can see this effort through to victory." Quoted in Ivo H. Daalder and James M. Lindsay, *America Unbound: The Bush Revolution in Foreign Policy* (Washington, D.C.: The Brookings Institution, 2003), p. 124. See also Walter Russell Mead, *Power, Terror, Peace, and War: America's Grand Strategy in a World At Risk* (New York: Knopf, 2004), p. 4.

50.   Sobel, op. cit., p. 3.

51.   John E. Rielly, "The Public Mood at Mid-Decade," *Foreign Policy* 98 (Spring 1995), pp. 79–80. For the argument that elite and public attitudes toward the world increasingly diverge, see Samuel P. Huntington, "Dead Souls: The Denationalization of the American Elite," *Foreign Policy* (Spring 2004). According to Huntington, "The public and elites agree on many foreign policy issues. Yet overall the differences between them far exceed the similarities. The public is nationalist, the elite transnationalist." Ibid., p. 13. "What emerges [from a 2004 survey of American oinion on foreign policy] is a picture of a political leadership that feels more comfortable than the public about using US wealth and power to spread American ideals." Edward Alden, "Poll shows gap between public and political elite," *Financial Times*, September 28, 2004, p. 2.

52.   Michael Mandelbaum, *The Ideas That Conquered the World: Peace, Democracy and Free Markets in the Twenty-first Century* (New York: PublicAffairs, 2002), pp. 93, 196–197.

53.   John Mueller, *War, Presidents, and Public Opinion* (New York: John Wiley and Sons, 1973), pp. 100–101.

54.   Ibid., p. 266.

55.   On World War II, see Alan Millett and Williamson Murray, *A War to Be Won: Fighting the Second World War* (Cambridge, Mass.: Harvard University Press, 2000), p. 545. "Over the course of the Cold War, between 1948 and 1989, the United States expended an average of 7.5 percent of its gross domestic product each year on defense." Aaron Friedberg, *In The Shadow of the Garrison State: America's Anti-Statism and Its Cold War Grand Strategy* (Princeton: Princeton University Press, 2000), p. 341.

56.   The "post–Cold War 'peace dividend' . . . reduced defence spending from 5.8 percent of GDP in 1988 to 3.1 percent in 1998." "Lexington: Divide and Rule," *The Economist*, October 23, 2004, p. 33.

57. Niall Ferguson, *Colossus: The Price of America's Empire* (New York: The Penguin Press, 2004), p. 277.

58. "Yet the public now attaches nearly as much importance [as protecting the United States from terrorist attacks] to the goal of protecting the jobs of American workers—84% say this should be a top foreign policy priority." "Foreign Policy Attitudes Now Driven by 9/11 and Iraq," Washington, D.C.: The Pew Research Center for the People and the Press, August 18, 2004, p. 18.

59. Peter G. Peterson, *Running on Empty: How the Democratic and Republican Parties Are Bankrupting Our Future and What Americans Can Do About It* (New York: Farrar, Straus and Giroux, 2004), p. 94.

60. "Economics focus: Trade disputes," *The Economist*, September 18, 2004, p. 80.

61. Mandelbaum, op. cit., pp. 363–364.

62. The enlarging impact on American security policies of traumatic attacks by foreigners is the subject of John Lewis Gaddis, *Surprise, Security, and the American Experience* (Cambridge, Mass.: Harvard University Press, 2004).

63. American history offers a precedent for a policy of intervention and nation-building for the sake of international order. In 1904, President Theodore Roosevelt announced that "chronic wrongdoing, or an impotence which results in a general loosening of the ties of civilized society, may in America, as elsewhere, ultimately require intervention by some civilized nation, and in the Western Hemisphere the adherence of the United States to the Monroe Doctrine may force the United States, however reluctantly, in flagrant cases of such wrongdoing or impotence, to the exercise of an international police power." This became known as the Roosevelt Corollary to the Monroe Doctrine. Quoted in Walter A. McDougall, *Promised Land, Crusader State: The American Encounter with the World Since 1776* (Boston: Houghton Mifflin, 1997), p. 115.

64. During the first Gulf War, for example, "people found oil issues and the restoration of the Kuwait government to be far less compelling reasons to go to war than doing something about Hussein's chemical and nuclear capability." John Mueller, *Policy and Opinion in the Gulf War* (Chicago: The University of Chicago Press, 1995), p. 39. See also p. 118.

65. Greg Jaffe, "In Massive Shift, U.S. Is Planning to Cut Size of Military in Germany," *The Wall Street Journal*, June 10, 2003, p. A1.

66. Quoted in Peter Spiegel, "US troops withdrawal part of a plan to revamp cold war military infrastructure," *Financial Times*, August 16, 2004, p. 3.

67. On the Korean peninsula, because of the large North Korean non-nuclear forces, the United States was practicing deterrence whether or not the Communist regime actually had nuclear weapons.

68. The best account of this subject, on which much of the analysis that follows is based, is Peterson, op. cit.

69. Ibid., pp. 57–59. "All federal retirement and disability programs now [in 2004] account for more than 40 percent of the budget. By 2030 the number of elderly beneficiaries is reckoned to rise about 80 percent ... the Congressional Budget office projects that spending on these programs will increase roughly 75 percent by 2030 (as a share of national income)." Robert J. Samuelson, "Same Old Evasion," *The Washington Post*, September 8, 2004, p. A23.

 "According to Goldman Sachs' economic team, 'Medicare is the much bigger problem. It accounts for more than four-fifths of the projected increase in entitlement spending in coming decades, and its costs—unlike those of Social Security—are largely immune to an increase in the retirement age.'" Irwin M. Stelzer, "Social Security Snares and Delusions," *The Weekly Standard*, January 17, 2005, p. 26.

70. Paul Krugman, "America's Senior Moment," *The New York Review of Books*, March 10, 2005, pp. 10–11.

71. Peterson, op. cit., p. 33. The lower figure is twenty times the 2004 federal budget and more than four times the nation's gross domestic product. "Hidden dangers," *The Economist*, August 2, 2003, p. 65.

72. Peterson, op. cit., pp. 39–40.

73. In fiscal 2003, the cost of federal benefit spending in the United States was $1.349 trillion. The defense budget totaled $0.376 trillion. Ibid., p. 111.

74. One national poll "found 76 percent agreeing with the suggestion that less attention should be paid to problems overseas and more to those at home." Ash, op. cit., p. 120.

Chapter 5: The Future

1. See Daniel Pipes, *Militant Islam Reaches America* (New York: W. W. Norton, 2002), Part I.

2. Iranian nuclear weapons ambitions received assistance from a loophole in the Nuclear Nonproliferation Treaty, which Iran had signed, which permitted the operation of facilities to prepare fuel for nuclear power plants. The process of fuel fabrication is the same as the process by which the material for a nuclear explosive is made.

3. Graham Allison, *Nuclear Terrorism: The Ultimate Preventable Catastrophe* (New York: Times Books, 2004), p. 8.

4. Ibid., pp. 77, 151.

5. According to the American economist Alan Blinder, a former vice chairman of the country's Federal Reserve Board, "For the US economy to go into a significant recession, never mind a depression, important policymakers would have to take leave of their senses." Matthew Bishop, "Capitalism and its troubles," *The Economist*, May 18, 2002, p. 18.

6. Jonathan Haslam, *No Virtue Like Necessity: Realist Thought in International Relations Since Machiavelli* (New Haven: Yale University Press, 2002), p. 25; F. H. Hinsley, *Power and the Pursuit of Peace: Theory and Practice in the History of Relations Between States* (Cambridge, England: Cambridge University Press, 1967 paperback), pp. 6–7.

7. Hedley Bull, "Society and Anarchy in International Relations," in Herbert Butterfield and Martin Wight, editors, *Diplomatic Investigations: Essays in the Theory of International Politics* (Cambridge, Mass.: Harvard University Press, 1968), pp. 36–37.

8. Michael Mandelbaum, *The Nuclear Question: The United States and Nuclear Weapons, 1946–1976* (New York: Cambridge University Press, 1979), pp. 23–27. In 2004, Mohammed ElBaradei, the head of the International Atomic Energy Authority, proposed that the process of fabricating nuclear fuel for power plants, the same process used to make the explosive material for nuclear weapons, be put entirely under international control. Allison, op. cit., p. 159.

9. Martin Wolf, "A global market economy needs a global currency," *Financial Times*, August 4, 2004, p. 11.

10. Stephen D. Krasner, *Sovereignty: Organized Hypocrisy* (Princeton: Princeton University Press, 1999).

11. Michael Mandelbaum, *The Ideas That Conquered the World: Peace, Democracy and Free Markets in the Twenty-first Century* (New York: PublicAffairs, 2002), pp. 190–193.

12. Hedley Bull, *The Anarchical Society: A Study of Order in World Politics* (New York: Columbia University Press, 1977), pp. 253–254.

13. Mandelbaum, *The Ideas*, pp. 193–197. For the contrary view, that "zones of chaos" ultimately affect the international system as a whole, see Robert Cooper, *The Breaking of Nations: Order and Chaos in the Twenty-first Century* (New York: Atlantic Monthly Press, 2003), pp. 6–9.

14. On the reasons that wars of secessions increased in number with the end of the Cold War, see Mandelbaum, *The Ideas*, pp. 184–186.

15. This is a principal theme of John Mueller, *The Remnants of War* (Ithaca: Cornell University Press, 2004). See, for example, pp. 2, 115.

16. "The best solution to the problems presented by civil warfare ... lies in the development of effective domestic governments ... " Ibid., p. 172.

17. Ibid., p. 180; Mandelbaum, *The Ideas*, pp. 186–187.

18. Cited in Timothy Garton Ash, *Free World: America, Europe, and the Surprising Future of the West* (New York: Random House, 2004), p. 149.

19. In the twenty-first century, it has come to seem all the less tolerable because the gap in economic well-being between the very richest and the very poorest of the planet had widened. "In 1820 the richest country in the world had a real income per head about four and a half times as high as the poorest. The ratio was fifteen to one by 1913, twenty-six to one by 1950, forty-two to one by 1973, and seventy-one to one by 2000." Martin Wolf, *Why Globalization Works* (New Haven: Yale University Press, 2004), p. 44. On the other hand, *overall* inequality was, by most measures, declining at the outset of the twenty-first century. Ibid., Chapter 9.

20. See, for example, Martin Wolf, "The future looks grim for the world's failing nations," *Financial Times,* July 16, 2003, p. 13.

21. Wolf, *Why Globalization Works*, p. 316.

22. Ibid., p. 115; Niall Ferguson, *Colossus: The Price of America's Empire* (New York: The Penguin Press, 2004), pp. 173–178.

23. Government is, by one definition, "a utilitarian device for ensuring a more efficient, less cumbersome social order ... " Leon

Mayhew, "Society," in *The International Encyclopedia of the Social Sciences*, vol. 14 (Glencoe, Ill.: The Free Press, 1968), pp. 578–579. Government, to put it differently, consists of a narrow set of hierarchical—that is, vertical—relations, while society consists of a far broader range of horizontal—that is, voluntary—relationships. Where government enforces, society harmonizes.

24. John Keane, *Global Civil Society?* (Cambridge, England: Cambridge University Press, 2003), pp. 4–5. On different aspects of international civil society, see Amitai Etzioni, *From Empire to Community* (New York: Palgrave Macmillan, 2004), and Anne-Marie Slaughter, *A New World Order* (Princeton: Princeton University Press, 2004).

25. "In his opening address as president of Europe's constitutional convention in 2002, Valéry Giscard d'Estaing, a former president of France, laid out his hopes: 'If we succeed in 25 or 50 years . . . Europe's role in the world will have changed. It will be respected and listened to, not only as the economic power it already is, but as a political power which will talk on equal terms to the greatest powers on our planet.'" Gideon Rachman, "Outgrowing the Union: A survey of the European Union," *The Economist*, September 25, 2004, p. 6.

26. Ferguson, op. cit., p. 227; Philip H. Gordon and Jeremy Shapiro, *Allies at War: America, Europe, and the Crisis over Iraq* (New York: McGraw-Hill, 2004), p. 172.

27. This is a major theme, for example, of Ash, op. cit.

28. Gordon and Shapiro, op. cit., p. 16; Ronald D. Asmus and Kenneth M. Pollack, "The New Transatlantic Project," *Policy Review* (October–November 2002).

29. For the contrary argument, that Europe will become a global rival to the United States, see Charles Kupchan, *The End of the American Era: U.S. Foreign Policy and the Geopolitics of the Twenty-first Century* (New York: Knopf, 2002), especially Chapter 4.

30. The first EU high representative for common foreign and security policy was the Spaniard Javier Solana, who had previously served as the secretary-general of NATO.

31. While France, Germany, Luxembourg, and Belgium adamantly opposed the use of force and worked to prevent the UN Security Council from authorizing it, in January 2003 the leaders of Britain, Spain, Italy, Poland, Hungary, the Czech Republic, Den-

mark, and Portugal issued a statement supporting the need for strong action to disarm Iraq.

32. Mandelbaum, *The Ideas*, pp. 121–128.

33. Rachman, op. cit., p. 8. On the transatlantic differences in attitudes toward war, see Robert Kagan, *Of Paradise and Power: America and Europe in the New World Order* (New York: Knopf, 2003).

34. Kagan, op. cit., p. 55; Ash, op. cit., p. 191. This is a major theme of Cooper, op. cit. See, for example, pp. 72–73, 78, 119, 145–146.

35. Mandelbaum, *The Ideas.*, pp. 53–68.

36. Ibid.

37. In December, 2003, the EU issued its first statement of a security doctrine. Entitled, "A Secure Europe in a Better World: European Security Strategy," it said "almost nothing about the use of force." Judy Dempsey, "Words of war: Europe's first security doctrine backs away from American style pre-emptive military intervention," *Financial Times*, December 5, 2003, p. 11.

38. Ash, op. cit., p. 121. Europe "would be hard pressed to deploy and sustain more than 6 percent of [its ground troops] abroad. In comparison, the United States can deploy and sustain some 62 percent of its ground troops." Gordon and Shapiro, op. cit., p. 57.

39. "... the entire British armed forces, slightly over 200,000 strong, number little more than the smallest of the American armed services, the Marine Corps." Eliot Cohen, "Thin Red Line, Getting Thinner," *The Washington Post*, August 13, 2004, p. A25. Britain and France's major unassisted post–Cold War operations took place in small, weak African countries—Britain's in Sierra Leone, France's in the Ivory Coast. When the British intervened in Sierra Leone in 2000, they asked the other EU members to contribute something to the military effort. All refused. John Newhouse, *Imperial America: The Bush Assault on the World Order* (New York: Knopf, 2003), p. 147.

40. Walter Russell Mead, "Goodbye to Berlin? Germany Looks Askance at Red State America," *The National Interest* (Spring 2004), pp. 23–24. This leads to the suspicion that, while many European governments refused to participate in the Iraq war because they opposed it, one of the reasons they opposed it was that they did not want to be susceptible to American requests to participate, and this because, given their meager armed forces, they could not participate effectively. Also relevant to the Euro-

pean misgivings about that conflict was the presence of large, at best partially assimilated, and in some cases potentially violent Muslim minorities in several countries, notably France and Germany. Gordon and Shapiro, op. cit., p. 90.

41. Bastian Giergerich and William Wallace, "Not Such a Soft Power: The External Deployment of European Forces," *Survival* (46) (2) (Summer 2004), p. 164.

42. Doug Bereuter, "Nato must try harder in its Afghan mission," *Financial Times*, June 29, 2004, p. 15; "Reinforcements needed," *The Economist*, June 19, 2004, pp. 41–42.

43. A number are listed in Giergerich and Wallace, op. cit.

44. John Micklethwait and Adrian Woolridge, *The Right Nation: Conservative Power in America* (New York: The Penguin Press, 2004), p. 392.

45. Ash, op. cit., p. 202. "Of the 71 percent who said they wanted the E.U. to become a superpower, 49 percent changed their mind if this would involve greater military expenditure. In other words, only 36 percent of all those asked supported the E.U. becoming a superpower with greater military expenditure." Ibid., p. 268.

46. Rachman, op. cit., pp. 9–10.

47. Peter G. Peterson, *Running on Empty: How the Democrats and Republican Parties Are Bankrupting Our Future and What Americans Can Do About It* (New York: Farrar Straus and Giroux, 2004), pp. ix, 66, 100, 101, 104. See also Peter G. Peterson, *Gray Dawn: How the Coming Age Wave Will Transform America—and the World* (New York: Times Books, 1999), pp. 6, 29–36.

48. One of the most internationally minded European countries is Poland, which sent troops to Iraq out of solidarity with the United States. Yet this deployment was not popular among the Poles. According to the director of a research organization on public affairs in Warsaw, "People don't understand why we should mess in other people's countries. These are not our problems, not our continent, not our issues." Ian Fisher, "Some in Poland Have Concerns About Nation's Expanding Role as a U.S. Ally," *The New York Times*, September 14, 2003, p. 10.

49. "Most analysts readily agree on what is wrong with the German economy. First and foremost, the labour market is far too sticky. Second, taxes and social-security contributions are too high and

profits too low. Third, and not unconnected, social-security payments, pensions and health-care arrangements are too generous." Xan Smiley, "An uncertain giant: A survey of Germany," *The Economist*, December 17, 2002, p. 10. The aging of the populations of the countries of Europe is also destined to reduce their potential for economic growth. Martin Wolf, "Europe must grow up if it wants to be taken seriously," *Financial Times*, November 10, 2004, p. 13.

50. Ash, op. cit., pp. 152–153. For the case that American economic assistance, properly calibrated, compares favorably with the aid provided by Europe, see Walter Russell Mead, *Power, Terror, Peace, and War: America's Grand Strategy in a World at Risk* (New York: Knopf, 2004), p. 39.

51. On the efforts to promote economic growth through loans and technical assistance by the principal international agency devoted to this task, the World Bank, see Sebastian Mallaby, *The World's Banker: A Story of Failed States, Financial Crises, and the Wealth and Poverty of Nations* (New York: The Penguin Press, 2004).

52. Ibid., pp. 154–156; Wolf, *Why Globalization Works*, pp. 212–218.

53. Kenneth W. Dam, *The Rules of the Global Game: A New Look at U.S. International Economic Policymaking* (Chicago: The University of Chicago Press, 2001), p. 80.

54. Clyde Prestowitz, *Rogue Nation: American Unilateralism and the Failure of Good Intentions* (New York: Basic Books, 2003), pp. 136–137. Ash, op. cit., p. 165.

55. Prestowitz, op. cit., pp. 124–125. Anti-American sentiment may also have played a role in designing the terms of the protocol. The chief American negotiator at a follow-up session to Kyoto organized to work out the details of the protocol said that he believed that "many EU negotiators wanted to force a change in the U.S. lifestyle and even to punish the United States. The European negotiators were all from the environmental ministries. [The American negotiator] noted that when he met with officials from the foreign ministries or trade ministries of Europe, they would roll their eyes over the positions of their own environmental ministries." Ibid., p. 138.

56. Scott Barrett, *Environment and Statecraft: The Strategy of Environmental Treaty-Making* (New York: Oxford University Press, 2003),

pp. 369, 371. See also Vanessa Houlder, "A change in the climate: will Russia help the Kyoto Protocol come into force?" *Financial Times*, May 20, 2004, p. 15.

57. Perhaps also relevant to the lack of appreciation of the American contribution to global peace and prosperity is the tendency to disbelieve good news and to concentrate on what is going wrong in the world even if much more is going right. See Gregg Easterbrook, *The Progress Paradox: How Life Gets Better While People Feel Worse* (New York: Random House, 2003), Chapter 3.

58. Borzou Daragahi, "France Steps Up Its Investments in Iran," *The New York Times*, June 23, 2004, p. W1.

Index

PublicAffairs is a publishing house founded in 1997. It is a tribute to the standards, values, and flair of three persons who have served as mentors to countless reporters, writers, editors, and book people of all kinds, including me.

I.F. STONE, proprietor of *I. F. Stone's Weekly*, combined a commitment to the First Amendment with entrepreneurial zeal and reporting skill and became one of the great independent journalists in American history. At the age of eighty, Izzy published *The Trial of Socrates*, which was a national bestseller. He wrote the book after he taught himself ancient Greek.

BENJAMIN C. BRADLEE was for nearly thirty years the charismatic editorial leader of *The Washington Post*. It was Ben who gave the *Post* the range and courage to pursue such historic issues as Watergate. He supported his reporters with a tenacity that made them fearless and it is no accident that so many became authors of influential, best-selling books.

ROBERT L. BERNSTEIN, the chief executive of Random House for more than a quarter century, guided one of the nation's premier publishing houses. Bob was personally responsible for many books of political dissent and argument that challenged tyranny around the globe. He is also the founder and longtime chair of Human Rights Watch, one of the most respected human rights organizations in the world.

For fifty years, the banner of Public Affairs Press was carried by its owner Morris B. Schnapper, who published Gandhi, Nasser, Toynbee, Truman and about 1,500 other authors. In 1983, Schnapper was described by *The Washington Post* as "a redoubtable gadfly." His legacy will endure in the books to come.

Peter Osnos, *Publisher*